Leisa

THE MAGIC OF
PROVENCE

D0951858

YVONE LENARD

THE MAGIC OF
PROVENCE

PLEASURES OF SOUTHERN FRANCE

BROADWAY BOOKS

NEW YORK

A hardcover edition of this book was originally
published in 2000 by Elysian Editions. It is here reprinted
by arrangement with Elysian Editions.

THE MAGIC OF PROVENCE. Copyright © 2000 by Yvone Lenard.
All rights reserved. Printed in the United States of America. No part
of this book may be reproduced or transmitted in any form or by any
means, electronic or mechanical, including photocopying, recording,
or by any information storage and retrieval system, without written
permission from the publisher. For information, address: Elysian Editions,
an imprint of Princeton Book Company, Publishers,
614 Route 130, Hightstown, New Jersey 08520.

Broadway Books titles may be purchased for business or
promotional use or for special sales. For information, please write to:
Special Markets Department, Random House, Inc.,
1540 Broadway, New York, NY 10036.

BROADWAY BOOKS and its logo, a letter B bisected on the diagonal,
are trademarks of Broadway Books, a division of Random House, Inc.

Many of the names and some of the identifying characteristics of the
individuals depicted in this book have been changed to protect their privacy.
A few are composite characters.

First Broadway Books trade paperback edition published 2001.

Designed by Elizabeth Helmetsie

Visit our website at www.broadwaybooks.com

Library of Congress Cataloging-in-Publication Data
Lenard, Yvone.
The magic of Provence: pleasures of southern France / Yvone Lenard.
p. cm.
I. Lenard, Yvone—Homes and haunts—France—Provence. 2. Provence
(France)—Social life and customs. 3. Cookery, French—Provençal style.
DC611.P958 L44 2001
994'.9—dc21
00-068075
ISBN 0-7679-0682-9

10 9 8 7 6 5 4 3 2 1

Contents

About Lavender

The sprig of lavender that opens each chapter evokes the flower whose pervading fragrance defines Provence and its sensuous appeal.

There, sachets of dried lavender are tucked between the folds of sheets in linen closets or hung from drawer pulls and bedroom window latches. Lavender soothes, heals, and helps to ensure a peaceful sleep. Mustiness of long-closed rooms will not resist a few drops of lavender oil. The fresh, innocent scent of lavender on sun-warmed skin is the breath of summer itself. It serves as the base of fabled perfumes, such as Guerlain's Jicky, a favorite of Jacqueline Kennedy, or the recently introduced Lavande Velours from the same house.

Lavender will grow almost anywhere but thrives best on the high plateaus of Provence (at lower altitude, it will be *lavandin*, a close relative, practically indistinguishable from *lavande* proper). Brave a July sun to visit Valensole fields in Haute-Provence, where carpets of mauve, purple, and blue stretch all the way to distant mountains. Deeply inhale their perfume to intoxication. Each flower is alive with bees brought there with their hives to collect heavenly scented lavender honey. After harvest, distilleries all over the countryside will waft their fragrant vapors into the air.

You, too, can grow lavender in a dry, sunny spot of your garden or terrace. Cut off the spikes and let them dry, then pull off the flowerets to fill your own sachets. If you tuck one of these under your pillow, you will fall asleep dreaming of Provence and its pleasures.

The Prince and
the Garbage Collector

*P*rovence smiled on us that first morning, and, seldom
drinkers that we are, we were both drunk before noon.

The night before, my husband and I had arrived at our
new hilltop village house in the Luberon, heart of Provence.
We slept fitfully, not yet adjusted to the time difference,
vaguely aware of roosters crowing most of the night. Their
enthusiasm rose to greet the day, and later the sun, streaming in through open windows, woke us up, as the belfry bell
rang eight times. When we rose, though, the rooms
remained night-fresh and the tiles cool underfoot.

No food in the house, but we were both too jet-lagged
to be hungry. Wayne left soon afterward to pick up a rental

truck and drive to Marseille, hoping to get there during the short hours the customs office opens to the public, to collect crates of belongings we had shipped from the States. Alone, I wandered from room to room, discovering our still-unfamiliar domain, exulting in this adventure. Bliss and expectation danced in the air, like the brilliant motes caught in bars of sunshine traced by the shutters I had half closed against the rising heat of the day.

Almost directly above stood the castle that had enchanted us on our first—and only—visit to the village, its red standard emblazoned with the gold lion of Provence, snapping in the breeze. Suddenly, from an open window way up in the towers, a cascade of piano notes burst forth and descended, floating down the battlements. Someone was playing Chopin. Not the hesitant fingers of a child. A sure, expert hand was spinning light, airy music. Transfixed, I stood lost in reverie. Had we, unknowingly, stepped straight into some Camelot?

The sound of the kitchen door, noisily opened, drew me out of my trance. I would learn later that, in Provence, callers walk in that way, ignoring more ceremonial entrances, not bothering to knock, simply calling out: *"Y a quelqu'un?"* Anyone home? I found myself face to face with a tall, handsome blond man in his thirties, carrying a small, wicker-clad jug.

He didn't introduce himself but took my hand and bent low over it. *"Salut,"* he said, "we heard you had arrived. *Il faut arroser ça,* one must drink to that. Do you have any glasses?" From the still-empty dish closet, I unearthed two jam jars and rinsed them, all the time thinking: This can't

be a village man, he is dressed much too casually. I suspected locals wouldn't come calling at the house of
strangers, wearing cut-off jeans and a shirt knotted at the
waist. Obviously, someone else. But who could that be?

He filled the glasses with rosé wine. "Taste this," he
urged. "Just picked it up at the winery down below. Our
rosé is the best in Provence. Can't travel, doesn't age well.
But when it's fresh, it's the Virgin Mary in silk panties. Like
it? It's still cool from the barrel."

The clear, pink wine smelled and tasted of fruit. It hit
the tongue with just a hint of sparkle and, indeed, slithered
down the throat as lightly as silk chiffon. "Well," added my
visitor, "to your health, and welcome. Hope you like it
here. Most Luberon villages already have a few American
residents, but it looks like we're catching up at last." *We?*
Him and who else, I wondered. *"Cul sec,"* he concluded,
"Bottoms up," and refilled our glasses.

I know enough to offer a seat to visitors, so I tried to
coax him to the terrace, where he could at least sit on the
low surrounding wall, or to the living room, maybe. But he
wasn't interested.

"Much better here," he declared. "The tiles are nice and
cool. Here, sit on the floor." And he showed me the way,
sitting in the kitchen doorway, feet on the stone steps, patting the place next to him, the rosé jug between us. Intimidated, yet entranced, I sat, too, on the kitchen stoop.

Who, *who* in the world could that be? His casually knotted shirt was *sans* buttons, but he wore a signet ring with an
almost worn-off engraving. No clues there. Obviously, I
don't know him, yet he seems vaguely familiar. A TV or

movie actor? I am not that up on French personalities. Blonds are rare in this Mediterranean land of dark-haired, olive-skinned people. Still, that profile, the clear blue eyes, the high forehead and slightly heavy jaw, why do I think I've seen it somewhere before? A chain hung from his neck, with a heavy gold seal attached. Twisting my neck as inconspicuously as possible, I tried to make out the engraving on the face of the seal. Perhaps there would be initials there, a clue of some sort? Pretending to squirm into a more comfortable position I managed to sneak a peak. Engraved on the face of the seal I distinguished something like a double-headed eagle, perhaps the emblem of some royal house.

Of course, now, I could figure out why that handsome face, with its square jaw, brought a vague feeling of déjà vu. In spite of the rosé's mounting buzz, I finally put it all together. Something aristocratic, as well as the man's very casualness, betrayed the highborn. Yes, yes: a couple of years earlier, a feature in *Town and Country* had caught my attention. The lead photo pictured a beautiful young girl, smiling a dimpled smile, strolling on the terrace of a castle in Provence, arm in arm with her fiancé. She was, told the story, the daughter of a great house, niece of a duke, and a budding concert pianist; he, the scion of the royal house of a neighboring European country. Although his father had, a decade or so earlier, lost his throne to a military takeover or some such political upheaval, *he* was still very much royalty. The wedding held at the Provence castle—the same one looming above and that I recognized from the images I had seen then—had gathered crowned and uncrowned heads, as well as the entire population of the village.

Festivities had culminated in farandoles in the meadow below, and fireworks that lit up the Luberon valley.

Given the uncertainties of politics, the man sitting now on my kitchen stoop, refilling my glass once more, stood in immediate line to a throne, and might very well, one day, become king in succession to his father. Impossible? Not if the citizens of his country tired of the military junta, or whatever system that governed them without the glamour of a royal court, and decided it would be more exciting to possess, once more, their own king and queen, princes and princesses, to enliven the pages of their tabloids, rather than having to rely on England and others for tales of princely scandal.

How does one behave in the presence of royalty? I guessed one, at least, gets off the kitchen floor, and I did. He looked up.

"What's the matter? You don't care for the rosé?"

I don't know how to curtsy. In any case, it would be hard to do in the direction of someone sitting on the floor.

"Monseigneur, Your Highness," I stammered, "I don't feel I should remain seated in the presence of a man who could be king." He laughed wholeheartedly.

"*C'est pas demain la veille,* That's not for tomorrow, or even the day after, so you can't very well remain standing until it happens. You'll have to sit down sometime. By the way, in French my name is Louis."

I told him my name.

"I know," he replied. "I understand you've been expected and everybody is curious. No one, though, would have had the nerve to barge in on you the way I did."

The piano, which had stopped playing for a moment, resumed its freshet of notes.

"Noise pollution?" he winked. "If it bothers you, I can tell my wife to close the window. She is practicing for a Chopin concert tour in the fall." He smiled. "And I'm told she's the best." No wonder that a moment earlier I had stood enthralled.

And then, he was ready to leave.

"By the way," he added, "I must not forget I was sent here on an errand. My wife's aunt, the duchess, would like to have you and your husband as her guests, for déjeuner at the château, a week from Wednesday. Quite informal, mostly family. I do hope you can come—and happy days in the Luberon," he concluded, pouring the last of the rosé into our glasses. Then he bent low over my hand again, and walked out, whistling along with the piano.

Call me a snob, but I felt there should be glass slippers on my feet instead of sandals, and the rosé did nothing to dispel the feeling that I had stepped through the rabbit hole, right into some fairy tale.

I was still shaking my head, trying to stop the spin of the rosé (No, I thought, I couldn't possibly be *drunk*. It's just a pleasant little lilt), when the kitchen door opened again. The prince back so soon? I should have at least fixed my hair. No. A small white truck had pulled up in the narrow, one-way street in front of our house. The word *Sanitation* under the lion coat-of-arms indicated this must be the municipal garbage conveyance. A florid-faced, stocky man in a béret, a Gauloise stuck in the corner of his lips, was standing in the doorway. He touched his béret, shook my hand, and informed me that he, Monsieur Bérange, with the assistance of a young helper (who didn't seem allowed off the truck), handled matters of garbage collection and public sanitation. He had noticed our *volets*, shutters, were open, therefore we were in residence and would need garbage pickup.

"We come by every other day, early A.M. Leave your *ordures* outside in a tightly lidded can, otherwise roaming cats and dogs will spill it all over, and, with the steep slope, empty cans and such roll all the way down to the lower village."

As I was thanking him, the arrival of Wayne's rental truck caused a major traffic jam in the narrow passage, and required a great deal of expert maneuvering on the part of both him and Monsieur Bérange. The latter came back inside, clearly to meet the man of the house and ascertain his message would be competently received.

On his way back, Wayne had stopped at a market to purchase emergency supplies, and when he put the grocery bags on the counter, Monsieur Bérange noticed the neck of a pastis bottle (the Provence aperitif of choice) sticking out.

"Getting pretty close to aperitif time," he remarked pointedly. Wayne, quickly picking up on local mores, rinsed the two jam jars. In each, he poured an inch of pastis, and filled them at the tap.

"I see you like your pastis light, just the way I do *sometimes*, like when I am working," commented Monsieur Bérange. They clinked glasses, and Monsieur Bérange, politely touching his béret in my direction again, drained his. Getting the hint, Wayne poured refills, with a good two inches of pastis this time.

"Whoa!" cautioned M. Bérange. "You want to make me drink like an *Américain?*" Nonetheless, he drained his second drink, smacked his lips, shook hands all around, and departed, assuring us he was *"A votre service."* No one had invited me to join in the libation, this was strictly a men's affair. Well-bred ladies don't quaff drinks with men in the kitchen. Unless, I thought smugly, it happens to be in the company of a prince. Just the same, my head was by now spinning fast, I seemed to have trouble standing quite straight, and, to tell the truth, was in no need whatsoever of a belt.

I couldn't wait to tell Wayne my story, which he just wouldn't believe. Jet-lagged, an inveterate light drinker—if drinker at all—quite unused to stiff drinks on an empty stomach at eleven A.M., his eyes were unfocused, he weaved on his feet, stood definitely off-kilter, and grabbed the counter for balance. I insisted:

"I'm trying to tell you that a prince came by this morning. He brought a jug of rosé and . . ."

"A jug of rosé? You drank rosé all morning?"

"No, not *all* morning. Just a few glasses, *I think.*"

"No wonder you look drunk."

"But listen, Wayne. He was a prince. He said . . ."

"You have to be very, very drunk," said Wayne severely. "Very, *very* drunk. A prince? That was *not* a prince. It was the garbage collector. I saw him. He just left."

And this is how we ended up laughing a lot, and sleeping off our liquor all afternoon. We woke up at six, sobered up and ravenous.

"Not just ravenous," yawned Wayne, pushing hair out of his eyes. "I am thirsty, too."

"A hair of the dog?" I teased, fully expecting a sermon on the evil of drink from my usually abstemious husband. I didn't know Provence was already weaving its spell, opening him to better enjoyment of each passing moment.

"As a matter of fact . . . no pastis, though, tonight. I'll leave that for earlier hours of the day. Tell you what: I'll fix us a *kir* while you get ready. Then, we'll go out to dinner someplace. I bet we won't have far to go to find good food. Now, hurry up, will you?"

Under the cool spray of the shower, I kept wondering whether or not I had had the visit of a prince that morning. One thing seemed clear, though: Chance had brought us to a place that might just be holding in store something very much like magic.

At aperitif time, drink pastis or . . .

The Kir *and Its Variations*

Aperitif is the before-meal drink that is supposed to stimulate the appetite, and while pastis is widely consumed in Provence, *kir* is served there, too, as well as everywhere else.

When Chanoine (Canon) Kir was elected mayor of Dijon, he saw it as his duty to promote the region's best products: Burgundy wine and cassis. Cassis (blackcurrant) is the berry that ripens on bushes widely cultivated in Burgundy. So he created a delicious drink of white Burgundy wine and cassis liqueur, the *kir*, which took the name of its inventor.

TO MAKE A CLASSIC KIR

In a footed wine glass, pour a generous tablespoon of crème de cassis. Fill to 3/4 with very cool, white Burgundy wine. (Chardonnay makes an excellent *kir*.)

THE KIR ROYAL

Use tulip or champagne flute glasses that you've kept in the freezer so they'll frost nicely. Pour in the cassis and fill with very cold champagne.

VARIATIONS ON THE KIR

L'apéritif maison (the house aperitif). In a good restaurant, one should ask: "Do you have an *apéritif maison?*" Many do, and it is often a variation on the *kir*.

In the Luberon, L'Auberge de L'Aiguebrun serves a combination of champagne and *fraise des bois* (wild strawberry) liqueur. In Châteauneuf-du-Pape, L'Hostellerie des Fines-Roches, a wine estate, uses peach liqueur. Our friends from Memphis, Tennessee, were hesitant at first (too sweet?) and ended up by stopping on the way back to buy champagne and a bottle of the same peach liqueur.

They thought the drink would go well for breakfast the next day, "for openers."

Roger Vergé, chef at the renowned Moulin de Mougins, suggests using *white vermouth* instead of wine, with raspberry liqueur.

A BISTRO KIR

The cardinal is made of *red* wine and cassis, served in heavy, bistro-type glasses. People who do not care for white wine or champagne may order a cardinal.

We Bought a House
in Provence!

W e live and work in California. Yet, almost inadvertently, we bought and restored a ruined house in a hilltop village of Provence. This left us as surprised as anybody else.

Just a year before, we had completed an assignment that had sent us to Aix-en-Provence for nearly a year. We didn't really know the region, as we'd driven through only a few times on our way to the Riviera, where, I must admit, a little of the ambient charm dissipated each year with the ever-growing crowds and traffic fumes. Oh, we had enjoyed the cool respite of *platane*-shaded roads, glimpsed rocky landscapes, crossed ancient cities, and sat for moments at cafés spilling their flowerlike umbrellas onto sidewalks. But we had not lingered—except for a brief assignment under a murderous sun. We had never experienced Provence, never shared in its life.

Provence? *The Provences*, rather, for the region has many faces. The fishing villages of the coast nestle in coves on an eternal Mediterranean, the "wine-colored sea," where sailed Homer's heroes. Resorts today though they may be, they still retain their village life, and locals sit, on summer evenings, on benches lining the quays. As for the cities, bustling as they are, they take pride in the glory imparted by their Roman conquerors: The ancient capital of Arles snuggles around its massive arena, still very much in use today for events such as bullfights. Well before even the Roman conquest, the Greeks had their trading posts there: Marseille was the sixth-century B.C. *Massilia* of the Phocaeans; Antibes—*Antipolis*—was thus named because it stood *before*, and protected the *polis*, the "city" of Nice, whose patron was Nike, goddess of victory.

There is rocky Provence, a sere land pierced by the bleached bones of its mountain range, the Alpilles, the little Alps. There is the Provence of high plateaus, where lavender fields spread their blue haze as far as the eye can see, for true lavender will not flourish below a fifteen-hundred-foot elevation (the lesser *lavandin*, on the other hand, will bloom anywhere). In the Provence of orchards, extravagant peaches and apricots ripen in orgies of sunshine. Don't forget the Provence of vineyards, where the *côtes*, the slopes of the Rhône Valley, produce the heady wines of Côtes-du-

Rhône, of which Châteauneuf-du-Pape is the most prized. In the Provence of gardens, early vegetables brave winter, purple stalks of asparagus poke through the ground in February, and the small Cavaillon cantaloupe perfumes summer meals with its pervading aroma. Today, sunflower fields—a rich cash crop—spread everywhere. The high-yield hybrids that turn their faces *away* from the sun (and not toward it, contrary to popular belief—we know, we have *watched* them, hiding inside our car) do not much resemble the wild, disheveled *tournesols* of Van Gogh's time.

And then, *then*, there are the perched villages, *les villages perchés*, which crown hilltops or spill down mountain slopes. Hard of access, they were built a thousand years ago by villagers seeking protection from the sudden terror of raids launched by Barbary Coast—now North Africa—pirates come from the sea.

The perched villages I discovered enchanted me; imagine them, clinging to their vantage points, huddles of pale tiles baked by centuries of sun. Fortifications encircled them. Their castle stood at the top, its keep the highest lookout point. Their church would ring the hours of prayer and toll the alarm in time of attack. Alas, although from a distance they had seemed fairly intact, a closer look revealed castles in ruins, silent churches, abandoned homes, rubble-obstructed pathways.

Danger of pirates long gone, it is no wonder that younger generations chose to build, instead, more comfortable homes in their fields down below. For the triple protection of ramparts, castle, and church had exacted a price: little living space, a long walk down in the morning, and, after an exhausting work day, the climb back, carrying heavy tools, in the face of a hot evening sun or the teeth of the mistral wind. So, as old parents died, their children removed supporting beams from roofs—a ploy that renders a house uninhabitable, and therefore free of taxes— and let the weather do the rest. They could, meanwhile, raise *their* own children in the comparative comfort of newer valley homes, with plenty of space around.

In spite of the desolation, I never tired of exploring the winding, narrow streets that lead to the heart of these villages, saddened every time to find decaying facades, crumbling masonry, caved-in roofs. Only a few houses remained occupied. And yet, signs of renewal already appeared: Rising among the ruins, a few beautifully restored homes, most often owned by foreigners, proved the villages' decline would soon be reversed.

I often wondered what it would be like to live in one of those self-contained villages that reminded me more of an organic structure, like a coral accretion, than of architecture. I fantasized looking down through one of those small windows set into thick walls—double protection against sun and wind—at a landscape of vineyards, olive groves, and sunflower fields. Or else, it would be the myriad hues of lavender fields, for the many varieties each produce a different tint. Would I grow frustrated, failing to find words better than those that mean mauve, purple, and blue, trying to name their hazy undulations? These thoughts, however, were never more than a passing reverie, for we *did* have a home already, and in a very different setting: by the Pacific Ocean, in Malibu, California. Still, the thought of life on a hilltop of Provence, fluttering in my subconscious, must have taken root there.

Living for ten months in the lively city of Aix-en-Provence was a rich experience. Most precious, we made friends there, such good friends that we knew it would be hard to leave them behind when the time came. Like Bill Hope, who signed his name *Bilope*, to reflect the French pronunciation, which ignores the *h* of *Hope*. Bill was an expatriate American, originally from the Deep South, a character that might have stepped out of Tennessee Williams or Truman Capote. Bill, who first came to Provence as a student and returned there to live—and die, as he eventually did. A poet and a musicologist, fervent afficionado of the opera, ready to fight anyone who failed to recognize Rosa Ponselle as the only true diva, he gave spine-tingling readings of Poe's *The Raven* and *Annabelle Lee* and imparted a Black Southern rhythm to the lines of Langston Hughes. He lived in a former monastery, more or less converted into apartments.

The first time we met, he invited us there.

"Come over some evening, around sunset. I'll make you my famous Manhattans, and show you the Cézanne on my balcony."

Bill's balcony, rather a wide stone terrace, faced full onto the Montagne Sainte-Victoire so often painted by Cézanne. The pyramidlike mountain filled the horizon, and we watched it pale from gold to ethereal azure as night fell. It felt, indeed, like stepping right into a Cézanne canvas.

Bill, associated with the Marseille opera as a music consultant, disposed of tickets for Sunday matinees. We'd never spent such music-filled winter afternoons. We saw *Faust*, *Carmen*, *Un ballo in maschera*, *Madama Butterfly*, and *Pagliacci*. Light operas, too: *Die Fledermaus* and *Der Rosenkavalier*. For *Ciboulette*, the director brought onstage a live donkey, a lobster, chickens, rabbits, and doves as part of the cast. After the show, we went for bouillabaisse or calzone in a little dive behind the theater where artists gathered after the show, and drove home in the dark, Wayne whistling, completely *on* key, his best-remembered arias. We often commented that Sunday afternoons back home loomed hopelessly dull in comparison. Paying bills and answering neglected mail, our usual pastime, would offer no match.

And then, it was in Provence that life brought me one of the best gifts ever: A true friend. Elisabeth embodies all the charm, the warmth, the heartfelt generosity of the land. Wayne, who always shortens names, immediately declared her to be *Liz*. I found in Liz the sister I never had, the best friend I dared not seek. Parting would create a painful void. Yet, we were resigned to the inevitable departure, even if we made vague plans to return to Provence "some day."

On our last day in Aix, we had decided to leave in the evening and drive all night to Paris to catch our plane home there, avoiding both traffic and daytime heat. Equipment was packed and the last piece of luggage snapped shut. Liz and I embraced, in tears, and Bill, for lack of anything to say, scolded everybody. Our friends gone, Wayne took the car in for service, and I remained alone for a few hours.

So, feeling very blue, and trying to make the best, somehow, of these last moments, I walked for the last time to the lovely Cours Mirabeau, sadly conscious I'd soon be gone from the town where I was leaving a part of my heart.

Cours Mirabeau is the enchanting center of life in Aix-en-Provence, a broad avenue shaded by a double row of stately *platanes* that form a cathedral arch overhead. Gurgling moss-encrusted fountains stand at intervals, dispensing thermal water. Cafés crowd on the left side, thronged with tourists and students, many students, for this is an ancient university town.

But instead of sitting for a leisurely, people-watching drink, as I had done many times before, I found myself walking, with unconscious purposefulness, onto the *right* side of the street, where no cafés spill onto the sidewalks. Only banks, offices, a few shops, line the Cours there. Before I knew it, I had stepped into the Agence des Thermes, a real estate firm I had never noticed before. To my complete stupefaction, I heard my own voice asking:

"Do you have any houses for sale? In a hilltop village?"

What in the world possessed me? We were leaving in three hours, with no prospect of ever relocating here, or even *returning* in the foreseeable future. I tried to reassure myself this must be a game I was playing.

"A hilltop village house?" breathed the realtor behind the desk. "Aren't you lucky! We happen to list something charming in Ventabren. Should be just right for *you*." We had been to Ventabren once, a picturesque village clinging to a hilltop between Aix and Marseille. Because of its proximity to two large cities, this one had been *overly* restored, leaning heavily to fake rustic and kitschy antique shops. "You'll love this house," enthused the lady. "There's even an American bar in the basement."

We're not buying anything, I told myself. Still, why not go look? It's not dinnertime yet. A phone call brought a puzzled Wayne, who generously chose to humor me, rather than embarrass me in front of the lady realtor.

Throngs of Marseillais cars were climbing to Ventabren like an ant caravan, jamming the winding road to the village. "Friday night," explained the lady. "They come here for the weekend, and you'll see, it's real lively, just like America, I guess."

Sure enough, rock blared from several sources, and a heavy-metal beat underscored Sammy Hagar's shouted warning of a *Danger Zone*. "It gets even better by Saturday night," promised the lady.

The house? Well, it *was* old, and certainly had been lovingly, if not wisely, restored. I counted ten different flowered wallpapers before I lost track, and so much fake Louis the Fifteenth woodwork that you'd have to tear down the whole place to get rid of it all. The terrace, way on top, could be lovely, once cleared of its plastic fountain and ceramic dwarfs, if you didn't mind climbing up three steep flights of stairs to reach it. As for the view, it boasted an unobstructed vista of the Marseille oil refineries, spewing smoke in the distance. I was waiting for the realtor to point out: "Just like America!" but she was already dragging Wayne downstairs.

The stone vaulted rooms over which the house was built had been cemented over, plastered, and painted a shiny brown, with lines drawn in green and black, hopefully suggesting a log cabin. Swinging saloon doors led to a "real American Western bar," complete with upturned whisky bottles. I knew perfectly well my mind harbored no intention *whatsoever* to buy. Why, then, was I getting almost angry?

"I'm afraid I don't understand what it is you might want," sighed the lady, puzzled and disappointed, on the way back to Aix. No wonder, we don't want *anything*, I thought. Now, Wayne, who is kind, is going to thank her and apologize. We'll say good-bye, and ouch, I'll be left to explain exactly what bit me.

To my surprise, I found that by now, *he* was leading the game.

"Don't you have anything else to show us?" he asked eagerly, oblivious to my kicks to his ankles.

"Nothing as perfect as that, especially for *Americans*," she repeated, perhaps aware by now that we weren't serious buyers. After a long silence, she added:

"There's a woman, in a village of the Luberon mountains, about half an hour from Aix, who restores ruined houses. We sold a few for her. She is a *maître d'oeuvre*, something between a contractor and an architect. You might ask her, that is, if you are really interested. But I seriously doubt you'll find anything like what I've shown you. And besides, that village is sort of out of the way, very restricted, because of the duke's castle there. No weekend action." She checked her watch. "In any case, it's almost dinnertime, please drop me off at the office. Should you decide to contact that woman, her name is Ariel Arnaz, and anybody in the village can show you where she lives. Well, good night, and good luck. Sorry I couldn't help you."

Now, I cringed, Wayne is really going to tear into me, and I'll have some explaining to do. Instead, to my surprise, he was unfolding his map of the area, and tracing the way to the village the woman had named.

It is true, I remembered, that he has a way of forgetting at times that he is playing a game, and grows so deadly earnest about it that he turns it into reality. *His* reality. I had seen this happen before, as when on the photo assignment, *On the Footsteps of Van Gogh*, he had *become* Van Gogh: lugging heavy equipment, limping from a sprained ankle under Arles's punishing sun, with such a visionary gleam in his eye that I had to threaten to count his ears every night. Now, he was truly *looking* for a house to buy and perhaps even *hoping* to find one. One of us would have to regain some grip on our true purpose. For, whatever that was, it certainly did *not* involve buying a house in Provence.

The realtor had no sooner stepped out of the car than we were fighting our way out of town through the evening traffic, to find ourselves, after a few miles, on a highway that soon led us to a narrow, almost deserted country road. It wound its way through vineyards and sunflower fields, into the foothills of the Luberon range.

As we rounded the top of a rise, the village appeared in the distance, small and golden against the purple mountains, a sight that took my breath away. A perfect self-contained jewel of a village, huddled on its own small peak, spilled its cascade of roofs down the slope. A majestic castle crowned it, windows aflame in the setting sun. "A living sculpture," murmured Wayne, always more poetic than I am. Why hadn't we come here before, during our months of exploring the region? Because it is removed from any main road? Doesn't harbor a recommended restaurant? Now, for some reason I couldn't understand, I felt I had come *home.* Home, in the absolute, Biblical sense of the word.

After we drove through the archway entrance and negotiated the narrow street that winds its way up, up to the Place du Château, it was easy to find Madame Arnaz's house. Smiling, she answered our unexpected knock, small and vivid in a narrow sheath dress, hair pulled back and tied with a silk scarf, a true Frenchwoman, in spite of her Spanish-sounding last name (due, we would learn later, to a remote Castilian ancestor).

She listened to Wayne's enquiry and shook her head.

"I am sorry you came all the way here, when there's nothing for sale in the village that you might want. Oh, there are ruins, plenty of them! Old folks die one by one. . . . Only last week we buried the widow Martin who cooked the school lunches. . . ." She stopped. "Wait! There might be just the place for you, after all. I heard it's for sale for next to nothing. A hovel, of course, but the location is marvelous and it could be restored into a lovely home. I'll show you."

At that point, I was going to interrupt her and confess we felt guilty taking up her time, since we weren't about to buy a house, let alone *restore* one. Why, we lived at the other end of the planet, might never even come back this way again. But Wayne was eagerly following her footsteps as she walked along. She pointed to a soaring watchtower, and we passed a massive, crenellated gateway closed by an iron portcullis, a *herse*, I learned, the vertically lowered gate that defends the entrance to a drawbridge.

"Not long ago, the duke and duchess celebrated the thousand years their family has owned the castle. The duke passed away since, but the duchess lives here most of the time. Her children visit during the summers, as well as many guests and relatives." We gazed in awe at the high, terraced battlements.

The widow Martin's abode proved *much* less impressive. Mean little rooms, two of them sharing a single window, a ruined terrace in front garlanded with crumpled chicken wire, shaded by a corrugated plastic awning held askew by two crooked poles. Boards leaning against the walls prevented more stones from rolling downhill. A sprung roof sank over a crumbling attic.

The whole wretched thing had been built centuries ago—the date 1539 was engraved on the lintel—above something even older, which must have long served as the village dump. A few goats now living there poked out their noses, bleating plaintively, and I fed them a handful of weeds growing underfoot. Wayne looked crestfallen. Meanwhile, Madame Arnaz, following her own thoughts, was drawing pictures in the air with small, expressive hands.

"As you can see, this is the best location in the village, right at the foot of the castle and overlooking the valley below, just like the prow of a ship. I suspect these goats are luxuriating in what must have been, at one time, the guard-room of the castle. After removing at least twenty truck-loads of muck, you'll find this peasant home was erected right over medieval stone-vaulted rooms."

"How would you know that?" asked Wayne, hopefully, I swear.

"These are common in places like this," she explained. "In fact, most of this village is built over such *voûtes*. These originated as quarries, dug out to obtain stone when the Romans erected the original *castrum*. Later, they were walled over and reinforced, their ceilings curved into Romanesque arches, to serve as storage and habitation for both the castle's garrison and the villagers.

She paused for an instant, then went on animatedly: "As for the house itself, we'll raise the roof, so you can have a second story instead of that miserable, half-caved-in attic. That pile of rocks in front will become a terrace again, your summer dining-room. I can just see it now." She eyed me suspiciously:

"Can you think in three dimensions?"

I shook my head helplessly: No. Ariel frowned:

"In matters of houses," she declared impatiently, "you *have* to think in three dimensions."

Wayne, for his part, was too spellbound to think, in any number of dimensions. He handed Madame Arnaz his pen and an old envelope. She went on speaking, drawing lines and squares:

"See? That's how it would look. I'm sure you can visual-ize it." I shook my head again, but she paid no attention, and instead beckoned us to follow.

"Look this way. While you're at it, you should buy this, too." She was pointing to a gaping space adjoining the house, half-filled with unidentifiable ruins.

"This used to be a *jas*, a sheep farm. The sheep lived downstairs and the shepherd above, in two rooms, with a terrace for drying herbs and skins. Now, the lower part could become a garage, with a great arched doorway. The floor above, we'd rebuild into a two-bedroom guest apartment fronting onto a sunning terrace.

"We'd break open the wall to unite the two parts. Quite a job: it looks to be at least five feet thick." More cabalistic gestures, more scribbles on the envelope.

"Do you feel it would be just right for you?"

My God, I thought, *who* will have the nerve to tell her we're *not* buying anything? We're *leaving* tonight, that's all we are doing.

"How long would it take to complete the work?" enquired Wayne.

"When are you planning to come back?"

Without blinking or missing a beat, Wayne replied:

"Next year, in June." (*What?* I never knew we were coming back at all, let alone next June. Perhaps we even have a *day?*)

"June fifth," specified Wayne, reading my thoughts.

"It would be finished."

"Now," said Wayne, "since you know the price of both properties, and the cost of the restoration work, can you give me a bottom line figure, all inclusive, ready to move in?"

The figure she quoted, after a moment's reflection, seemed quite reasonable, perhaps even within reach. In fact, it wouldn't even buy a one-bedroom condo in Los Angeles. . . . Oh, no, this is too ridiculous. What are we doing here?

Before Wayne could go any further, making it even harder to extricate ourselves, I stepped in:

"You understand, Madame, that this is quite sudden, and we'll need time to think it over." I was trying to soften the blow of our refusal. "We're leaving tonight, and we'll write you from the U.S. to let you know our decision. We *do* live very far away, it would hardly be a practical purchase for us." Indeed, I thought, we've already rejected the idea of a vacation home in Palm Springs, a two-hour drive away, as too far to drive on a regular basis.

We walked back to Madame Arnaz's home. Through her kitchen window we could glimpse her garden, where a cherry tree bent, so loaded with glistening dark-red fruit that its branches had to be propped up to prevent them from breaking. In the sink, a colander held a few handfuls of the thinnest green beans. A garlic braid hung on the wall. Unaccountably, I wanted to taste those cherries, and those beans, lightly cooked, flavored with fresh garlic, more than any food before. . . . Instead, I asked for a glass of water. She drew it from the faucet.

The water tasted startlingly pure. I drank religiously, handed the glass to Wayne. "Mystical," he said.

This is probably when the decision was made, at some deep subconscious level, and well before we knew about it.

I hurried the parting, and soon we were, in the gathering dusk, driving toward the freeway. A backward glance showed the village outline. Suddenly, as in a sign meant for us, an invisible switch was turned on, and the dark mass of the castle became illuminated, bewitched into an ethereal presence floating above a dark pedestal.

We stopped for dinner in Pertuis, the little market town that would be our shopping center if . . . I brushed the thought away as too ridiculous to dwell upon. Wayne scribbled figures on the paper tablecloth, absorbed and forgetting to eat.

During the long drive to Paris, we spoke little, and, next day, sitting in the airport waiting lounge, he suddenly stood up and walked away, to return with a postcard and a stamp.

"Here," he told me.

"Here what?"

"Don't you want to write a note to Madame A., telling her it's a deal? Isn't that what you want?"

I don't remember whether or not I hesitated, but I know the card was mailed that day from Charles de Gaulle Airport. Perhaps we'd fallen into debt, but much more important, fallen into something very much like love.

Back home, I filled pages of a yellow-lined pad with figures. After terms were agreed upon, we were left to stop our ears against the dire predictions of family and friends.

In October, a letter from Ariel—on a first-name basis now—informed us that work was progressing: The goats had found another home, and, just as she had sensed, cleared of all the muck, great vaulted arches were revealed. They formed a succession of three grandiose rooms, the last one completely hewn out of rock. "Once cleaned, the stones showed the rosy-blond color of local rock. And a date scratched on a broken lintel reads 1185."

In November, she reported that the house above was coming into shape. The ghost of the widow Martin, should it return, would never recognize the newly emerging rooms. The country kitchen, with its bread-baking oven, was left structurally unchanged, but antique doors found by Ariel would close the cupboards and hide from view both refrigerator and dishwasher, as required by the Office of Fine Arts in Avignon, who apparently kept a watchful eye on all restorations. A small annex kitchen would hold the freezer chest, a sink, and shelves for canning and jam-making, O! fantasies of cherry preserves. A mantel, contrived from a piece of sculpted wood, would top the fireplace. "Under the ruined ceiling, we found authentic lath and plaster, at least three hundred years old." Later: "You'll love your bedroom. A pair of French doors opens onto another terrace I was able to add. Lovely for breakfast." Later yet: "A village artisan made tile for the master bath—hand-glazed turquoise mosaic. Instead of a boring tub, we're building one of the same mosaic. And, oh, yes, I discovered the perfect pewter sink in a demolition yard."

Meanwhile, the mounting chorus of our friends and relatives was warning us: "Don't you believe a word of what you're told! Everyone has heard horror stories about enterprises of this kind. Nothing is done right, you'll find sinks installed at knee level and doors finished in yellow marine varnish." In one extreme case, reported in a magazine clipping pushed under our noses, the contractor neglected to install plumbing and electrical lines. Or else: "You'll arrive to find very little work done, and piles of materials lying about. You'll be told that's where your money went, and that more, much more, funds are needed if you want a finished project. And how about that case where all the work was done on property that hadn't been properly acquired under French law? How do you know she even *bought* that ruin?"

All agreed that, at best, we were in for a nasty shock one way or the other. "You'll discover the price you're paying didn't include a roof, or some such. The French are notorious for that kind of scam. You must admit they'd have to be *angels* to resist the temptation to cheat, with owners as naive and trusting, and so far away."

Yet, we could detect, beyond claimed sympathy for our impending discomfiture, the vague, or perhaps not so vague, hope that they might come over and check for themselves how bad things really were in that village. Stay a few days, a week, maybe?

By Christmas, scribbled on a greeting card:

"Remember that half-empty place, next to your house? According to the plans you approved (on the back of that envelope?) you will have a garage, with a big arched portal. This is rising now. And before going further, it has occurred to me that you might like a pool, a mini-pool, on the terrace above. Nice to cool off after sunbathing. My men can carve a little fountain, so you'd have the sound of tinkling water. Your guests might enjoy that, since the two guest rooms open directly onto the terrace. Of course, there'll be planters all around, which I'll fill with dwarf cypresses and geraniums."

Next, Ariel wondered: Since U.S.–made filters were the best, but terribly expensive in France, could we ship one over. Wayne could only find a regular-power type, fit for a good-sized pool, so our mini would bubble and swirl like a Jacuzzi.

Where, O! where is the catch? "You'll find out soon enough," predicted our friends, "and you won't be amused. Surely a great story to tell later, *much* later. Meanwhile, we promise not to laugh when we come over to see how you're doing. Did you say *two* guest rooms?"

No news for several months. Meanwhile, we dutifully sent our final payment according to schedule. We also made plans to take delivery of a small Renault car in Paris, on June fourth.

Finally, in May, a note, with a fabric sample: "Two walls of the living room will remain stone. I thought of covering the others with this tweed. It is woven out of rough fleece yarn by a local hippie, turned *tisserand*. And while I am at it I could have forms cut out of polyurethane for a pair of couches and fireside chairs. Very comfortable. I'll cover them in the same tweed. That way, your room won't look cluttered. And you'll be able to sit down, at least, the moment you arrive."

(God bless you, Ariel, but you can't be for real. There *has* to be a catch somewhere.)

———

A few days later, a postcard: "I've been looking for a few pieces of antique furniture in scale with your rooms. I'll have the dealers put them in place. If you like them, you can buy directly from them. If not, they'll take them back. None are expensive. All will be ready for your arrival."

And finally, *the day* was there. We flew to Paris, picked up our Renault. It looked like a Disney-designed, friendly, crouching little animal. The color we'd picked, as the most Provençal-looking one, was called *Chipper Orange* in the catalog. So, it became Chipper, a good name for a modestly powered but spunky little car, which purred down L'Autoroute du Soleil.

We rounded the top of the hill in the summer evening light, just as we had a year earlier to see the village suddenly revealed, profiled in its jewel-like perfection by the setting sun. My throat tightened: We had a home there now. We were coming *home*. Wayne took my hand. "I'd forgotten how beautiful it really is," he murmured to himself.

We drove past the stately plane trees and the flower gardens of the château, entered the village through its archway. The new sign limiting access to *riverains*, residents? It meant *us!* We were indeed *riverains* here, unless we'd dreamt it all. Chipper growled bravely up the narrow street named Grande Rue that leads to the high village.

The house was there, finished, perfect, and I started to cry. We could see the blue light of the pool reflected in the dwarf cypresses of the terrace. An exquisite jewel of a home, both very old and quite new, with all its lights on for us. A fountain *did* splash into the pool. The linens I had sent from California were in place, towels draped in the turquoise bath. Champagne cooled in a bucket.

I cried and laughed, my heart bursting. Wayne turned lights on and off, opened doors, checked the interior of closets. Was he perhaps looking for the catch and not finding it?

We walked up and down, exploring the three levels: the cool, noble, vaulted rooms down below, the country kitchen, living room and dining space above, with master bedroom and study on the top floor. Through the newly pierced door—yes, the wall turned out to be at least five feet thick!—we penetrated the guest wing, and found two bedrooms and a bath, complete with an amusing fresco decorating a blind wall. It showed what the view would be, should the wall not be there. Ariel, I remembered, had mentioned something about an artist friend of hers. All was finished, ready to be lived in.

"Box springs and mattresses are more useful there than in my storage. Return them when you've replaced them. Curtains and bedspreads? I made them myself," explained Ariel later. "I'll tell you how much the fabric cost as soon as I find the bill. Labor? I thought we were friends."

We picnicked on the terrace, on fragrant cantaloupe, sliced salami, a jar of *tapenade*, and a baguette we'd bought along the way. The champagne? We poured some in the pool and drank the rest, standing waist-deep in the luminous water and hugging a great deal.

Later, we slipped between pale sheets and slept to the cicadas' sawing melody and the muted crowing of roosters, to awaken to brilliant sunshine and the visit of a prince.

Other foreigners who moved in later were less fortunate, and their house-restoring experiences, far from dreamlike, took on the features of a nightmare instead. So, our California friends were right, after all. The worst could, and *did* happen. But they were right, too, when they predicted that, given a few years, all these new village homeowners would laugh heartily about their misadventures. Especially at cocktail time, on their *terrasses* overlooking the mauve Luberon.

But for us, as the years pass, this dream of a house and of the village around it we haven't awakened from yet. The catch? There was no catch. As inadvertently as we'd bought the house, we'd tapped into Ariel's wellspring of taste, talent, and generosity. Innocents that we were, we'd had the rare luck to chance upon such a priceless offering.

The salsa of Provence . . .

Tapenade

  Tapenade (from the Provençal word for *capers*) is used very much like salsa in the United States. It was created, more than a hundred years ago, in a Marseille restaurant called La Maison Dorée. It keeps well in the refrigerator, so you can make it in double batches.

I cup pitted black olives, coarsely chopped
I 3-ounce can tuna, packed in oil or water, drained
I can flat fillets of anchovies, cut in pieces
2 Tbs Dijon mustard
$^2/_3$ cup capers
3 Tbs wine vinegar
I ounce brandy (optional)
Black pepper
Hot sauce (optional)
Olive oil

Place all ingredients except olive oil in mixer, and pulse just long enough to obtain a coarse paste (not quite a puree). Remove to a bowl. Add a little oil, a few drops at a time, until your *tapenade* is smooth enough to spread.

Use *tapenade* at aperitif time, on toasted, buttered baguette slices or crackers; or to fill celery sticks; as a filling for hardboiled eggs, mixed with the yolks; or (add a little more oil) as a vegetable dip. Offer it also as a condiment with cold meats. (You'll probably think of other uses.)

Days of Pastis
and Lavender

By July, lavender (or rather *lavandin*, but the two are hard to tell apart) planted in great clumps on the terrace has already put out long spikes. A few days later, these are tipped with ears of violet blue, intensely aromatic, rugged little flowers, whose perfume begins to rise under the morning sun and wafts through our open window.

We know bread was baked earlier, in the lower village bakery. We could smell it just about the time the six peals of the belfry bell rang out. We also know one should not tarry too long before the croissant run, for by eight, they'll all be gone. The baker still hasn't adjusted to the influx of newcomers like us who are beginning to descend upon the village, so his output remains stubbornly too low.

Walking barefoot on the terra-cotta floors, Wayne brews espresso on a machine imported from Italy to California, that he, in turn, shipped to Provence. The espresso machine's travels could have been considerably shortened, since here we are not much more than a hundred miles from Italy. But such are today's wasteful ways. Sitting on our terrace we sip, and scatter croissant crumbs for insistent sparrows, who scoop them right off the table. On a nearby tower, one of the few still standing out of the fortification's original twenty-two, a pair of magpies raucously yells at us greetings, or, more likely, warnings. A calico cat sits on the very edge of the overhanging roof and stares down at us with total concentration.

Yet, breakfast can be only so languid, for there are inflexible rules to be learned. Everything will close down at noon sharp, except food stores, which *may* remain open a little longer: shops, post office, gas stations, garages, city hall, banks will shut tight, since their employees shall be going home for *déjeuner*. And *déjeuner*, as practiced in France, holds nothing in common with what we Americans know as lunch. Some places will re-open around two, or two-thirty, or three, some not until four, and others not at all. So, all errands should be completed before closing time, and if you have plans for the afternoon, or guests over for dinner, get going before it is too late. Besides, nobody wants to miss out on the best part of the morning in town: the hours devoted to food shopping.

In Pertuis, our nearby shopping *bourg*, the streets are hosed down in the early A.M., so they stay wet and cool all morning. Doors are wide open for business, and great displays of fruit and vegetables crowd the sidewalks: lush tomatoes picked with their vine; tightly bunched pink radishes; varnished *courgettes*; new onions like white jade veined in celadon; strawberries glowing scarlet; and the small, musky cantaloupes with an aroma you can smell from the end of the street.

Bakeries are crowded, because the second batch of the day has just come out of the oven, and everyone is stocking up for the day, carrying away baguettes and *ficelles*, the thinner, crustier version of the baguette, in a thousand imaginative ways: tucked across a baby carriage; strapped over a backpack; firmly grasped with a briefcase handle; or brandished like a conductor's baton, the better to point to a direction, or stress a point in conversation.

In the *charcuterie*, which, according to an age-old royal edict still in force, is privileged to sell only pork meat and pork-meat products, *jambon de Paris*, cooked ham, and air-dried *jambon de Bayonne* are thinly sliced, giant salami are unhooked from the ceiling with a hooked pole, chunks of pâté are wrapped in wax paper.

We hurry from shop to shop, composing menus as we go. We'll have tomato salad for *déjeuner*, followed by *ravioles de Romans*—tiny goat-cheese raviolis you just dip in boiling water and serve with a touch of butter and cracked pepper—fruit for dessert. Since we expect guests for dinner, we'll need some of the paper-thin *jambon de Bayonne* to drape over slices of cantaloupe, *courgettes* for a gratin, a lamb roast and mesclun salad to drizzle with dark-green olive oil from the village mill. Mesclun is composed of baby leaves of all kinds: lettuce, escarole, arugula, romaine, endive; some sweet and some bitter. We are all set now, except for dessert, and for that, we know exactly where to go.

We return to our car, parked in the parking *payant*, where one always finds plenty of space, since the French prefer to park more creatively—on sidewalks, in front of doors, or even double park on the street—to save a few francs, yes, but much more likely to exercise that Gallic sense of indiscipline that brings zest to their life.

We are already opening our doors, when, from the terrace of the Café Thomas, someone waves energetically and calls out to us. We recognize Monsieur Estain, one of our neighbors, sitting there with a friend he wants us to meet. Everybody shakes hands. Custom demands each man buy a round of drinks, and what would anyone drink near noontime in the summer but pastis?

Bébé, the owner's great white poodle, ambles over to identify these newcomers, gets a sniff and a scratch on the head, then languorously paces over to the next table. The waiter brings a tray with glasses, ice cubes, a carafe of water, and a bottle of pastis. It seems that, sitting in a café, ladies may accept *one* drink with the men. Refusing refills shows good breeding. We beg for a pastis *léger*, just a little of the golden liquor poured in before the glass is filled with water. It is lovely to watch the yellow liquor turn into swirls of milky opal as it mixes with the water, and a strong *anis* aroma fills the nostrils. No *léger*, though, for the natives. The recommended formula is one part pastis to five parts water, but they prefer their own *tassé*, practically half and half.

At other tables, they're having *perroquet*, parrot, the same as ours, but with the addition of a dose of cream of mint. Others tint their pastis red with grenadine: that's a *tomate*. Adding almond syrup, called *orgeat*, makes a *mauresque*. Even so, pastis is never sweet; it remains briskly tart and truly refreshing.

In the middle of a pastis-induced euphoria, I idly observe a young parking officer examining cars, but I fail to connect his interest with any potential problem. As he leans over Chipper, M. Estain calls out: "Eh, Lucien! How about a drink?"

The officer walks over, removes his cap, wipes his brow, shakes hands all around, and sits down. "I wouldn't mind," he allows. "The sun's beating down." He turns to us: "Isn't that your car, over there, by the fountain?"

M. Estain interrupts:

"Lucien is from the village. I've known him since he was that high. His dad and I go hunting together." He turns to Lucien, roughly jocular: "So, you rascal, you found a job, at last? About time, too, I'd say. But don't you go bugging honest people, now. Try and catch some criminals, instead. Plenty of those, I hear. Right here, though, I don't see any crimes being committed."

"Ah, but," stammers Lucien, "it's not crooks that I chase. I am a parking officer. And their car, over there, it's overparked by fifteen minutes." You feed coins into a meter that delivers a ticket stamped with date and time, to be placed on the dashboard. Ours obviously shows overtime.

"What," roars M. Estain, turning red in the face. "And so what? This isn't the Lord's good earth anymore? You have to *pay* to just sit on it now?"

Lucien tries to argue. He's got the law on his side, after all, as well as a job to do. "*They* can sit all they want," he insists, fairly. "It's only their *car*. The parking time has expired. . . ."

Monsieur Estain is now purple with righteous indignation, and makes it abundantly clear that if Lucien, that good-for-nothing strippling, thinks he can bother good, honest *Américains*, yes, the same who landed in Normandy to liberate us in '44, and personally vouched for by Monsieur Estain *lui-même*, he'd better think twice. M. Estain happens to be a municipal councillor, don't you forget, and he'd have only one word to drop in the proper ear to send Lucien right back to unemployment.

We try to protest.

"No, no, Lucien is right. He's only doing his job, nothing personal. Give us the ticket, Lucien, we don't mind at all, we'll pay it. Come on, Lucien."

But M. Estain's hand clamps over my wrist. He's teaching us a lesson in village life and doesn't mind at all displaying, in the process, the awesomeness of his authority. Meanwhile, Lucien's drink arrives, glasses are clinked: "*Santé!*" and M. Estain mock-angrily crams the ticket pad into Lucien's uniform pocket, as Lucien protests he would never give a *contravention* to friends of M. Estain. Now that he knows our car, he'll tell his colleagues to watch for it. . . . By the way, he's heard we're from California. Is it true he looks like Tom Hanks? His girlfriend swears he's a dead ringer.

The resemblance is far from striking at first glance, but now, in profile, I can see something indeed of the character Tom Hanks created in *Forrest Gump*. So, I assure him truthfully that, yes, his girl is right, he does have that certain look about him, especially the right profile.

"Maybe you should go to 'Ollyvood and become a movie star, eh?" suggests M. Estain scornfully. "But you see, these guys, they may *look* dumb, but they're *smart*. So, you're better off here."

No hard feelings. Lucien turns his profile to me even as we shake hands all around. And we rush to Chipper, now over an hour overparked, but unpunished, thanks to powerful protection.

Now, for the dessert run.

A couple of miles out of Pertuis, in the midst of verdant vineyards pruned to manicured perfection, and where fat grape clusters are already taking color, a sign at the corner of a dirt road announces: *Michel Perrière, L'Art Glacier*. This is a clue only initiates could find or follow, but we have already joined the number of those lucky few.

The road is narrow, banked with rosemary bushes; grass grows in the center, leaving a deep rut on either side. Chipper bumps along, scrapes once or twice his low-slung muffler on treacherous rocks or snaky roots, catches sprigs of rosemary in his windshield wipers, until the road finally veers into a spot cleared for parking under tall pines. It faces a lovely house stuccoed in deep ocher, with white shutters and geranium boxes. Outside, in the shade, sits a group of young people, some hulling strawberries, others peeling and slicing ripe peaches from crates piled beside them, filling great white vats with the dripping fruit. They are English and Dutch, they tell us, camping nearby and earning a little vacation money this way.

Michel Perrière and his son are *Maîtres Glaciers*, yes, Masters of Ice Cream—making, for there is indeed such a title, recognized by the government and granted upon completion of demanding courses in nutrition science and, of course, in ice cream—making. Something like an M.B.A., perhaps its acronym could be M.I.C., should such a degree exist in America. Except that, instead of facing a computer screen, here in Provence, Michel lords it over his vats of fresh fruit and frosty, steamy-cold stainless-steel vats.

Elfin Sissi Perrière rushes in, kisses us effusively: "You came just in time to taste our new sorbets!"

The Perrières make ice cream and sorbets to sell from their home factory, as well as to deliver in larger quantities to the top restaurants, select shops, and tearooms of the region. Their installation on the ground floor of the big Provençal house is unexpectedly state-of-the-art, while piles of apricot, pear, berry crates, boxes of eggs, containers of cream still frosted from the refrigerator truck bear witness that only natural products are used.

One could die, of course, for the many ice-cream flavors, so smooth, so true to the fruit, yet never too sweet.

However, we are known here as dedicated sorbet afficiona-dos. So far, Wayne's favorite has been *cassis*, the tart, black-currant berry. Mine is a toss between apricot or the bitter black chocolate (yes, chocolate sorbet).

"We've been experimenting and working out recipes with new flavors all week," explains Sissi as she brings out tiny ceramic cups. "We just made batches of rosemary, tomato, and lavender sorbets. You'll be the first to sample them."

Three cups are placed in front of us, with small dollops of two of them. The verdict: The red tomato sorbet is full-bodied, very tomato-y, spicy. I can feature a scoop of this topping a bowl of iced gazpacho. Next, the blueish rose-mary. It tastes aromatic, slightly bitter, startling. Might go well with a chicken and pineapple salad, but it needs to be studied at leisure. Last, after a pause, Sissi, with eyes shin-ing expectantly, places a teaspoon of blue lavender sorbet in the third cup.

I watch Wayne sniff first, run the dish past his nose, taste with the tip of his tongue, looking introspective. Finally, he smiles, eyes crinkling, and finishes the sample with a rever-ence one would bring to communion. "Let's take a *quart* home," he requests, "unless you have it in larger containers." We end up taking the entire pre-production batch. And, of course, a Gâteau Sissi to enjoy with our dinner guests.

Gâteau Sissi is the latest addition to *L'Art Glacier*'s reper-toire, and we find that it solves any dessert problem for a dinner party. Named after Sissi, who created it, it consists of a thin base of hazelnut ice cream covered with neat lit-tle scoops of *all* the sorbets and ice-cream flavors of the house. Pastel tints of pink, cream, rose, and green are set off by the dark tones of chocolate, cassis, and black grape. Each ball is decorated with an edible, almondy, little green leaf. Spectacular and delicious in everybody's opinion.

All those samplings, following the pastis aperitif, have dulled the edge of our appetite. But what is there to do during the noon hour? Everything is tightly shut, even museums and monuments are closed. The French are at home, celebrating the ritual of *déjeuner*. Better join them. One could wander through deserted streets, drive traffic-free roads, but who wants to?

So we eat, slowly, relishing the flavors, in the breezy shelter of our covered terrace. The lavender-*lavandin* plants, under the full sun, distill an intense perfume. Wayne stretches his long legs and sighs:

"I've been thinking of doing something orgasmic."

And he brings out dishes of lavender sorbet. He sits on the edge of a planter, flower spikes brushing his face, and takes one taste, then stops for a whiff, then a taste again . . . closes his eyes, smiles his ecstasy . . . another sniff, another taste.

Flavor and flower, taste and fragrance, cool ice under a hot sun distill the very essence of this summer day. Silence is palpable, etched only by the buzz of a bee, who circles Wayne's nearly empty dish, and finally lands near its edge, glad to have found, perhaps, something sweeter than pollen to enjoy as a break, or else mistaking the trace of lavender sorbet for the flower itself.

The essence of a Mediterranean diet . . .

The Salads of Provence

All these salads use the same basic vinaigrette dressing. It is very simple, with only three ingredients.

VINAIGRETTE DRESSING

1 cup olive oil
½ cup wine vinegar (preferably white balsamic)
3 Tbs Dijon mustard
(Salt and pepper may not be needed, since the mustard is usually sufficient. It is better to add those directly to your salad, to taste.)

POIVRONS À L'HUILE (ROASTED SWEET RED PEPPERS)

This is a classic of Provençal cuisine and very easy to make. You can prepare a larger quantity than you need, since it only gets better as it marinates longer.

4 plump, shiny sweet red peppers
1 clove garlic, minced
Salt and pepper
Vinaigrette
A few leaves of basil
Rolled fillets of anchovies and capers (optional)

Cut off stem end and cut a slice off bottom of each pepper. Slit it open, remove seeds and white membrane. Flatten out on a cookie sheet. Slide under the broiler.

When skin is charred (approximately 10 minutes), take out, wrap in towel, and let the peppers sweat. When they are cool, it is easy to remove the tough skin membrane. Cut peppers in long strips. Arrange in oblong dish. Sprinkle with minced garlic, salt, and pepper. Add vinaigrette. Scatter leaves of basil over top.

Optional: You might arrange the peppers around a mound of well-seasoned green salad and sprinkle them with pieces of anchovy and a generous scattering of capers.

TOMATO SALAD

Few meals are served in Provence during the summer months without a bowl of tomato salad on the table.

    5 vine tomatoes (slightly underripe)
    1 sweet onion, very thinly sliced
    Vinaigrette
    Salt and pepper

In a salad bowl, slice tomatoes into thin slices with a sharp or serrated knife. Add sliced onion. Toss with vinaigrette. Season with salt and pepper.

CUCUMBER SALAD

Another staple. It is excellent alone, but goes particularly well with fish, especially cold poached salmon.

4 or 5 cucumbers
I Tbs coarse (kosher) salt or *sel gris*
Vinaigrette
Salt and pepper to taste
Yogurt or sour cream or *crème fraîche* (optional)

Lightly peel cucumbers with a vegetable peeler, leaving a little green. Cut in half lengthwise, and with a teaspoon scoop out the seeds. Slice cucumbers thinly, on a slight bias. Place in a colander, and mix in 1 tablespoon salt. Cover with a weighted dish to press down on cukes, and let them drain off their bitter water and their "burp" (at least I hour).

Press cukes between paper towels to remove last of excess water. They should be sort of limp, but crunchy. Season with vinaigrette, salt, and pepper. Add yogurt or sour cream or *crème fraîche*, if desired.

MUSHROOM, TOMATO, AND GREEN-BEAN SALAD

This makes a tasty first course, but it is also often served as a main dish, followed by a tray of cheeses and a basket of fruit.

I pint fresh mushrooms
Olive oil

1 pound whole green beans (fresh or frozen)
4 vine tomatoes (slightly underripe)
Vinaigrette
Salt and pepper
Minced fresh herbs (tarragon, chervil, or chives)
   (optional)

Clean, slice, and sauté the mushrooms in very hot oil, so they brown quickly without rendering their liquid. Cook green beans until just tender in boiling, salted water. Refresh and drain. Cut tomatoes in quarters, then each quarter in half. Toss together mushrooms, tomatoes, and green beans. Add vinaigrette, toss again, and season with salt and pepper. If desired, sprinkle top with minced herbs.

Déjeuner at the Château

Unless the rosé played tricks on my memory, invitation for *déjeuner* is today.

After agonizing over what to wear, I finally settle on my red and white silk-look dress, white sandals with heels, and no hose. Wayne wanted to go in jeans, but he gives in after a furious argument. He'll put on a dress shirt, open at the neck, slacks, and a light summer coat. We can only hope that this is the way one dresses to mix with aristocracy and even, yes, royalty.

The château looks impressive enough, seen from below, as it looms over us. But walking through its great portals crowned with the lion coat-of-arms, and under the gate that creaks up and down, guided by an ancient mecha-

nism—dare we fantasize it was raised today in our honor?
—is frankly intimidating. The wide stone stairs climb
steeply, angle twice, and climb some more. Finally, out of
breath, we stand in the honor courtyard shaded by geo-
metrically pruned chestnut trees, facing the ornate door,
with its lion brass knocker. A lion is carved, too, above the
lintel, and, overhead, the red flag bearing the same heraldic
lion snaps in the wind.

Am I certain about the date?

Our knock resounds inside, and we wait for what seems
like a long time, before a maid in a white apron opens the
door and escorts us up more wide stairs, flanked by carved
stone banisters, and shows us into a salon.

The duchess stands up and walks over to welcome us,
taking my hand in both of hers, assuring us that she is glad
fate brought us here, and that she sees the restoration of
our house as an omen of good things to come for the village. "Tell your friends in America that they must come,
too." She speaks with an elegant British accent that Wayne
remarks on. "Always had English governesses growing up.
Last luxury my family could afford." She is somewhat past
middle-age, a bit stout, with pure white hair, no trace of
makeup, and the most crystalline voice I've ever heard.
Right away, I like her simplicity and the humor in her eyes.
In spite of—or perhaps even *because* of—her worn shoes,
simple dress, and plain steel watch, I easily recognize a true
grande dame, and my admiration for her will grow from that
day on.

She introduces us to a pale young man, a distant cousin,

visiting, I understand, for a few weeks. We also meet a few local dignitaries, the mayor of a nearby village, and a judge, who all seem as impressed to be here as we are. The maid brings aperitifs, a tray of simple glasses of rosé.

There are superb antiques and family portraits all around, all priceless without doubt. But the upholstery is tired and sagging. The Savonnerie carpet shows worn spots and several poorly mended tears. The conversation might be strained, except that the duchess keeps it going with effortless grace. "Mr. Mayor," she tells one of the dignitaries, "please, do not take that chair. It has a broken spring and it wouldn't do to hurt your . . . seating arrangement." This breaks the ice, everybody laughs and feels more relaxed.

And then her niece, the princess, comes in.

Now I know what one wears for *déjeuner* at the château.

One wears a simple cotton dress, so washed-out the color runs in streaks, sleeveless, with a low neck and full skirt, in a shade that might have been turquoise, flat espadrilles laced up tanned ankles; one wears a twenty-inch waist, small round breasts, blond hair tied back with a ribbon. One also wears a delicately turned-up nose and a pair of angelic dimples. She is absolutely ravishing, unmade-up, like her aunt; but who needs makeup with apricot-tinted skin? I feel overdressed, overmade-up, and awkward. She hugs me, extends her hand to Wayne, who, to my surprise, kisses it, and I can see him suddenly spellbound, as unfocused as the other day after those glasses of pastis. It has happened in a flash: Here should now be a scene in this script for the Fairy Tale Princess and the Silly Handsome

American. The scene is missing, but the princess is here and Wayne cannot take his eyes off her.

Her husband comes in a little later, with one of the duchess's sons. They both bow low over my hand. It turns out that Wayne, in his linen jacket and slacks, is perfectly dressed, since that's the way the other men are dressed. With the exception of the prince, that is. He is unshaven, a blond stubble blurs his jaw, his hair is tousled. His blue work shirt, minus torn-off sleeves, hangs over a pair of very short shorts. I notice that the duchess purses her lips, but she says nothing. The prince insists that I should accept a glass of rosé: "First time you're tasting our rosé?" he smiles conspiratorially. "You'll see, one can grow to like it," embarrassing me with the implication of something illicit between us, since he can't have forgotten his visit on that first morning, and the jug he brought.

As the butler—I have seen him busy with masonrywork on the battlements and also tilling the flower garden, so he must do multiple duty—opens the double doors leading to the dining room, a little scene occurs, probably often repeated, but unfamiliar to Wayne and me and the dignitaries too, I guess. The duchess bows in the direction of the prince, who in turn bows to his wife. The latter indicates with a gesture that her aunt should go first. It is all very understated, barely indicated and easy to miss. But the little scene reveals a world we know nothing about: The prince, of royal blood, outranks everyone here and is privileged to walk first into a room. Out of courtesy, he invites his wife to precede him, but she, in turn, defers to her aunt, the mistress of the house. A charade? Probably, but in this setting and present company, I find it evocative of centuries of tradition, a tradition whose evidenced survival today enchants me. It is a flicker of grace in an increasingly graceless world.

The dining room is magnificent. Great tapestries cover the walls, telling the mythological story of Orpheus and Eurydice, we're told. They, like the salon carpet, could use repair and restoration, for either moths or time or both have been at them. Over the table, a gigantic crystal-and-silver chandelier spreads its twelve branches. The duchess points to it.

"I polished it myself before you arrived," she tells her niece, showing her hands still etched with faint black lines. "Yes, standing on top of this table for most of the morning. Maria can't do everything, the poor woman is overburdened as it is. As for Carlos, between the garden, the grounds, and all the repairs that constantly need to be done, he has more than he can possibly attend to."

The meal is served by Carlos, the butler-of-all-work, wearing a white jacket. First, he passes a beautiful molded aspic, a mosaic of sliced boiled eggs and bits of colorful vegetables in an evanescent gelatin. "My own recipe," says the princess. "And so inexpensive to make."

The conversation revolves around the tours of the château. Every afternoon it is open to visitors, at five dollars per person, with reduced rates for children, students, and groups. So, someone must always be available to serve as a guide. It is understood that Maria and Carlos just cannot do it more than occasionally; that is why the young colorless cousin had been invited: He guides tours every afternoon.

The main course is roast chicken, carved to perfection and presented with the traditional Provençal *tian* of tomato, sweet pepper, and eggplant in the center.

"All the vegetables come from the garden. And I keep thinking we should try and raise some fowl, too," comments the duchess. "It would be a savings."

Discussion of the tours continues. Each lasts about half an hour, although you can draw it out longer, with more detailed information, or shorten it, if the group you're leading shows little interest. Only representative rooms are included in the visit, not the intimate salon where we were received today, and none of the fourteen family bedrooms. On good days—Sundays and holidays, especially during the summer—there are often enough visitors, streaming in all afternoon, for five, maybe six tours. The duchess, incognito, regularly leads tours herself. They must be the most interesting ones, but I can't help noticing how heavy and tired her legs seem to be. These tours must be killers, with a dozen staircases to climb, and mind-numbing as well: Fascinating as the castle's history is, repeating it ad nauseam must take its toll.

"I guided a visit yesterday," boasts the prince. "Made fifty francs in tips, too. At the end of the tour, I stood, barring the exit, extended my hand, and told the group: I am Prince Louis, of a royal house. I don't accept tips, but I have my charities. Most of them didn't dare give me less than five francs."

An animated discussion of tips and the best way to procure them follows. The duchess remains silent, directing the service with barely raised eyebrows. She turns to me:

"You must think us quite petty and mercenary. The fact is, those tours are one of our main sources of income."

Plates are cleared and dessert is presented on a large, footed crystal dish. It is a chocolate cake, impeccably turned out. Sliced, it reveals a moist, almost puddinglike interior. Its flavor brings to mind the term "profoundly chocolate." I exclaim: "This is delicious!"

"I made it myself," the duchess tells me. "I adore chocolate, could live on it. If you like, I'll share my chocolate cake recipes with you. I have a collection with some dating back almost two hundred years, when chocolate was a great novelty. They called it 'colonial chocolate' then, because it came from colonies in the Caribbean."

The conversation now turns to Monaco. The duchess is a great friend and a relative of the reigning family. Each year, she is invited to spend a week at the palace.

"I love going there," she confides. "The moment you arrive, a maid is attached to your service. Your clothes are pressed, cleaned, altered as needed. A dressmaker and a cleaner are in residence. Shoes and luggage are checked, polished, repaired if necessary. Every morning, a printout of the day's activities is brought to your room with breakfast. . . ."

"You cannot bring your dog," warns the prince, interrupting. "They've just put in new carpeting throughout, and dogs are not allowed. Rainier is very strict about it."

"Didn't you take yours when you stopped by there the

other day?" The princess's dog is a nasty, minuscule Yorkie, which she carries everywhere. He is, right now, sitting on her lap, alternately eating tidbits out of hand and snarling every time the butler ventures near.

"That is an entirely different matter," corrects the prince. He winks at us. "Your dog is only a *ducal* dog while ours is a *royal* dog. That makes all the difference." And, warming to the subject: "Anyway, I'd like to see Rainier Grimaldi trying to tell me what I can and cannot do."

Once more, the duchess purses her lips and keeps quiet. It is clear that a certain animosity reigns between her and her royal nephew-by-marriage. Because he outranks her, he seizes every opportunity to annoy her. That's why he comes to the table unshaven, in disreputable clothes, and is now teasing her with matters of rank and etiquette. These are important to both of them in spite of the duchess's obvious simplicity. But now, suddenly, he goes on:

"Those Grimaldis were nothing but lesser nobility from Genoa. Only, *they* managed to cling to their rock. *We* are the descendants of seven centuries of royalty, allied to all the crowns of Europe. . . . And today, Rainier still sits on the throne of his pocket-size principality, which grows wealthier with every new building that goes up there. Meanwhile, *I* am looking for a job."

All this time, the princess is either feeding her Yorkie or—is she, or do I imagine it?—exchanging sidelong glances with Wayne that hint at some secret between them. He asks about her piano practice, so she invites him to accompany her to the top floor of the keep, where his "mechanical genius" as she puts it, might be put to use fixing a stuck piano pedal. He springs to his feet, she hands the Yorkie over to the pale cousin, who immediately gets bitten, and they leave, *not* hand in hand, but that's how it looks to me.

Not put off in the least, the prince offers to lead me on a tour of the castle. So he takes my arm and steers me through a grand salon, much larger than the one we sat in earlier, with gigantic life-size portraits of cavaliers on horseback and crinolined ladies. Then, a library, and formal, never-used canopied bedrooms: a duke's and a duchess's, a "bishop's," and a "king's." Francis the First slept here, legend has it, on his return from the Wars of Italy in the 1500s. Then stairs going down, weapons' rooms with armor, pikes, muskets, pistols, and sabers. We finally step into a winding, stony passage leading to the private chapel. He allows only a glance at the lined-up prayer chairs, all tapestried with the lion coat-of-arms in petit-point by duchesses of an earlier century. The black marble altar was a gift from the Vatican, I learn.

Back in the long passage, he points to a small door, shoulder high, in the wall. "Look," he pulls it open, though it resists and creaks. He flicks his lighter: "This used to be the prison." The room is maybe five by five feet. A stone floor, a small stone bench built into one of the walls. No air, no window, permanent darkness. I protest:

"But there wasn't even enough room for a man to lie down in there!"

"Probably not," shrugs the prince. "But then, they were not put in here for comfort." I shudder, so he puts his arm around my waist. "You realize, of course, that it hasn't been used for quite some time." He leads me farther down the passage.

"Now, look at this." He points to a spot where several stones have been removed, revealing a hiding place hollowed out of the wall. "There's quite a story here, and one that happened very recently." He picks up and drops moldering pieces of a broken chair, then rubs the dust off his fingertips. "My wife was giving a concert in South Africa last winter. An elderly blind gentleman asked to be led to her dressing room afterward. He held her hand, and told her that, while listening to her play, he had a vision: She was connected, somehow, to a house in a high place, on a mountain, perhaps, and in that ancient house, a long passage leading to a holy room held a dangerous and accursed object, which should be removed and exorcised.

So, she immediately called her aunt, who exclaimed that she wasn't surprised: Her dog barked every time it walked with her down that passage. It would always stop at the same place, she said, and growl ferociously at the wall. She'd never understood why, but now she'd try and find out.

The duchess, then, had Carlos break up the mortar there, and pull out a few stones. Sure enough, there was this hollowed-out hiding place you see now."

"And . . . was anything in there?" I ask a little tremulously. Do I feel a chill, and an eerie presence in this dank, confining passage? And by the way, is Wayne still up there in the tower with the princess?

"Yes, there was. First, this broken and disintegrated chair here, and also a portrait, long fallen off. But I don't want to tell you about it, it would make you nervous. No, no, I won't. Just ask the duchess if you're interested. I'm sure she'll show it to you—that is, if you're *sure* you want to see it."

I don't know what could be so awful about a portrait, but by now, I am frankly ill-at-ease. I suppose it shows, for the prince playfully raises my hand to his lips and kisses the palm, looking into my eyes.

"How old was that portrait?" I ask, hoping to diffuse the charged atmosphere. Old enough, I wish, for whatever was wrong with it to have evaporated, so it would be harmless today.

"Oh, maybe four hundred years old or so. The duchess keeps it in a locked room, on the upper floor. But she tells us that her dog still carries on the same as it did before, whenever she walks down the passage with it. I guess some of the aura lingers."

By now, I'd frankly prefer to move to some more cheerful spot, and I tell the prince, who, his arm tight around my waist, leads me to more stairs, more halls, and finally to the Saints' Chamber.

This stark, spacious room, dimly lit by stained-glass windows, formed, centuries ago, the heart of the medieval fortress. Here lived Amat and Eliabel, ancestors of the family. It was in the thirteen hundreds . . .

"The king felt that Amat, the young heir, should make a rich marriage, for the family, loyal servants of the throne, needed an injection of capital. . . ." He pauses. "An endemic problem. That hasn't changed today."

So, when the orphan boy reached the marriageable age of thirteen, the king directed that he should marry Eliabel, an orphan, too, and heiress to a vast fortune. Eliabel had been raised by a relative, abbess of a convent. Under that sainted woman's guidance, she'd made God a gift of her person, vowing to remain a virgin for life. She had to be forcibly dragged out of her convent and married off, despite her tears and protestations.

"But on their wedding night, she confessed her vow of chastity to her adolescent groom. Touched, he agreed to respect it for two years. After that time, her piety had apparently won him over, for he now accepted a perma-nently imposed chastity. In time, his grandfather, surprised that no offspring was born to that young couple, was prompted to send a servant to spy on them in this very chamber.

"The servant discovered that they spent their night hours kneeling on either side of the bed, lost in prayer. She even reported in wonder that she had seen an angel hover-ing above, holding wreaths of roses over their heads, a sure sign of God's grace. Thus, the grandfather became aware that chastity had replaced carnal desire and, probably at that point, gave up hope for an heir.

"Later, Amat performed the miracles prescribed for his admission into the ranks of recognized saints. As when, during a period of famine, he ordered the doors of the cas-tle's granary thrown open: Lo and behold! Wheat rolled out in great billows at the feet of the starving villagers. His feast is celebrated every year, the second Sunday in September."

"And what about his wife, Eliabel?" I want to know.

"Oh, her," the prince dismisses poor Eliabel with an airy gesture. "She only reached blessedness, a much lesser rank in paradise. Normal, don't you think? After all, *he* did most of the suffering. But out of courtesy we call her a saint, too."

I tease, unwisely:

"Is chastity an enduring trait in the family?"

This time, it seems he has tightened his hand a little higher than my waist. I move aside slightly.

"No," he laughs. "Just that one time, it seems. Never heard of another case. It's definitely *not* a family problem."

But it seems that, before dying, both Amat and Eliabel distributed their fortunes among the poor in order to leave this world in gospel-recommended poverty. Only the castle, an inalienable property, remained, and passed into the hands of a cousin of the same name.

"Always an eye for the grand gesture, but no head for business," concludes the prince.

We have reached the bottom of yet another steep staircase, which ascends higher than any of the others.

"Goes up to the room at the top of the keep. Want to run up?"

Arriving there, he pushes a door, and here are Wayne and the princess. She is sitting at the keyboard, striking isolated notes, while Wayne, hair tumbling into his eyes, is leaning over, peering into the piano. He looks up, totally innocent:

"I can't find what's wrong with that pedal. I am afraid it will take a specialist."

The princess pouts, then dimples: "What an angel! He's been trying so hard to help!" As for me, I try not to wonder whether he's kept his head inside that damn piano *all* this time. And I succeed—reasonably so.

"Do you feel like climbing up this ladder to the terrace on top?" suggests the prince.

All four of us troop up the straight ladder, to emerge to dazzling light on the topmost part of the castle: the terrace on top of the keep. It is a square space, surrounded by a crenellated, shoulder-high wall. In the center, on top of a steel pole, the red lion flag snaps so sharply that it hums in the wind, a wind to cut your breath away.

From this elevated vantage point, the view is awesome, and snowcapped summits of the Alps emerge beyond the hazy distance. This is where, a thousand years ago, sentries stood, surveying the circular horizon for signs of approaching enemies. But there are more promising signs today.

"Look at those tour buses! Three of them, all heading in our direction! Business will be brisk today," rejoices the prince.

When we come downstairs, I ask the duchess about the portrait. "So, Louis told you about it! Yes, a strange story. Come with me, I'll show you." More stairs, more halls, and more stairs again, which she negotiates tirelessly. In a room almost empty of furniture, a portrait has fallen to the floor, next to a low table. The duchess reaches down, picks it up, lays it back on the table. Then, she pushes the wooden shutters open.

The painting shows a man in ecclesiastical garb who, holding a small, open box in his right hand, seems to be staring into it. Except that his eyes have been gouged out, leaving only jagged holes. The heart has been pierced, too, and random stabs slash the entire canvas.

"I suppose somebody had reason to hate him, whoever

he was," comments the duchess. "It would be interesting to know what he did and what's in that box."

Does she have any idea why the portrait was stabbed and immured in stone? She shakes her head, no. She adds, though, as if speaking to herself: "It's strange. Every time I come in, I'll find him fallen to the floor. I'll lay the portrait flat on the table, and the next day, it's fallen off again. . . . I have thought of burning it, but the priest who exorcised it advised me against it. You never know, he tells me, what you might release. The fumes, you know. It might set free evil forces better kept prisoner."

All this, actually frightening to me, seems an everyday matter to her, and she obviously takes the malevolent portrait in stride: "Why, this is just one of those things you'll come face to face with in a place like this. In a thousand-plus-year-old castle, you should expect a few unexplained events now and then."

We walk downstairs, and she peers through a window, counts tourists pressing into the courtyard. "Quite a crop, today," she remarks with satisfaction. "We'll have many tours."

The prince and princess want to walk us down, and accept Wayne's invitation to see our house. After all the grandeur of the castle, I am almost embarrassed, because it suddenly seems so small and modest.

But the princess looks around, taking in our newly rebuilt and decorated rooms: "Can you imagine," she sighs, "being able to *buy* this! It must be nice to be American!"

Deep, velvety, and rich . . .

The Duchess's Chocolate Cake

This recipe gives proportions for one cake, baked in a 12-by-1½-inch-deep pan. The secret lies in not letting it bake too long, so that the center retains some creaminess.

> 1 box, less 1 square, Baker's semisweet chocolate
>   (7 ounces)
> 1 box, less 1 square, Baker's unsweetened chocolate
>   (7 ounces)
> 12 eggs, separated; keep whites at room temperature
> 2 cups sugar
> 3½ sticks butter, room temperature
> ½ cup flour

FOR DECORATING
> Powdered sugar
> Slivered almonds
> Maraschino cherries

Melt chocolate, *completely and without stirring,* in a double boiler (or a saucepan resting in 2 inches of water). Cream the egg yolks with the sugar until almost white. Add luke-warm chocolate, then the butter, soft but not melted. Add the flour, and mix well.

Whip the egg whites to form peaks, and fold in, lifting the mass from bottom to top.

Butter a nonstick 12-by-1½-inch-deep pan. Sprinkle it with granulated sugar and shake off excess. Pour in batter, leaving a ½-inch margin on top.

Bake in a preheated oven at 300°F. The cake should not rise, only swell some. If it rises too much, lower temperature. After 30 minutes, start testing with your fingertip: Exterior should be firm, inside elastic. The crust should enclose a creamy, *not liquid* center. If in doubt, turn off oven and let cake stand inside for a few minutes.

To decorate: Sprinkle with powdered sugar. Make a ring of daisies on the perimeter with petals of slivered almonds, and a red maraschino cherry at each center. Place a few daisies in center of ring.

Don't Ever Go to
Saint-Tropez

Now it seems that every afternoon, Wayne can't wait to walk out of the house.

He has an important errand in Pertuis, perhaps, or else he needs to take some air, he tells me, although air, fresh and lively, is plentiful on our terrace. Or perhaps he has spotted a scene earlier that he wants to photograph in the afternoon light. Unfortunately, even though he may delude himself, I know exactly where he is going.

Off the Place du Château, beside the church, the *remparts* form a recessed nook, shaded by an ancient olive tree with a forked trunk that children sometimes like to climb. People will linger there, afternoon and early evening, enjoying the breezy shade, gazing at cascading rooftops

and, way down below, the checkerboard countryside: vineyards, melon and sunflower fields, the latter in blinding
chrome-yellow bloom right now. Farther out, other villages
emerge from the greenery: Cucuron, with the ruins of its
two hilltop castles—Vaugines, Fontjoyeuse of the felici-
tous name. The Aigues River, a torrent in spring, barely
trickles in the summer, but more villages line its valley: La
Tour d'Aigues, Peypin d'Aigues, all huddles of sun-baked
tile roofs. The Luberon range bars the horizon, its slopes
always tinted purple through some play of light.

But it is not the storybook landscape that attracts
Wayne to this half-hidden spot. Quite inadvertently, I
glimpsed him the other day leaning against the tree, while
the princess sat on the low wall, legs dangling in the void.
No reason for anyone to feel guilty, heaven knows, and I
am sure neither one did. It was all quite innocent.

For one, it is certain that the princess would not be
interested in someone as obviously plebeian as this tall
American photographer. She is, after all, descended from a
long line of great aristocrats, and married into the even
higher ranks of royalty. Could it be that she feels obligated
to be as charming to him as she is to everyone else? That
she enjoys his obvious admiration? Is she bored? Come to
think of it, there may not be much entertainment for her
in the château—except, I suppose, when fascinating guests
are staying. The village would have little to offer this beautiful young woman. She does have a handsome husband,
and I have seen them holding hands, but he is absent a
great deal, having, no doubt, obligations to fulfill elsewhere.

So now, almost every afternoon, Wayne finds himself distracted on the way to his car, or else he casually ambles through the village, presumably intent on filling his lungs, camera slung around his neck, seeking "wild" shots to grab. But his rambles invariably bring him back to that low wall and the shade of the olive tree. Is it because the princess might be sitting there, swinging her slim ankles over the rampart wall, in conversation with this or that villager? And her conversation, I'd be the first to admit, *is* charming. She knows everybody—she has been coming to the château since she was a little girl, for all her summer vacations. Unfailingly, she remembers ailments, problems, and joys; to enquire about the grandmother's rheumatism, the grandson's exams, and the daughter's promotion. She knows that the age-old wisteria, savaged last year by the mistral, is blooming again along the Perrons' terrace, and that twins were born to Angèle, who works at city hall.

When old Madame Oraison hobbles by, leaning on her cane, she rushes over, hugs her, clucks sympathetically over that troublesome leg, and helps her up the church steps. Her Yorkie may snarl at all comers, but *she* radiates smiling warmth and concern. This could be her way of holding court, prompted by genetic memories. In any case, I don't believe for a moment that she could be waiting for someone.

When Wayne appears, playfully aiming his camera at her slender figure, she couldn't very well turn suddenly ungracious. Instead, she compliments him on his new shirt, or his extravagant head of hair, speaking to him in her hesitant, primitive English, which, I am sure, he finds irresistible. She'll indicate a spot for him to sit, and they remain there, her exquisite profile turned to him in utter fascination. All quite innocent, as I said before, but, for reasons I don't need to explain, I don't like it at all.

I know I must find a distraction. The prince has already left, invited by some other royalty for a yacht cruise in the Greek islands, said the duchess. As for the princess, she is due, it seems, to leave soon to attend a society event. It is a ball in Deauville, I think I heard, in connection with the racing season. If I manage to get Wayne out of here for a few days, she'll be gone when we return.

So, I brightly suggest a trip to Saint-Tropez, the fabled Riviera resort, about two hours away. Just a spur-of-the-moment idea, I tell him. It takes a struggle, as expected, to convince him. He prefers to stay right here, and cannot think of any place he'd rather be. Don't we find everything we *want* right here? I refrain from saying that's precisely *why* I am trying to get him away and, instead, bring up that powerful argument: photo ops. Wouldn't it also be a shame to be so close and not even know what it is that others find so attractive in Saint-Tropez? Anyway, we don't need to stay there *forever*! Just as long as we feel like it, and not a second longer. He relents at last, so I make hotel reservations and pack my new bathing suit.

Saint-Tropez sits at the tip of a small peninsula, well removed from any freeway or main road. That very isolation led to its fame when, in the sixties, Brigitte Bardot, then at the height of her fame, sought refuge in that fishing village bypassed by the rush-to-the-Riviera craze. The easiest way to get there in the summer, we were told, is to take the ferry that crosses the bay from Saint-Raphaël, so crowded is the only access road. But we shrug off the suggestion. How bad can driving eighteen miles on a picturesque route be?

After leaving the autoroute, you engage on a narrow road that winds its way through the Estérel range. It crosses grove after grove of cork oaks, most of them raw and naked, their thick bark stripped off and lying by the roadside tied in great bundles, waiting to be picked up by the cork factories. The road hairpins sharply, veers this way and that, climbs up and descends to climb again, passes the fortified village of Lagarde-Freinet, where the last pirates held out for centuries, before it descends to the coast. This could be a beautiful drive, and surely is, off season.

But in summer, it is a nightmare.

Cars, trailers, campers with plates of every European country, trucks bringing supplies, stand immobilized in giant *bouchons*, bottle stoppers, as the French call traffic jams. You wait there, motor heating up, until you decide to turn it off since you are as motionless as a fly in amber, with little hope of moving at all for the next half hour. Then, suddenly, you are rattled by a terrific roar and engulfed in a cloud of dust: German motorcycle clubs have discovered Saint-Tropez, and apparently chosen the place as a preferred destination. So, their giant Harleys effortlessly weave their way through the stalled traffic. American Hell's Angels are a tame bunch compared to these *mensch*: sleeveless leather shirts, chains wrapped around bare arms over deathheads and swastika tattoos. The girls, riding pillion, hug the men with massive bare thighs, tangles of blond hair flying under horned helmets, like Valkyries on a rampage. A threat emanates from daggers stuck in boots and steel-spiked spurs as they pass in a raucous blast of hard rock and guttural shouts, wave after wave, on their way to sweet Saint-Tropez.

Saint-Tropez, when we get there, after covering eighteen miles in six hours, is indeed a lovely, small fishing port, which its city fathers have managed, through some miracle of zoning, to keep apparently untouched. Little shops line its rectangular harbor, just as they always did, except that now, cheek by jowl to the grocery and the bakery, designers' boutiques offer more expensive necessities: a mango chiffon wraparound skirt, for instance, for three thousand dollars. The string bra and panties, the latter revealed at every step, are sold separately. Where are the customers for this attire?

On the yachts.

Because yachts are now moored along the quay, where fishing boats used to unload their catch of sardines or *rascasse* for the bouillabaisse. Not the ordinary, cabin-cruiser type. Only the largest, most luxurious, some almost ocean-liner size, all reeking of boundless fortune and the quest for extraordinary pleasures, share the privileged front row. It is clear that some sliding scale, based perhaps on mooring fees, relegates the plainer ones to the anonymous mass of bobbing masts and antennas further back.

And now I learn why one should *not*, ever, go to Saint-Tropez.

Girls.

Girls are everywhere in Saint-Tropez: lying nude, like adolescent, tide-washed goddesses, on the top deck of yachts, or standing, drink in hand, on the lower one, clad in three strategically placed fabric flowers, or else draped on lounges, displaying endless tans. They parade along the harbor, wearing not much more than a G-string, or in long, diaphanous skirts that open as they walk, or else they sit at café terraces bare, or better than bare-breasted. Farther into the village, they play *boule* under the plane trees, wearing nothing but bikinis, to the delight of pot-bellied locals, who sit on chairs lining the *boule* grounds, commenting on the sights. They shop at the open-air market in abbreviated, clinging shorts and unbuttoned shirts, breasts revealed each time they reach for a peach or weigh a pound of tomatoes on the hanging scales.

Breasts are everywhere in Saint-Tropez, either bare or concealed for revelation. Not the massive silicone or saline type, for cleavage is out, out, out. The breasts of Saint-Tropez are the kind you cannot *buy*: small, firm, upturned. They resemble, if anything, lemon halves, or better, pointed hyacinth bulbs. None sag, or even hint at the onset of gravity. Rib cages are delicate, waists round and narrow, bellies taut with sweetly coiling navels. Thighs are long and slender. Hair is four feet long, straight and sweeping, raven or else a frosted taffy blond. It seems that red and platinum are out this year. Any woman, proud of her good figure and smart hairstyle, suddenly feels like her own grandmother.

And all these girls appear to be on the prowl, displaying their arrogant young flesh, on a hunt for . . . sex? Probably.

But sex as a means to an end, I'm sure. After a moment at Café Sennequier, the premier girl-watching spot, one becomes aware that this is no innocent display of youthful, exuberant high spirits. All this nudity isn't meant as a glorification of nature, either. Leaning on their railings, the middle-aged yachtsmen, tufts of white hair on sagging torsos, are not seeking a purely aesthetic experience, nor are they looking for college roommates for their granddaughters. This activity along the quay may not be a slave market, but it *is* a market: a flesh market. "Here is what we have to offer," wink the upturned breasts. "Look us over, and let us know what you'll give in return. Plentiful as this merchandise seems here, you won't find such choice and quality elsewhere. So, *messieurs*, what am I bid? Decorating the lounge for your next cruise may come high, but surely you can afford the best. How much is it worth to you to see the yacht-club members' eyes pop when they spy on your deck what you brought in, better than naked, next time you moor in Portofino?"

A fool's bargain, in any case. Whatever baubles from Cartier, Hermès, or Tiffany may serve as currency, they're a cheap price for this elusive loveliness of youth. One more deal where these good businessmen will get the better value for their money, *hélas*.

Wayne has been rather silent, this trip, and there didn't seem to be much that we needed to talk about. Now, as I look over, I find him, not raptly watching the passing parade, but instead engrossed in a day-old issue of the *Herald Tribune* someone had abandoned on a neighboring chair.

A little later, when we look for a restaurant, it seems that every place is either already crowded or *réservé*, or they simply won't serve you for reasons of their own—like if they don't recognize you, I suppose. In desperation, we end up in a small divey place, on a back street behind the harbor. After being made to wait, standing for the longest time, we are grudgingly waved to a table right by the door—unoccupied the whole time—where everybody bumps into the back of our chairs.

When she finally approaches our table, our waitress, an insolent girl with enormous, made-up green eyes, the deepest tan, and a top so skimpy it reveals rings in her nipples and navel, doesn't even glance at us as she drops menus in the general direction of our table. After an endless wait, she negligently brings *fromage aux herbes*, a watery cottage cheese with chopped herbs that nobody would touch at home. Another eternity, and, after we remind her twice of our order, she brings us, instead of the grilled lamb chops we had ordered, two lukewarm dishes of an insipid ratatouille. We wouldn't mind that much, if it was a *good* ratatouille. But this one is as watery as the *fromage* and frankly inedible. No point in complaining. Clearly not looking for a career in food services, she sneers at customers at large and loses any shred of interest in our area after two South American types in yachting caps stroll in. So, after more waiting, we are left to figure out the bill ourselves and leave the money on the table. Wayne, usually so slow to anger, flatly refuses to leave a tip.

By then, it is late, and the harbor scene is teeming with strollers, even more exotic-looking than the earlier ones.

Hordes of German bikers lean on their machines, swilling beer and schnapps, passing joints, leering at the crowd like predators. Transvestites have now appeared in large number, and patrol among the girls, making the afternoon display seem tame by comparison. The height, outré makeup, jewelry, extravagant wigs of the *travelos* parody the real girls, who now seem almost demure. The flesh market is turning into a caricature of itself, with undertones much more disquieting than just a quest for sex.

"Let's get out of here," suggests Wayne, "and don't you think we should forget about that room we reserved?" I don't need to answer. "Let's get out of this circus," he repeats, "and walk a little. Then, we'll drive home. Traffic might have thinned out by now."

So, we leave the harbor, where yachts, all lit up with fairy lights strung along their masts and railings, are rocking with crowded parties, to stroll along a deserted part of the shore. Wayne's arm is draped around my shoulders and he doesn't speak. His camera hasn't been used once today.

We walk in silence for a while. Finally:

"No need to spell things out," he whispers. "I just want to say I'm glad to share my life with you, and damn lucky, too. I hope I'm not too much of a fool for you."

We walk on, waves gently lapping at the pebbles. A small, sandy spot nestles among the smooth stones. I slip off my sandals and step into the shallow water, surprisingly cold for such a balmy night. The lighted yachts and cafés glow in the near distance; music, voices, and shrill laughter carry over the water. But here, it is quiet. A wavelet washes over my feet.

"We are happy," I say. "Let's keep it that way."

From one of the yachts, lines from a popular song waft across the harbor:

> *Ah, ah, ah, ah, mon amour,*
> *Ah, ah, ah, ah, à toi toujours . . .*

and as I hum the tune: "Sickening," says Wayne. "Let's go home."

Summer in your plate . . .

Tian (Ratatouille)

Baked in a shallow earthenware casserole called a *tian*, the ratatouille takes that name, just like a casserole dish takes its name from its container. The secret of a good ratatouille: Start by cooking the vegetables separately.

2 eggplants
Olive oil
2 sweet red peppers, roasted and peeled (see p. 47)
3 sweet red onions
5 zucchini
8 or 10 Roma tomatoes, cut in half and squeezed to expel water
2 Tbs vinegar
1 Tbs sugar

3 cloves garlic, minced
1 bay leaf
½ tsp thyme
½ tsp paprika
Dash Tabasco
Salt and pepper

Peel and slice eggplant into small slices. Brush slices with olive oil, and grill under broiler until tender (this way, you'll avoid frying them in oil, which eggplant absorbs like a sponge). Set aside.

Cut your roasted and peeled peppers into strips (roasting will also avoid frying them in oil). Set aside.

Slice onions and zucchini. Cook them together in a little olive oil until tender and *very lightly* browned.

In a large skillet, mix all vegetables. Add tomatoes, well squeezed. Add all seasonings and cook, uncovered, until excess liquid has evaporated. Taste, and correct seasonings as needed.

Remove to a *tian* (shallow baking dish) and bake loosely covered at 300°F for 30 minutes for the flavors to mellow and blend.

TIAN D'AGNEAU (RATATOUILLE WITH LAMB)

Lamb is the best meat of Provence. Try this delicious dish, slowly baked until the meat is fork tender.

Brown 2 pounds of lean, cubed lamb meat in a little olive oil. Season with salt and pepper and mix with your ratatouille *before* baking it. Bake at 300°F until lamb is tender (1 to 1½ hours). Uncover, sprinkle top with bread crumbs, and bake some more until top becomes a little crusty.

TIAN AUX OEUFS (RATATOUILLE WITH EGGS)

In your *tian* of ratatouille, make nests with the back of a spoon. In each nest, break an egg, season it lightly with salt and pepper, and bake uncovered until eggs are set.

This addition of eggs turns the *tian* into a full-meal dish, often served in the summer.

The Wine Connoisseurs

*U*naware that our wine education will progess by a giant step tonight, we simply look forward to a delightful evening. Ariel and Christophe, her companion, are coming for dinner, as they often do.

We have learned that, when invited to dinner in Provence, you shouldn't ask: "What time?" This apparently silly question will puzzle your hosts, who may answer: "Oh, about dinnertime." Similarly, in restaurants, you reserve a table without specifying the time. You should know they start serving after seven-thirty or eight, depending on their particular custom, and the table is yours for the evening. Show up whenever you like, but not too late, or it will be near closing time. In other words, be civilized, and show up at *dinnertime*.

As we found out, dinnertime is about eight-thirty, but there can be enormous variations. Here, like everywhere, people are punctual or they are not. For instance, Ariel, who finished our house to near perfection on a tight schedule, has never been on time since. It might be that she compensates for the exacting demands of her professional life by the relaxation of her personal timetable. If she asks you to dinner, and you show up a little after eight-thirty, she may not be home yet, or else seems so surprised to see you that you panic, fearing to have come on the wrong day. So, next time, you plan for a nine-thirty arrival time, just to receive a frantic call at eight thirty-five: "What's the matter? Did you forget? Did something happen?"

As a guest, Ariel's punctuality is just as erratic. She and Christophe may arrive two hours later than expected. We find them easy to excuse: Christophe, an electronics engineer, works in Marseille, and faces a long, traffic-heavy commute. As for Ariel, she may have spent the afternoon supervising the tearing down and rebuilding of a doorway, because she didn't feel it arched with just the right curve; or else, in knee-high boots in an ocher quarry, selecting, with her workers, the best tint of tawny gravel for the stucco of a new house's walls, oblivious to any other concern. But when they finally show at the door, attractive, lively, and energizing, all is forgiven, and I hurry to slip dinner into the oven.

Ariel makes her own clothes, and always surprises us with numbers of her own creation, often worked out from fashions bought at the Pertuis open-air market. Tonight, she is playing Provençal peasant in a lavishly tiered skirt, cleverly contrived, she happily confesses, out of *three* petticoats from the market racks. The blouse is a plain white one, from the same source, only she cut off the top and gathered it with a velvet ribbon, to shrug off one shoulder. Her rich, dark hair is pulled back under a starched man's handkerchief that looks just like a peasant coif. She looks ravishing, and carries in a basket under a checkered cloth her offering of the day: A large jar of *Confiture de Vieux Garçon*, says the handwritten label.

We need to be told, since we know so little of real value in this world of Provence, that *Confiture de Vieux Garçon*, Bachelor's Jam, is actually fruit preserved in eau-de-vie.

"Take a nice jar that you'll keep on the sink, and whenever you refill your fruit basket, cut up a peach, a pear, a couple of nectarines, plums, a dozen cherries, a handful of white grapes. No berries, they turn mushy. Pour enough eau-de-vie, white brandy, to cover, drop in a few spoonfuls of sugar. Continue as summer progresses, until the jar is full. Then, cover tightly, and let it stand in a cool place until December. *Alors*, you can uncork it, breathe in the delicious aroma, and serve your *confiture* in brandy snifters with coffee, in place of dessert. The traditional time for that is Christmas Eve, when you return, half-frozen, from midnight Mass. It's guaranteed to help you warm up."

"Why do they call it *Confiture de Vieux Garçon?*"

"Because it is much less trouble to make than real jam, and since bachelors are notoriously poor cooks, they're supposedly incapable of going through the precise steps of jam-making."

"And some are said not to mind a nip, too," winks Christophe.

I carefully put the jar away. Shall we be lucky enough to return here next Christmas? Why, this might be the perfect excuse: We have to fly back to Provence, otherwise our *Confiture de Vieux Garçon* might go bad after midnight Mass.

Christophe, for his part, is a man given to hobbies. Each time we return, we find him deeply involved in a new one, in which Ariel follows him enthusiastically and even tries to surpass him. One year, it will be astronomy so they scan the night skies with a newly acquired telescope. They're sure they've discovered uncharted stars and sighted numerous UFOs. Ariel has even renamed their house *Orion* after the constellation. Another year, they will be into sound, with a brand new lexicon of tweeters, woofers, and baffles, plus a state-of-the-art system on which they play, to our surprise, dusty and warped CDs. But this year, they are into wine expertise, lyrical vocabulary and all.

"What are you serving for dinner? Would it be red meat by any chance?" Ambitiously, I have tried my hand at filet of beef *en croûte*, praying that it will come out just right. Christophe beams:

"Perfect, perfect. I brought just the right wine, then. Look: A bottle of Côte-Rôtie, and the best there is, Condrieu. You're in for a treat, wait and you'll see."

We dutifully exclaim over the understated label, and respectfully caress the coat of velvety dust. "Côte-Rôtie is one of the few Côtes-du-Rhône wines that ages well. As for others, I'd say throw them away after two years. But Côte-Rôtie gets better for ten years or more, depending on vintage."

We know all about Côtes-du-Rhône, the wines produced along the slopes of the Rhône Valley. Most are
excellent when drunk fresh, but, except for a few like
Châteauneuf-du-Pape and, apparently, Côte-Rôtie, they do
not age well.

Christophe describes the Côte-Rôtie vineyards: "They
are planted on almost vertical cliffs overlooking the Rhône,
just south of Lyon. Extremely difficult to work, as you can
imagine, but perfect for grapes, since these grow best in a
well-drained, rocky soil. And those cliffs are *that*, to the max.
So sun-roasted, too, that they're called just that, Roasted-
Hillside. Condrieu is at the center, not as well known as it
should be. Unfortunately, people traveling from Paris to the
South miss it, because the freeway is on the other bank of
the Rhône. Worth a detour, though, and a little shopping."

Then, we learn about the importance of temperature.
The wrong temperature can spoil a wine, no matter how
great it is to start with.

"I took care it shouldn't be too warm," explains Christophe. "We put the bottle on the bottom shelf of the
refrigerator for an hour, so it should be just about right
now: 64 degrees Fahrenheit, which is best for a full-bodied
wine like this. For a lighter red, 63 is better. You can't be
too particular about temperature, I tell you. I'd never drink
a very light red, say a Beaujolais, for instance, above 59.
Now, a rosé just cannot be served above or below 54—
that's a must. For white wines, it's a terrible error to chill
them. They should be cool, *not* cold, so 50 is about right.
Of course, champagne should be colder: 43, I'd say, but
certainly not below that."

Ariel nods solemnly. Wayne and I look at each other, aghast: Think of all the bottles we've served and consumed over the years . . . all at the absolutely wrong temperature! Reds at California temperatures of well above 63, and whites chilled all day in the fridge. The fact that we and our friends enjoyed every one of them only goes to show how ignorant we stand. Shall we ever dare serve another bottle, for fear of confusing temperatures? We are in awe.

Christophe checks the wall thermometer on the terrace. It is still 75 degrees Fahrenheit on this warm, still night. "Let's wrap the bottle in a damp towel, if we're not going to drink it right away. This will prevent it from warming too much."

The time has finally come. The bottle is ceremoniously unwrapped, carried to the table, uncorked with the utmost care, all the time resting in the wicker wine basket. Christophe looks around the table, screws his face in pain:

"Please, oh, please, take away those tulip glasses. We want footed ones, yes, but big and round."

The proper glasses are found, and an inch of wine poured into each.

"Admire that robe," recommends Christophe. "See the onion-peel tint?" Indeed, the wine looks like garnet shot through with amber. A lovely, clear, red-gold color. "Now, swirl it around and then hold it at eye level. See the drips inside? Those are the tears."

"Some call it *la cuisse*, the thigh," interrupts Ariel. "For that particular wine, I'd call it that. Sexier, because *this* is a sexy wine."

"Whatever," continues Christophe, "it tells you a lot about the body of the wine."

Next, the bouquet must be sniffed at length to evaluate the nose.

"Wine contains esters, similar to those found in fruit, flowers, woods, spices—any vegetal substance. One can easily identify scents of two or three flowers: This is known as the "floral" bouquet. The fruit aromas you detect in wine are the *fruité*.

"Côte-Rôtie is well known for its violet scent," puts in Ariel. "Quite distinctive, as a matter of fact."

I deeply breathe in the wine's rich aroma. Violets? I couldn't tell. Must admit I haven't smelled a bunch of violets in a long, long time, and I regret it now.

"In this particular case, I'm sure you can't fail to recognize the scent of geraniums, too. It's a distinctive undercurrent."

"*Pink* geraniums," specifies Ariel. "It would have to be, for God's sake, it's much too complex for a red one, and not bland at all like white geranium."

"Hmmm . . ." Christophe sniffs again. "You're right," he concedes, "pink geranium." Another long sniff: "And then you cannot miss a hint of peony."

Ariel frowns. "Of course, of course, peony. No doubt there. As a matter of fact, it is more than a hint. A definite statement. But it is *white* peony."

"Are you certain? I'd say peony, peony in general."

"Are you out of your mind? Lost your sense of smell, perhaps? I smell *white* peony, and that's quite different from the other colors. I said *white* peony." Ariel is ready to fight for her white peonies.

The *fruité* brings the same distinctions.

"Raspberry accent? You mean, Christophe, *wild* raspberries. Surely not the cultivated ones. They don't have that hint of musk wild raspberries do. Wild, Christophe, *wild*."

Or:

"Apricot? Perhaps. Yes, yes, that's right. But it is a spicy apricot, not a regular one."

"I agree," concedes Christophe, deep in concentration. "There are cloves under that apricot."

"Not under, Christophe. The cloves are not under, they stand right alongside."

But Christophe returns to the floral scents of the wine:

"Look here, Ariel, as far as those peonies are concerned, I wouldn't swear they're white. They could be any color. Don't you agree they all tend to smell alike?"

But Ariel stamps her foot. Those peonies are white, and no other color.

By the time we've learned that wine experts can distinguish up to fifty different fruit scents in vintages (and I have in vain tried to conjure up in my mind how many fruits I could even *name*; even with exotics like star fruit and guava, I'd never approach that number), tasting is mercifully allowed.

The bite, the palate, the swallow, the aftertaste are dissected. The verdict, arrived at after lengthy discussion between Ariel and Christophe: This wine is long in the mouth, quite rounded and full. It shows verve and distinction, perfect balance, and a steadily developing aroma. A real presence.

Ariel is still frowning, totally absorbed in her sipping:

"White peonies," she mutters. "White."

I must say that, once we can finally *drink* the wine, it is rich in taste and body, smooth and fragrant. So who could object to a little lyrical display of wine connoisseurship?

"There is a great deal more to identify," Christophe lectures. "Undercurrents of mint, *anis*, moss, oak, walnut or hazelnut, even orchard flowers—you name it. And if you learn how to concentrate your senses, you can find any of those and much more in a good wine. Putting the right name on your sensations helps their enjoyment."

No doubt he is right, there.

The filet has turned out perfect: rosy pink and tender in its golden crust, with an in-between layer of chopped shallots and mushrooms sautéed in butter and then *déglacé* in port. It slices beautifully, and little new potatoes, lightly browned, provide the perfect accompaniment. The night, on the terrace, has cooled down to sweet and balmy, cicadas are winding down the day's symphony. A silver half-moon hangs over the belfry where the bell has just chimed eleven. Time for the cheese tray, and we are such modest drinkers, there's enough left in the bottle to go with a sliver of chèvre and a taste of Roquefort. We savor the perfection of the moment. Ariel is less talkative than usual and seems lost in her thoughts.

"Something on your mind, Ariel?" Wayne wants to know.

"It's not just any kind of peonies in the wine. It is white ones, I'm sure."

Christophe pinches his lips. He doesn't quite agree, but is careful not to anger Ariel, who can be quite opinionated. As for Wayne and me, we frankly don't care. It was a great wine, good food, lovely company, and the perfect setting to enjoy them all. We say so, wholeheartedly.

Dessert is served, a Sissi, of course, with its multitude of flavors and colors. With it, Wayne guilelessly brings out from the fridge a bottle of Beaumes de Venise, a wonderful local muscat—great with sweets—and proceeds to serve it, chilled, just the way we've always liked it. "Too cold," chorus Ariel and Christophe. "*Much* too cold. Let it stand."

Wayne tries to protest. "We can't wait, or the Sissi will have melted. I'm sure it's going to be all right, especially since we're having it with an iced dessert."

While they argue, I panic slightly: How long will it take until they've identified the mango (wild), the passion fruit (the really passionate kind, not just the warmly affectionate), the musk rose (white, English, and of course, a moss rose), the acacia touched with mimosa, and hyacinth (pink or blue? With cinnamon under or right alongside?)? Should the Sissi meanwhile return to the freezer? But they relent, since the muscat is so obviously at the wrong temperature, it's not worth bothering with. They just drink it, stoically, having given up on trying to educate us.

"What a shame. Might as well kill it dead. Ten degrees too cold," sighs Christophe.

"Don't take that bottle of Côte-Rôtie away," begs Ariel as I clear some dishes away. "I want to triple check."

She pours the last drop onto her fingertip, sniffs, tastes with the tip of her tongue, concentrates.

"White peonies," she smiles at last, relieved of all doubt. "I knew it all along."

Christophe remains pointedly silent. Might be any color.

Later, as we walk with them to the gate, they notice, in a far corner of the terrace, a small bush, still in its plastic container. I bought it this morning at the Pertuis market, seduced by its elaborately lobed leaves and its giant, rounded yet disheveled blooms, white, lightly veined with pink. It is a sturdy, prolific-looking plant, and I'll set it in one of the planters now that the lavender has begun to fade.

"Nice flowers," remarks Ariel. "Never saw those before. Where did you get that plant?"

"Must be something tropical," suggests Christophe. "I don't remember seeing those before, either. Do you think they could live here? What are they called, anyway?"

Without blushing or stammering, I affirm that I just don't *know* the name. Perhaps I was told, but if I was, I forgot it. I bought the plant as a gift for my friend Liz to plant in her Aix garden, I add, thinking fast. Wayne will bring it to her tomorrow when he drives into town.

It is a peony plant. A white peony. But I *do* want to keep my friends, especially if they're wine connoisseurs.

Don't wait until summer . . .

Pruneaux au Rhum (Prunes in Rum: a variation on the Confiture de Vieux Garçon)

This version of the Confiture uses dried prunes, so you can make it any time of the year. The method is different here, because *dried* fruit must first be plumped in hot liquid, otherwise it will harden and shrivel in alcohol.

Use large, pitted prunes. Place them in a bowl. Pour enough *strong, hot, well-sweetened* tea to cover. Let stand, covered, overnight, unrefrigerated.

By next day, most of the tea will have been absorbed. Pour out any leftover liquid. Place prunes in jar and pour enough dark rum to cover. Close with lid.

Your *pruneaux* will be ready to eat in three days. They will keep for months in a cool, dark place.

You can serve the *pruneaux* in brandy snifters, with coffee. You can also serve them with ice cream or in pastries.

Note: In the southwest of France, Armagnac is used, and *Pruneaux à l'Armagnac* are a specialty of the city of Agen.

The Miracles of
Saint Amat

*I*nnocently, on one of our first summers, I decided to plant flowers around the foot of the six mulberry trees that shade the little square facing our house.

I dug out circular beds, set in petunia plants, which I fed fertilizer and watered in abundance under the critical eye of three elderly pensioners who spend their afternoons sitting on one of the stone benches there. Although I greeted them each day as I went by, they didn't return my *bonjour*. Not out of hostility, I guessed, or surliness, but simply because they didn't know me, or what I was about. Can't be too cautious with foreigners, so let's just wait and watch.

As I straightened out my back to survey, with some satisfaction, the results of my gardening efforts, one of them spoke up:

"You cannot plant here," he warned me gruffly. "This land doesn't belong to you."

"I know that," I replied. "This is municipal property. But flowers here cannot hurt. On the contrary, they'll make the square nicer for everybody."

"Kids will ride their bicycles right over them, or else trample them playing ball," volunteered another.

"They'll all be pulled out and stolen, with none left by morning," predicted the third. "Mark my word. You don't know about all the *bad* people here."

I assured them I stood ready to accept the worst. I'd just give it a try, all right? Whatever happens, happens, no skin off anybody's back. They all shook their heads morosely: A bad idea, since no one had ever done it before, this was enough reason not to do it now.

Nobody trampled the petunias, and they weren't stolen, either. Under my care, they prospered in scarlet and purple profusion, a nice note of color on the little *place*. When we went away for a few days, I worried that, on my return, I'd find them wilted for lack of water.

But, surprise! When we pulled up near the square, the day we came back, I spied from a distance all three gents busy weeding, pinching, and watering the beds. They had rigged a length of hose to the drinking fountain, and were soaking the ground around the plants. They didn't see us as we parked and went inside. After they had returned to their bench, hands clasped over walking sticks, I came out of the kitchen, smiling, carrying a tray of pastis glasses, ice clinking. They shrugged, grumbled, and grudgingly accepted the drinks. Then, they made room for me on the bench.

"You have no business planting anything if you can't be here to take care of it," one scolded. "Easy to see you were never a *farmer*! A good thing we were around. Otherwise, your flowers would all be dead. A fine sight that would be."

Next day, we all worked together, and they even showed me a pile of small rocks, half-hidden under weeds, that we could use to edge the beds, a very nice improvement. Of course, we relaxed from our labors with a pastis again. A week later, one of them brought me a bunch of pink and orange dahlias from his garden. "Here you are; since you like flowers so much, you should have those. Don't care for them myself. My poor wife planted them the year before she passed away."

This was several years ago, and the planting has now become a yearly ritual. My three friends have, *hélas!* dwindled to two, but together we keep the little square abloom all summer. If my arrival is delayed, then they go ahead without me, and I swear they almost smile when they see my surprise. But they shrug and grumble: "Someone's got to do the work, since *you* cannot be counted on."

So, in this way, and many others, we have become part of village life. Everybody seems aware of our schedule of arrival and departure. "Shouldn't you have been here last week already?" asks the bakery lady on my first croissant run. I even perform an important civic duty, serving on the *Comité de la Fête des Fleurs*, a municipally appointed group who, on the second Sunday in June, walks through the village, notebook in hand, granting points for the most flowery balcony, the best climbing vine, or the nicest use of plants and greenery. I always give top marks to Madame Amory, who grows incredibly lush, salmon-pink geraniums in a row of plastic motor-oil containers, labels and all, in front of her house.

Afterwards, the mayor distributes prizes, and treats the whole village to a *vin d'honneur*—in this case, *kir* of white wine and cassis liqueur—served on trestle tables under the mulberry trees, in the glory of the petunia beds. Wearing his Stetson by popular request, Wayne photographs the event for the municipal newsletter, and each year gets complimented on his progress in French.

But that June, to my chagrin, I wasn't asked to serve on the *comité*, and I felt quite disappointed not to be importantly pacing the village with the other members . . . when suddenly cries erupted in front of our windows:

"Are you home? Come on outside!"

"Come out, come out, you won first prize!"

Everybody was gathered on the square, glass in hand, beaming. The *comité* had excluded me, they explained, because had I been a judging member, I couldn't very well have been awarded this highest distinction. But now they were here, *comité*, municipal council, and the whole village behind them, holding forth our prize: a magnum of the village *mousseux*, a sparkling wine brewed from the famous rosé. Tears in my eyes, I swore we would *never* drink it, but instead cherish it forever as a keepsake of this most happy day in Provence. I presented my two friends and collaborators, who grunted, shrugged, and made as if to walk away, but were coaxed by unanimous cries until they reluctantly posed, scowling, for the camera. The mayor made a little speech, even throwing in a word or two of English, about international understanding being fostered through a common love of beauty.

Was this one of those miracles that, long ago, helped propel the good lord Amat into the ranks of sainthood? The duchess assures me that they continue to occur to this day. She is certain that the happiness of our village seems to dispense is only the fruit of benevolent grace this kindly saint bestows from heaven onto his former home.

The thought came to me as I was baking a *pissaladière* tart, its crust filled with golden onions and olives. Hadn't Saint Amat helped me find my way through petunia beds, into the heart of the village? And what of that joy our home obviously distills. Nothing, of course, but signs of the saint's mercies.

As I took the tart out of the oven, all brown and bubbly, I knew what I must do. I walked over to the church and lit a candle of gratitude. Better make that two, I thought, just in case someone equally blessed might not think of expressing appreciation.

In the flickering light of the two little flames, I could almost swear I saw a smile on the painted lips of the wooden statue.

Easy as pie . . .

Tartes Salées (Vegetable Tarts)

We attended a luncheon in the Luberon where food was set out, buffet style, in the lacy shade of an olive tree: three salads, three vegetable tarts (big ones), a tray of cheeses (Camembert, chèvre, Roquefort), and a fruit salad splashed with champagne at serving time. Petits fours were passed with coffee later.

Asked for her recipes, the hostess confessed she buys the dough for all her crusts from the frozen foods case at the market. But you might prefer to use your own pie crust recipe.

I suggest making *big* tarts, they go fast. Serve as a first or as a main course, or even in small slices, as an appetizer with drinks.

TOMATO TART

Spread crust with Dijon mustard. Cover with thin slices of Swiss cheese. On top, arrange overlapping slices of unpeeled tomato (squeeze tomatoes first, to expel excess liquid). Salt and pepper well. Sprinkle with chopped black olives, a little thyme, and more cheese, grated.

Bake at 350°F until tomatoes are done and cheese is lightly browned and bubbly. Lower temperature if crust browns too quickly.

PISSALADIÈRE (ONION TART, THE PROVENCE PIZZA)

Thinly slice 5 or 6 onions—you'll need a good quantity as they lose a lot of volume in sautéing. Cook them in a little olive oil until soft and lightly caramelized. Season well with salt and pepper, and a little nutmeg if you like. Spread evenly on crust. Beat one or two eggs (depending on the size of your tart) in ½ cup of cream and pour over the onions. Scatter a handful of black, pitted olives on top and sprinkle well with grated cheese. Bake at 350°F until set. Slide under broiler for just a moment to brown.

(Traditionally, the *pissaladière* is baked in a shallow rectangular dish. A cookie sheet works out well, too.)

Pass a bottle of Worcestershire sauce with the *pissaladière*.

TARTE AUX COURGETTES (ZUCCHINI TART)

Slice zucchini, unpeeled, and sauté in olive oil until soft and just *a little* browned (this caramelizes the sugar in the vegetables and brings out their flavor).

Spread crust with Dijon mustard. Place zucchini on top, in an even layer, about 1 inch thick. Season well with salt, pepper, and a little thyme and tarragon. Arrange small cubes of Gouda or Swiss cheese on top, so they form a pattern as they melt.

Bake at 350°F until the crust is browned and the cheese has melted and browned slightly.

The Saturday Ghostbusters

*I*f there existed an organized men's club in the village, its meetings would be held on Saturday mornings at the winery. Men congregate there then, as it is the preferred time to stock up on the week's wine provision. Women abstain, shrugging they have more important things to do, like cooking, cleaning, taking care of the kids, balancing the checkbook. Men, for their part, are certain that wine purchase is far too serious a business to be entrusted to females.

The winery is the *Coopérative Vinicole*, an official-looking building just outside the village, where local vineyard owners truck their crop of grapes at harvesttime. Weight and quality are measured, and each owner paid accordingly.

Grapes are pressed in great vats, their juice fermented according to government-prescribed laws, and the wine is sold year-round thereafter, at the *Coopérative*. Each Luberon village owns such a cooperative winery. They were built in the 1920s, after the government granted local wines the prestigious and lucrative appellation of Côtes de Provence or Côtes du Luberon.

So, male crowds gather under the jolly, if calculating, eye of the director, Monsieur Gendre, Robert to everyone. Robert is careful to watch his step: Although he's run the *Coopérative* for well over twenty-five years, he is not a true villager, doesn't even speak with the local accent, coming, as he does, from some *city* up *north*. So, what he lacks in inbred trustworthiness, he tries to make up in good cheer and an even better business sense. A stocky five-foot three, wearing a Stetson that Wayne brought him from the States, he looks like a teapot with a mismatched lid. Together with tall, lanky Wayne, of whom Robert is fond, calling him John Wayne, they make a Mutt and Jeff or Don Quixote and Sancho Panza pair.

Robert keeps the conversation going, serves abundant samples, entertains with jokes, and pushes sales, while his wife, silent and attentive, fills out stacks of government-required forms and collects money in the isolation of her glass-enclosed cubicle. Wayne's presence will often bring to mind stories about Americans. Quite a folklore has grown around those Americans eagerly awaited during the war and stationed in France for years after World War II. The passing of time has turned them, by now, into larger-than-life characters.

"When I was a boy," tells the baker, "American forces were still in Marseille, and they had their own cinema where they could go for free. I was apprenticed to a baker in town who furnished bread for their messhalls, so a supply sergeant gave me a pass. Was I happy to be allowed to go to the American movies! Next Sunday afternoon, it is freezing cold, and there's that long line of GIs stretching way down the block. Freezing, I tell you, with a mistral to blow the mast off a ship. Yet, they all stand and wait patiently. *Peuchère!* You'd never see the *Marseillais* stand like that. They'd push and shove and crowd at the door instead. Well, the line is barely inching, and there's that tall MP standing by, feet apart, a little ways off, watching, chewing his gum." The storyteller puts on a wooden expression, mimics the gum-chewing, watching MP. "While his back is turned, quick, I run and sneak up to the front, oh, maybe third in line or so. Nobody says a word. They all just stand there, chewing their gum, so I think: 'Hey, I guess I am smarter than they are, but they don't seem to mind.' Then, just as I reach the window to show my pass, a hand comes up, grabs my collar, lifts me off the ground, and that MP carries me back to the very end of the line. Not a word is said, mind you, they don't laugh or jeer, they all just go on chewing their gum. *Des drôles de gaillards, ces Ricains,*" he concludes, half admiring and half uncomprehending. "Funny guys, those *Ricains.*"

This brings forth more reminiscences of weird American behavior.

The U.S. Fleet occasionally makes port in Marseille, and when it does, the Shore Patrol, the SP, is there to check on the good manners of sailors on the town.

"It was late, my wife and I were walking out of a restaurant right on the Vieux Port," tells Victor, a young man who works for Air France. "We saw two American sailors having a fight with a couple of Arabs, and they were good fighters, too, mind you, using only their fists, but with those Arabs, you never know; they're quick at pulling a knife out of nowhere. Meanwhile, the Shore Patrol jeep is parked along the sidewalk, not far off, with two SP sitting in it, helmets pulled down to their eyes, looking asleep, except they're chewing their gum. When they've seen enough, they just look at each other, swing their legs over the sides, and amble over to the fighters. Each drops one of their boys cold with his baton, drags him by the shoulders to the jeep, and they take off. It all happened so fast, the Arabs just stood there, openmouthed."

Everybody laughs but wishes the Arabs, too, had been given a chance to wake up in the brig. Those talkative, exuberant, volatile Mediterraneans are impressed, and at the same time puzzled, by phlegmatic Anglo-Saxon behavior. How can anyone remain silent in situations that involve emotions? In any situation, in fact? Does gum-chewing replace words for those *Ricains*? Would they, perchance, feel no emotions? Have nothing to say? Still, one must admit they have a way, *toc!* to deal with situations, that you have to admire.

The postmaster was ready to leave, his twenty-liter jug hoisted over his shoulder. But he, too, remembers an America-connected story, so he puts the jug down.

"This takes place in *Amérique*, in the *Farouest*. There are these three *coboys* in a saloon: an Englishman, an American, and a *coboy* from Marseille. They're fighting and carrying on about who is the best shot, and raising such a ruckus that the bartender gets fed up, so he shoves all three through the saloon doors and they go sprawling in the dust. As soon as they've picked themselves up, they resume their arguing, and they're so loud, a crowd gathers.

" 'I'll show you, mates' the English *coboy* says. 'Just watch.' And he throws a shilling into the air, draws, shoots. The shilling falls to the ground, pierced clear through the middle. The crowd whistles and applauds.

" 'Next, the American *coboy*, he shifts his gum, waddles in his chaps to the center, folds a dollar bill lengthwise, throws it up into the wind, and shoots. The two halves of the dollar flutter to the ground. The crowd gasps.

"'Now, the Marseille *coboy*, he is a short, bowlegged little guy, he hitches up his pants and crouches in the middle of the town square. 'See that mosquito buzzing, over there? About forty feet away?' Everybody peers, squints, and finally, yes, they can make out the mosquito.

"*Bang!* goes the Marseille *coboy*'s gun. 'See?' he calls out to the crowd triumphantly.

" 'But your mosquito is still there! It's not dead at all. It's still flying!' protests the crowd.

" 'Ah, flying, yes' retorts the Marseille *coboy*. 'Flying, that he is. Only, he'll *never* make love again.' "

This brings roars of laughter, for they're all familiar with the Marseillais' reputation as braggards and probably liars. Robert takes advantage of the good feeling to push his last year's red. Everybody agrees that it is not all that great, and the sooner it is drunk, the better, before it turns to regular vinegar. Still, the price is right, so several ten-liter jugs are quickly moved.

But the belfry bell reminds everyone that the morning is well along. Aperitif is uncalled for, since wine sampling has been going on throughout. Now, wives soon will have *déjeuner* ready, and it would not do to be late. Monsieur Fabre shakes hands and leaves: His wife is baking her special eggplant dish, the *Demoiselles d'Aix*, so he is eager to get home. Time only for a last story, this one from Robert.

"God created the world, and after he finished, he thought he could rest at last, but instead, he heard a great yelling coming from *everywhere*. All the countries he'd created were complaining, saying he'd given way too much to France, and not enough to anyone else.

" 'Look at what you've done, Lord!' they cried. 'The Eiffel Tower, the Loire castles, the Riviera, the cheeses, the wines, the three-star restaurants, beautiful women. It's too much. It's *unfair*. Do something to even things up.'

"So, God looked over what he'd done. They are right, he thought. That perfect hexagon: seas, oceans, mountains, fertile plains, great food, Provence, yet! France has it all. I must do something to spoil it some, so other countries won't feel cheated.

"*Alors*, He thought about it all day Sunday, and on Monday, he created the *French*."

———

Laughter is polite, pointedly less hearty than before. Of course they'd all agree that God gave all that to France, too much, perhaps, and not enough to lesser countries. But what's wrong with that? And what's wrong with the *French*, pray? Not one of them would trade his nationality for any other, nor can they think of a single negative trait attached to it.

As everyone is getting ready to carry purchases away, the curé pants in, greeted by a semirespectful silence and a few touched caps. He has served this parish for years, knows all his parishioners, has baptized and married most of those present, and remembers each of their youthful pranks.

"*Bonjour, bonjour,*" smiles the curé, wiping his brow and laying his jug on the floor. "Glad I found you still open," he tells Robert. "Just finished catechism. Say, Antoine, that boy of yours, he's no better than you were, and just as hardheaded, too. Can't recite a single prayer yet, but I caught him shooting his slingshot at pigeons on my windowsill. He breaks the panes, you get the bill."

"Punish him, *Monsieur le Curé*," retorts Antoine. "I can only make him do what he *wants* to do. Takes after his mother. The way she talks back to me. . . ."

A moment of reflective silence. It seems Antoine's wife isn't the only one talking back.

"Have you heard about the cemetery?" asks the curé.

No. No one has heard anything concerning the cemetery, where exciting events are, after all, rare.

"Well, last night, Lodie Babin came running to my house. *Pauvrette!* Crying, she was, almost fainting, and trembling all over, could hardly get hold of herself. Scared out of her wits. Seems she'd been out to the cemetery, after sunset, to tend her family tomb—daytime's too hot right now—when she saw ghosts."

"What kind, boy ghosts or girl ghosts?" leers Robert, looking around for guffaws.

"Must have been large for old Babin to see them, blind as a bat as she is," chimes in the postmaster, who's not from the village, either. Glances silence him.

"Says they were dancing all over the grave of Julien Delmas; you know, the Delmas grandfather who died not long ago. The tombstone was put in place last month, and they piled up all the wreaths on top. Well, she claims she watched ghosts jumping up and down, tossing wreaths up in the air. She saw the tombstone pushed from under, like old Julien was trying to get out. . . ."

Nobody here believes in ghosts, of course. Yet the words bring an unmistakable *frisson*. Better be cautious in cases that involve the dead. You never know. No snickers are heard.

"Could be some kids playing? Trying to scare her, maybe?" ventures Robert.

"She says no, no kids. These were *real* ghosts. Don't you think a few of us should go over to the cemetery tonight, after sunset, and find out just what kind of ghosts these are, and what's going on?"

Victor volunteers first, and he quickly forms a posse. Each will bring his hunting rifle, because there's no telling what you're going to find in a cemetery after dark. The hunting season hasn't begun yet, but should the gendarmes happen by, why, they'll be enlisted in the ghostbusting expedition. If any mischief is going on there, then it's their job to make arrests.

"Hey, Wayne, want to come along? Bring your six-shooter?"

Wayne returns home in a state of high excitement. He doesn't have a gun here, of course, since transporting firearms is not encouraged by Air France. No hunting rifle, either. Anyway, he wouldn't kill a living thing, and always escorts lurking spiders out of doors. He takes from the wall the antique dueling sword we bought at a flea market and is examining the blade, but I am so convulsed with laughter at the idea of skewering a ghost, or even several, on that rotisserie implement that, his dignity ruffled, he abandons the idea and replaces the weapon on the wall.

All afternoon he tries to tackle this chore or that, waiting for the day to drag itself into evening, and as time goes, I am getting restless, too. Finally, the sun has set, and here they are, all four of them armed to the teeth, knocking on the *volet*. With Wayne, plus the curé, it will be a fearsome six.

Rifles are stood inside the kitchen door. I serve pastis with slices of tomato tart. Those brave men will need sustenance tonight, and the next refill goes quickly down, too. Now, they're on their way to meet the curé, who's waiting for them in front of the church, where he went to get his *goupillon*, the holy-water sprinkler. After they leave, I see the sword is no longer on the wall. Wayne must have taken it after all, while I wasn't looking.

Twilight is gathering. All alone in the darkening house, I'm not laughing anymore. Excitement, touched with a thrill of fear, has taken hold of me, and I'm eager to know what kind of ghosts the men are going to find down at the cemetery. Could these be dangerous? Will they be captured? Scared away? Is it all just a prank? Or is there really *something* supernatural going on? What could the old lady have seen there last night? Although it is still too early to turn on the lights, I feel better with them on. A moment passes. I turn on the TV, and then turn it off. I want to hear whatever is going on outside.

A shot, followed after a pause by three more, startles me. My God, it sounds as if someone might be hurt. Then silence, nothing but silence as I strain my ears, silence with only the pounding of my heart, and half an hour passes, which seems like an eternity.

Finally, I hear voices and laughter outside. The troops are back, all accounted for, unhurt and rather thirsty. Wine is brought out, this time, with a crock of pâté, a jar of cornichons, and baguettes to slice on a breadboard. After they have sufficiently recovered, I get to learn the story.

First, they walked single file, stealthily, into the cemetery, stepping carefully so gravel wouldn't crunch underfoot. They soon found the aisle where the Delmas tomb would be, and spotted it, a brand-new black marble slab shining between old mossy ones. Wreaths were indeed piled up on top: some made up of real flowers, now all dried up; others, those big bright plastic arrangements people bring nowadays; and even a few of the old-fashioned kind they used to make, with little glass beads strung to form flowers. And they'll be damned if these wreaths were, if not quite dancing, at least lifting, moving sideways, and occasionally being tossed aside.

"It looked just like someone was underneath, reaching through the marble slab, pushing the wreaths away," says Victor, putting down his glass for a refill. "Old Lodie Babin had it right."

So, they stood there watching, frozen on the spot, not daring to come closer. A sight to chill anyone's blood. Surely someone, or something, was pushing at those wreaths. Was old Julien trying to get out? In the evening silence, they could hear muffled little cries. And if it wasn't old Julien, then, was it his ghost? Or his spirit? Something supernatural was happening right under their eyes.

The curé reached for his rosary, held it up, to no effect. A sprinkling of holy water from a safe distance didn't stop the saraband, either, or the cries that were enough to break your heart. None of them dared move closer. Suppose a ghostly hand were to suddenly reach out and. . . . So they waited, holding their breaths. What should they do now?

Finally, Victor shouldered his rifle, raised it, and at a loss for better action, fired a shot into the air.

And just then, believe it or not, a whole flock of little birds took off, as if they, too, were shot into the air, dozens of finches, in a great flutter of wings, chirping in terror, and began circling above in a panic. It seems they've built nests under those wreaths and, in the evening, they're all there, feeding their young, lifting the wreaths as they move back and forth underneath, before getting settled down for the night.

"So, we fired a few more shots into the air for good measure, and we decided to leave the finches alone. Let them return to their nests. At least now we know what causes the commotion."

I'm glad the birds weren't hurt.

"No, no, not worth shooting them. Much too small to eat."

Wayne swears he cannot remember a more intense adventure than ghostbusting in the village cemetery. Still he regrets not coming home with a *brochette de fantômes* speared on his sword.

Madame Fabre's secret recipe . . .

Demoiselles d'Aix (Eggplant Rolls)

"This," declares Monsieur Fabre, who, after a half century of his wife's superlative cooking, knows a thing or two about *good*, "this is *excellent*. I call it the haute cuisine of Provence." Monsieur Fabre is right. The dish takes some preparation, but the result is entirely worth it.

Serves 4

2 or 3 eggplants
Olive oil
½ pound Emmentaler or Comté or other
　Swiss cheese
1 pound thinly sliced cooked ham
Tomato sauce (recipe follows)

Peel and slice eggplant in long strips, about 3 inches wide. Broil or fry in oil, in batches, until just tender, and lay them flat to drain on paper towels. Cut cheese in 3-inch-long sticks, ½ inch in diameter. Cut ham in 3-inch-wide strips. Wrap a stick of cheese in each strip of ham, and wrap, in turn, each in a slice of eggplant.

Arrange rolls standing up in a baking dish (a *tian*). Pour enough tomato sauce over to cover, leaving only the tips of the rolls showing.

Bake at 350°F for 25 minutes. Lower heat and continue baking at 300°F for another 30 minutes or longer.

TOMATO SAUCE

For 1 pound of tomatoes, you'll need: 1 pound of onions, 5 cloves of garlic, 1 bay leaf, salt and pepper, basil, 1 Tbs sugar, 2 Tbs vinegar.

Cut tomatoes into eighths (press them first to expel excess liquid), and slice onion. Cook in heavy saucepan with garlic and bay leaf, covered, until they have become a compote. This will take at least 1 hour. Add salt, pepper, basil, sugar, and vinegar. Stir well.

In your blender, mix at high speed until the puree is

smooth. It should be thick. If too watery, return to saucepan and boil, uncovered, until it reaches desired consistency. Verify seasonings.

Wine: A red Côtes de Provence, Vieilles Vignes, for instance, would do justice to this savory dish.

Not All Stings Are
from Mosquitoes

There are few bugs in our part of Provence—as opposed to the more humid Riviera—and whatever there would be are gobbled up on the wing by *hirondelles d'église*, small, wedge-shaped swallows that nest in cracks and holes between old stones in the church walls, castle towers, and fortifications.

Seldom seen during the day, they surge forth in droves at twilight, flying in great swooping arcs, just for sheer exuberant joy, it would seem. However, this is not fun, but dinnertime: They catch a myriad of insects, and when a storm threatens, dive low enough to graze the ground, because, we are told, the change in atmospheric pressure drives the bugs lower.

One evening, sitting on our terrace in semidarkness, enjoying the last of a new dessert I'd just learned how to make, a violent thud startled us. An *hirondelle* had hit the wall, and, stunned or dead, fallen to the floor. Wayne tenderly gathered it and carried it upstairs, wrapped in a tissue, when we went to bed. During the night, the bird recovered enough to slip between the wall and the phone jack, tightly folded into an impossibly thin wedge, the way they probably do in their nests.

Early the next morning, Wayne was ringing the bell at the Pertuis vet's door. The vet, a gentle young Vietnamese, examined the bird, stretched its wings, ascertained no broken bones, gave it water through an eye dropper, and instructed Wayne to bring it home, try feeding it boiled egg yolk—which was refused—and to launch it into the air, the only way *hirondelles* can take off.

So, Wayne, heart in his mouth, positioned himself on the top terrace, carrying the little bird folded inside his hand, unhooked its claws from his ring, and, finally, threw it up in the air, dreading to see it drop, helpless, to the ground. Instead, the *hirondelle* extended its wings, and, flying fast and high, took off, arcing in the direction of the church.

"I felt like I was bestowing life, or flight, in that case," confessed Wayne afterward. "Just like God on the Sistine ceiling, reaching out his hand to touch Adam's to give him life."

But if we are spared mosquitoes, other stings aren't unknown, victims usually unsuspecting foreigners, naively lulled into a dreamlike trance by the charms of Provence, or simply hoping to avoid hassles and enjoy their vacation.

We had become friends with Derek, an Englishman, who'd discovered the village just as we did, and fell in love with it, just as we had. A ruin was found for him, and Ariel drew lovely plans. Work had progressed well, when, *hélas!*, the two had a falling-out over design: Derek wanted the fireplace in the *center* of the back wall. Ariel insisted on placing it in the *corner*, her trademark being dramatically slanted staircases angling across living-room back walls. Unfortunately, Ariel, who is gifted and generous to a fault, can be pigheaded stubborn, especially in matters of her own taste versus anyone else's. When she angrily dropped out of the project, Derek found himself left to deal on his own with suppliers and artisans.

"First, there was that beautiful stone, which had served for centuries as a doorstep to the ruined entrance. More than five feet long, worn in the center, seasoned by time, it would, with just a little carving at both ends, make a perfect mantelpiece, since the entrance door would be moved.

"So, I asked François, the stonecutter, to haul it over to his workshop, store it there, where it couldn't be stolen, and work on it as agreed. When the house was ready for it, he would haul it back and install it, just the way we'd discussed it. I even gave him a handsome advance payment.

"When I came back six months later, the fireplace was ready for its mantel, and I looked for François. He dodged me for days, but I finally cornered him in his workshop. There, he showed me a nondescript piece of rock, newly cut from some quarry, white and crumbly.

" '*Voilà* your stone,' he tells me.

" 'No, no, it's not that one at all. Mine is old, seasoned, and *much* bigger. That's the one I want. Where is it?' " Derek may be new to Provence and country life, but through the construction of his house he's already learned that the value of a large, genuinely antiqued stone can reach several thousand dollars. So, he's not going to accept that . . . that quarry reject.

Or is he?

Derek's old stone is nowhere in sight. François swears to high heavens that *this* is the one he was asked to haul and store. Furious but helpless, Derek conducts his own investigation and learns that his beautiful stone has indeed been finished by François, who sold it and installed it as a mantel in a new home nearby. Derek fumes, swears he is going to sue François and drag him through the courts. But first, he'll march in to confront the new house's owners.

Sleepless through the night, he thinks better of it: These people are probably in good faith, they've honestly paid François and would no doubt take Derek for a crank or a madman if he barged in, babbling about owning their mantelpiece. So, by next morning, he's decided nothing could possibly be gained that way. He'd only create a useless scandal and ridicule himself in the bargain.

Meanwhile, every villager, of course, knows exactly what happened, but not a single one would testify on Derek's behalf. Not because they love François so much. They don't even *like* him, and he has a bad reputation for being dishonest, a drunk, perhaps even taking drugs. But here, that kind of silence is called *minding your own business.*

Besides, village solidarity is stronger than loyalty to us newcomers.

A scalded cat, Derek is now watchful. When he next returns to the village, a truckload of roof tiles has just been delivered. So, first thing, he checks the delivery against the invoice.

"Terra-cotta roof tiles come in great packages of one hundred, held together with metal bands. I arrive two days after they've been dumped at my construction site, and count twelve such packages, therefore *twelve hundred* tiles. The invoice reads *fifteen hundred*. Next, I measure a tile: *Fifteen inches* long, at *seven* francs each. The same afternoon, I call at the tileworks, inquire about size and price. A *fifteen-inch* tile retails at *five* francs, and the *eighteen-inch* size at *seven* francs. I was charged for the larger size.

"I raised a big stink, but both the tileman and the trucker agreed I'd been delivered exactly what the invoice describes: fifteen hundred tiles. More sleuthing shows that, indeed, some of the stacks had been stolen before my arrival.

"Who stole them? Some gypsy-type people who live just below took some. They are, at this very moment, repairing their shack's roof with brand-new tiles, right under my nose. . . . A neighbor, too, hinted that she *might* have observed boys pushing a wheelbarrow loaded with tiles, coming from the direction of my construction site. The thefts, though, probably don't account for all that's missing. I'm certain they shorted me on the delivery. But the consensus seems to be: 'You ought to have been here. With no one around, who's to tell?' "

Wayne is sympathetic to his friend's plight. "It still leaves the matter of size and price. You were overcharged there by several hundred dollars. Did you straighten that out?"

"Oh, that," Derek admits ruefully. "You see, both the tileworks and the trucking office closed down on Friday, to go on their summer vacation. They won't reopen for at least six weeks, and their phones are not answered. I might as well admit that I was so worn out and felt so inadequate in dealing with the matter, that I decided to drop it. I paid the bill. Why? I want the damn roof to be up before I leave again. Otherwise, work will be delayed until next year, and with the interior almost finished now, I'd find it all ruined after being exposed to weather all winter long."

This is the heart of the matter. Someday soon we'll be leaving for our nebulous foreign land, and we are eager to see our work done before. But *they* are staying, village life will go on, and they'll continue dealing with one another.

Wayne and I aren't immune to that particular facet of the Provence spirit.

Mélanie, our cleaning lady, never a model of grace even on her best days, had become, over the years, truly venomous. When we first hired her, presented by our neighbor, Madame Oraison, who praised her honesty, my intention was to pay her for so many hours a week when we are here and a lower fee just to look after the house the rest of the year. But Wayne, always concerned about the welfare of others, felt that fairness demanded, instead, that we pay her the same summer salary all year long. He reasoned that, if we expected her to be available at our convenience, we must pay her as well the rest of the time, make that in three-month installments, payable in advance, so she'd never have to worry about an unpaid bill. Far from recognizing this arrangement as fair and even generous, that charmer reads in it only weakness and stupidity on our part. So, to test our limits she lets us find increasing sloth, cobwebs, unwashed windows, and dust everywhere when we arrive. She'll even write to complain if her advance is a few days late.

For several years, I carried on endless arguments with the phone and electric companies, for bills impossibly incurred in an unoccupied house. French phone bills, unless specially requested to do so, show no detail on calls, only the total amount due. When I eventually filed the request, we found numerous phone calls made to Corsica, Tunisia, and other places where Mélanie's relatives live. I even learned that she'd housed visitors of hers in our home, for the better part of a winter. Still, we decided to let that pass, rather than face the scene of recriminations that would be sure to follow.

Encouraged by such kindness, which is in fact inexcusable cowardice, for I'll admit I am a little afraid of her, she took to viciously displaying her much vaunted "honesty." This honesty applies to two pet subjects: Foreigners are poison to the villages of Provence; and our house, in particular, is an eyesore. I listened with one ear, controlling my exasperation, continued tolerating her . . . and paying her, like the idiot I am.

Further testing our limits, in spite of repeated entreaties, she even stopped watering plants altogether. Since it is easier for us to clean a house ourselves than to replace dead plantings, we explored other avenues and discovered that a Monsieur Autessier who ran a garden service nearby might be available for a weekly visit.

Monsieur Autessier waxed lyrical on his love for anything that grows out of the ground. He even owned a *book*, he told me in confidence, with names of plants. I explained that I didn't expect such erudition, just a weekly, year-round watering as needed, plus, perhaps, a little weeding thrown in. I love gardening, so I could interrupt the service when we are there, but fairness demands, etc. There is a French term to describe people like us: *bonnes poires*, juicy pears. In other words, easy marks. Mélanie became furious when we hired Autessier, perceiving him, perhaps, as a spy who would report on her. But then, she is furious more often than not.

So, all year, every month, we dutifully paid Monsieur Autessier's bill, and rejoiced that our problem had been solved.

In the spring, we learned that our work would require our presence in Europe in late September and again in early November. So we decided to postpone our summer trip and instead spend September, October, and November in the village. Fall in the Luberon is beautiful, and we can seldom be there to enjoy it.

There had been rains when we arrived, so the planters on the terraces were wet. Still, I found a suspicious number of overgrown, disheveled plants, and among them a number of dead ones. Deadest were the chrysanthemums, which should have been in bloom right now. Must have been a long, hot summer, I thought, while I threw away the corpses and pruned the rest. I'm sure M. Autessier did his best.

A week, two weeks, passed, and then another. No M. Autessier. I watered regularly, but kept wondering when I was going to see my gardener. Perhaps he happened to show up while we were out? To be certain, I tied a thin thread to the latch of a terrace gate that only *he* would use. The thread remained intact to the day we left.

Back in California, what sits right on top of the pile of mail? Autessier's bills, of course, for three months' service, with a touching little note, deploring the fact I won't be there to enjoy the chrysanthemums' blooming season, since they are particularly *jolis* this year.

I am shaking with indignation. I'll *joli* you, I think, and in a rage, I dial Autessier.

"I am calling you from California, where I have just returned after three months in the village. Your bills are here, but I shall not pay them, because you never came *once* during all the time I was there, and probably not much the rest of the time, either."

A silence at the other end of the line. Ah, ah, I thought, gotcha. I'd like to see how you're going to explain *that* one away. But instead, M. Autessier was gathering *his* righteous anger.

"Did you say you were in the village for three months? Is *that* what you said? I call that nerve. And you never had the courtesy of letting me know! You couldn't be bothered to call and say *bonjour*? That's a low trick if I ever saw one. You *spied* on me, that's what you did. And here I trusted you, never dreaming you'd be the one to pull such a dishonest one on me. After all the *work* I did for you!"

I tried to put in a word edgewise, but Mr. A. was too wound up. My anger was no match for his.

"One would think you'd have the decency to call, rather than sneak in like a thief! With that kind of behavior, what did you expect?"

I managed to sputter:

"I expected, Monsieur Autessier, one thing, and one thing only. I expected you to do the job you're paid for."

"*I* am an honest man, madame," Autessier declared grandly. "If I had even *suspected* that you were there, I wouldn't have missed *once*. That's the kind of person I am."

Bravely, then, I didn't pay those last three months' bills, and that was the end of Autessier. Plants continued to die, poor dried-up little mummies, right next to the water source. We tried plugging in an electric timer, but that didn't work because power surges and failures are frequent and it turned off right away.

Finally, on the next trip, I found the planters turned to mud and overflowing. Mélanie *had* turned on the water . . . and forgotten to turn it off, letting it run for how long? A week? A month? Longer? Mildewed stones, ruined upholstery, and puddles of rank water greeted us in the vaulted rooms below.

When I attempted to confront her, she let out a barrage of rantings, raving about supposed leaks in our pipe system and complaining how nothing ever works right here, in the first place. Furthermore, she had thought up a new one this year:

"Now that you have arrived, I'm taking the six-week vacation that you owe me. I hope you'll know how to clean house, and if not, perhaps you can learn." We didn't owe her a vacation, for she held a regular job elsewhere and only "worked" for us, as we call it, in her spare time. Besides, she always could, and did, take weeks and weeks of vacation in our absence. Yet, angry as I might be, I was also somewhat relieved. Better let her go; I'll be rid of her over the summer. But, magnanimously, she was going to "work" before leaving, and as she vaguely dusted around she treated me once more to an even more fervent version of her favorite canto: Foreigners—and that includes Parisians as well—are the ruination of Provence villages. Perhaps in the past I did answer that replacing bramble-infested ruins with beautiful, authentically restored homes, employs numerous artisans in the process and creates substantial tax revenue. The people who occupy these homes come here to spend money in shops, restaurants, garages, and pay *help*, too. But I was past that point. This time, I'd had it. And I listened, livid, with clenched teeth, waiting for a pause in which I'd fire her for good.

Instead, she segued into her second stanza: Our house is an insult to her aesthetic sensibilities as well as a blight on the village. One of our windows, in fact, looks more Italian than Provençal to her expert eye! Why bother to tell her that the National Office of Fine Arts had to approve every detail? "It would take foreigners to ruin Madame Martin's place. She kept the most beautiful chickens you ever did see where you have that . . . that terrace, as you call it. I look the other way when I'm walking by. Inside . . . well, I pray

God to help me tolerate what I see, but it just turns my stomach." This went on and on. She was in fine form that day, even more lyrical than usual.

Except that she'd managed to truly enrage me. Replacing *that* can't be too hard, I thought.

"Leave this instant," I hissed, "and don't you ever dare come back." (Still, I let her keep the three months' wages paid in advance.)

Wayne and I celebrated that night with a special dinner at the Cheval Blanc, our favorite restaurant, and clinked our glasses, basking in a feeling of joyful liberation. If we didn't find another cleaning woman, it wouldn't make much difference, anyway. We were rid of her at last. How could we have tolerated her for so long?

Still, timid people can be pushed too far, and I was now vindictive. The sluices of my pent-up anger were wide open, and I wouldn't rest until I had some sort of a revenge. Firing is too good for that shrew. She needs a better lesson. Let's take a stroll down the warpath. I might know just what to do.

The next day, carrying two generous helpings of double chocolate-raspberry, I knock on the door of old Madame Oraison, who lives across the street from us. She loves ice cream, but doesn't own a fridge. I remember how she introduced us to Mélanie, when the latter was still an almost nice girl. I know she keeps in close contact with her as with everybody in the village. She walks with difficulty, but a telephone sits at her elbow, she receives numerous visits from the ladies, and enjoys a place of distinction at the hub of the local grapevine.

"Too bad we can't have Mélanie anymore," I comment. "But I understand that now I owe her a six-week vacation, and just when we are here. . . ."

"You don't owe her *any* vacation," interrupts Madame O. "Must be an idea she got into her head, that's all."

Well, I explain that poor, overworked Mélanie *does* need a summer vacation, after all, but since *I* need service, we decided to come to a parting of the ways. "Still," I go on, "I was lucky to have her all these years. . . ."

I am sure Madame O. knows I have *fired* Mélanie, but she doesn't let on.

"There aren't many like her," I say, truthfully. "Honest as the day is long! Always speaks her mind, tells you what she thinks and nothing else. . . . How many times did she tell me that foreigners like us are a plague on villages? Who else would have been frank enough to tell me to my face?"

More meditative licking of spoons. Madame Oraison is poised, knowing some juicy gossip is coming her way.

"As a matter of fact, that honesty did us a great service. Because she also told me many times how much she hates our house. Probably told you, too."

"Perhaps she talks too much," ventures Madame O.

"Well, she tells it the way she sees it. Doesn't look Provençal to her and the bathroom window has an Italian feeling . . . so awful, she has to look the other way. . . . And the inside of the house just turns her stomach."

I continue slowly, so not a word will be missed.

"You see, we were going to leave her that house in our wills, or perhaps even give it to her *much* sooner, when we don't feel like coming here anymore. Yes, with everything in it. Everything. Both my husband and I felt she should have it, after working in it so hard and for so long. . . . So, we wrote our wills some time ago, making her the beneficiary of *everything.*" I stress the word again. "With enough regular income, of course, to maintain it. But you see, we finally came to our senses."

Inheritance matters a great deal here and is taken most seriously. Entire lives are spent waiting for a legacy.

Madame O. nearly drops her ice cream. Openmouthed, she is trying to take in that prime information. Now, that will nourish gossip for the rest of the summer. Might even pass into the village lore. Did she understand correctly?

"You're leaving her your house? With everything in it? Even that washer-dryer from America?"

"Why, yes. That is to say, we *were.* But now, thank God, that we understand at last how she really feels about it, we are changing the terms of our wills. Can you imagine saddling the poor girl with something she hates so much?"

Madame O. gazes through her open window at our gated entry, the arched doorway. She can hear the fountain in the terrace pool. And then, there is that washer-dryer from America, not to mention that refrigerator with the ice-making machine. . . .

"Maybe she just talks. I know she liked it better in Madame Martin's time . . . and then, she can be ornery," protests Madame O. feebly. I can see she fervently rejoices over what she's learning. Village solidarity fades before news of such quality. Oh, what a story to tell! and to Mélanie first, of course.

"Oh, no," I interrupt. "She told me quite plainly how

much she hates it. As you know, she *always* speaks the truth."

"Foolish girl," reflects Madame O. "Would have changed her from that hole she and her father live in."

She is now eager for me to leave, for she can't wait to tell her friends: "Can you believe those Americans were going to *give* Mélanie that house they paid so much for?" (The price, never announced in the village, has been magnified in consequence.) "With money every month, too, so she could afford to maintain it. But that stupid girl couldn't keep her mouth shut and had to blab to them that she hates it. So, now, they've changed their wills. Serves her right, don't you know. When you think that washer-dryer from America could have been hers one day! The American woman even told me that they would probably have given it soon, because they won't be coming here much longer."

The next morning, I heard noise in the kitchen and found Mélanie standing at the sink, arranging a dozen store-bought carnations.

"I went to Pertuis and picked this color, because it goes so well in your beautiful living room," she said. "It's like this kitchen: Working here is more like pleasure, it's so nice! I always meant to tell you. And, by the way, I came to inform you that I have changed my vacation plans. I'll be here all summer, *à votre service*," and she concluded, with great effort, "*Madame.*"

I'd had my revenge, but I remained firm, refused the peace offering, and Mélanie stayed fired. As it turned out, we had no trouble at all replacing her. The very next day, a nice lady volunteered to help, a lady who thought enough of us to have her hair done and wear her pearl necklace whenever she came to work. She did wonders with the silver. And, when she had to leave, she brought us Dolorès, a smiling young woman who's been with us to this day.

Still, the summer wouldn't be complete without Derek's latest.

He arrived for dinner, convulsed with laughter.

"You know that, three years ago, I ordered a special chest of drawers from Monsieur Brun, the cabinetmaker near Aix."

Indeed, we'd received periodic reports about the chest of drawers. First, M. Brun played hard to get. Finally, he'd relented, and showed up with wood samples and a book of different styles. The new piece had to fit a certain spot and serve as a companion to an antique armoire Derek had recently acquired.

Monsieur Brun took elaborate measurements, discussed every detail at great length, even called a few times to verify this or that point. A design and price were finally agreed on. Now only remained the vital question: "When will it be ready?"

"When are you coming back?"

"Next year, early June."

"It will be ready then. Not to worry, that leaves me plenty of time."

The year passed, and Derek looked forward to the sight

of the new chest of drawers on his return. But, *hélas*, the place it was to occupy still gaped, sadly empty.

"My mother-in-law took sick," explained Monsieur Brun. "And then all my *ouvriers* had the flu. A bad year. . . . But now, just tell me: When are you coming back?"

"Next year, early June."

"I give you my word of honor. It will be ready by then. And a beauty, too. You'll see, you won't be sorry you had to wait."

Thus another year went by, and still nothing on Derek's return. Monsieur Brun was most apologetic, dreadfully sorry. Still, it wasn't *his* fault.

"I feel very badly on your account. But the right wood I was promised didn't come along. I wouldn't dream of palming second-quality materials on *you*. . . . When are you coming back?"

"Same as every year. Early June."

"Well, no excuses this time. I'll drop everything else if I must, but *your* chest of drawers will be ready, and in place."

When Derek returned, and still found nothing after three years—one learns patience in Provence—he felt the end of the road had been reached. He tracked down Monsieur Brun and demanded to know whether or not there would *ever* be a chest of drawers.

Monsieur Brun sat down, took off his cap, wiped his brow, placed his hands palm up on the table.

"I'd better tell you something *right off*," he said. "Nothing like being honest *from the start*, that's my motto. I have too much esteem for you to be anything but frank with you *from day one.* Chests of drawers? I just don't know how to make them. Never have."

Derek is laughing so hard, he has to wipe his eyes and sip some water.

"No chest," he finally manages to sputter. "No chest, and there won't be one. But isn't it all worth a giggle?" Clearly, he is now attuned to the spirit of this land.

Easy to see why we all have such a good time in Provence.

Where Provence and Alaska meet . . .

Baked Alaska à la Manière d'Apt

The city of Apt, in the Luberon, is famous for its candied fruit. This recipe combines them with the traditional Baked Alaska.

I lb pound cake
I½ cups brandy, rum, or fruit liqueur
I pound brick of vanilla ice cream
6 egg whites, room temperature (reserve half a shell, as neatly broken as possible)
I tsp cream of tartar
½ cup sugar
I cup chopped candied fruit

Slice cake in half lengthwise (like splitting a layer cake). Place halves side by side, touching, on an ovenproof flat serving dish. Sprinkle with ½ cup brandy, rum, or fruit liqueur.

Working fast, divide brick of ice cream to cover cake. Place in freezer until ready to serve.

Just before serving, warm I cup of brandy, rum, or fruit liqueur in a small saucepan, just long enough to *warm*, but not to boil or evaporate. Whip egg whites to peaks. Add cream of tartar and sugar, beating just enough to mix. Take out cake–ice cream preparation. Scatter candied fruit over ice cream, pressing it down. Slather on egg whites to cover completely, top and sides. Slide under broiler just long enough for top of meringue to brown lightly.

Push eggshell into top of Alaska. Turn lights low, pour warmed brandy, rum, or fruit liqueur into eggshell, light, and bring flaming to the table. Pour remainder so it spills, flaming, down the sides of Alaska. Create fireworks by tossing some sugar or grated orange peel into the flames. Serve immediately.

Note: Be sure that serving dish is large enough to contain run-off of flaming liquid.

Only Hot Thing in a
Frozen Landscape

That winter, we couldn't get away for Christmas. Wayne was busy elsewhere and not expecting to be through for weeks. I waited until after the holidays, but Provence nostalgia finally got the better of me, and I decided to fly over. I'd stay six weeks, and while there, alone and undisturbed, try to complete a pesky project I'd been putting off for too long. So she wouldn't stay alone, with only daily visits from the cleaning lady, I took along Truffles, my little yellow mongrel, who's been there many times and is well acquainted with the more disreputable local canines.

At the Paris airport I learned that the dollar, usually hovering around five francs, had been allowed to float to its real value and could now be exchanged at the rate of *ten* francs to the dollar. Armed with my pinch of traveler's checks, I suddenly felt rich.

I also found out that I had arrived just at the onset of the worst cold spell in well over a century.

Now, the only real source of heat in our village house comes from the fireplace. Its warmth rises to our bedroom, and since it had never been truly cold on previous winter holidays, we'd always been comfortable with the addition of an electric heater in the bathroom.

Only now, Siberia had descended. Opening my front door on the first morning, I stepped into a thick, frozen mist that seared my lungs and sent Truffles scurrying back inside, shivering in her thin yellow fur. I went to light the fire, but found that, while we still had a few thick logs I could barely carry, only a few pieces of kindling remained at the bottom of the box. I built a fire using some twigs, but leaving enough for the next morning, just in case. It took a long time, and a lot of smoke spewed out of the cold, damp flue, half choking me, before the fire finally caught. But it wouldn't burn bright, only smolder. And it didn't seem to warm up the house at all. When I touched the stone walls I found them covered with a thick sparkling frost, and more cold seeped through cracks I never knew were there: under the doors, windows, even, I swear, through the walls. I stuffed towels wherever I could to stop drafts, piled on three sweaters, and, still shivering, added anorak, muffler, and furred boots. Still, my hands and feet remained numb. Then, as I was going to make coffee, the electricity went off.

There are no gas lines serving villages, so electricity is the only source of power. But the new surge in restoration, and sharply increased use of appliances, bring constant outages. On top of that, most year-round residents now have a full complement of electric radiators, going full blast, I'm sure, on such a day.

So, overtaxed, the system just shut down. This meant no light, no cooking, no hot water, no space heater, no radio, no television, no typewriter.

I can deal with the situation, I thought. First, I'll drive to Pertuis and the car heater will defrost me some. Then, I'll have breakfast at the Café Thomas, with a giant café au lait, and I'll share with Truffie all the croissants they have left. Afterward I'll feel better, and I'll run to the market for candles, groceries, and dog food. On the way back, I'll stop to order a firewood delivery and fill the trunk with kindling and faggots. In any case, it cannot stay that cold for long. Electricity surely will return, so I might get a couple of small heaters, too.

Chipper, the little Renault of early years, had been replaced with a larger Citroën with one of those diesel engines—widely used in this country of five-dollar-a-gallon gasoline. I couldn't understand why it stubbornly refused to start, but when the battery began to gasp, I quit and called Monsieur Giano, the garageman who looks after the car.

"Diesel fuel is frozen! In cold such as this, it turns thick, like vaseline, and clogs the lines. This very minute, trucks are being stalled along all the autoroutes. My service truck is frozen, too, since it's diesel. Even if I managed to thaw it out enough to start, like with a blowtorch, it would freeze again as soon as I've driven a mile, and I'd be stuck on the road. Sorry I can't help you, but you're better off at home than anywhere else, believe me."

Frozen diesel? Never heard of such a thing at home. Yet, I'm sure some parts of the U.S. occasionally endure temperatures as low, and even lower than are being registered now in France. And what about Canada, Russia, Siberia? Only later was I to learn that, since France prides itself on a temperate climate, regulations allow commercial-grade diesel to contain a relatively high level of water-based additives. Only military and emergency vehicles qualify for a higher, no-freeze grade.

Power didn't return. So, I made instant coffee by pouring the last of the faucet's lukewarm water into hardened powder at the bottom of a jar. Later, for lunch, I opened a rusty can of tuna, lacerating my finger in the process, since the electric can-opener was dead, and shared the treat with Truffles.

In distress, I did what I had always done before in emergencies: called Ariel.

Instead, I found Christophe at home, swearing at *his* diesel. He'd given up hope of driving to his Marseille office, but Ariel, who'd been in Paris for a week, was due to return today. He couldn't very well leave her stranded at the airport, so he was considering pouring *gasoline* into his engine, at the risk of ruining it for good, since he *had* to start the damn car one way or the other.

I arranged the logs end to end, so they'd burn slowly, coaxed Truffles into a basket lined with an old blanket, for she was inching so close to the embers that I feared she'd singe her coat. Then, I wrapped a woollen scarf around my head and face, and, looking like a terrorist, set out in search of whatever the village could provide. The frozen mist clogging the air was so dense, it almost obscured daylight. All the foreigners' houses were tightly shuttered, of course, everyone gone back home after the holidays. But, heaven be thanked, the bakery remained open. "We still have one small woodburning oven," the lady told me, "but not much wood left. After that's gone, we'll have to close down, unless we run out of flour first. All deliveries have stopped."

By the light of a single, flickering candle, I bought all the bread they'd let me have, and from the severely depleted grocery chest took milk, cheese, butter, a little sliced *jambon* in a vacuum pack, and the last bag of dog kibble on the shelf. By the time I'd trudged uphill, bread and milk had frozen solid.

At least now we had food. Truffles devoured her kibble and retreated immediately to the comfort of her fireside basket. The afternoon passed slowly in the cold dark room, lit only by meager embers.

And finally, long after night had fallen, excited cries at the door. Ariel stood there in her wolf-fur coat, opening her arms wide, happy to see me, anxious to help. I kissed her ice-cold cheek as Christophe trailed in, loaded with a cold roast beef and a cake. I brought up a bottle from the cellar, where I found that most of our stores had frozen and burst, shattering to the stone floor in puddles of purple ice. We thawed the wine by the fire, and nobody complained about

its temperature, which certainly remained well below optimum. Ariel described how Paris had come to a standstill.
She'd been lucky to catch the last Air Inter flight, for there
would be no more as long as the cold wave lasted, which
caused ice layers to accumulate on the wings of airplanes.

Huddled by the smoldering fire, we devoured our picnic, and by the time I was dipping pieces of cake into wine,
my hands and feet had almost regained feeling. Suddenly,
Ariel cried:

"No wonder it's freezing here! You don't know how to
build a fire. Here, I'll show you."

Before I could stop her, she'd grabbed all my precious
kindling and thrown the whole handful into the fire.

"Now," she exclaimed, "you'll see it blaze! And you must
pile those logs on top of each other, *not* end to end, if you
want a *real* fire. See? Now, that's the way to get it roaring."

My heart sank. My few remaining logs were massive, at
least a foot in diameter; there was no way at all I could
hope to start a fire tomorrow morning if I let this one go
out. Slipping into a caveman's mentality, I thought: I must
keep this fire going all night or I'll be frozen stiff in the
morning. Tomorrow, I'll try to find more wood.

So, after they left, I allowed the fire to dwindle to
embers, again carefully laid the logs with ends barely touching. Wrapped in blankets, I settled on the couch, my travel
clock set to go off in two hours. This is going to be a long,
lonely, silent vigil, I shuddered. Very silent and dark.

I had no idea that it would turn out to be anything but
a *silent* night.

Jet lag, or else the eerie surroundings, kept sleep at bay.

An hour passed, ringing louder from the belfry in the frozen air. And then, strange sounds rose: cracking, breaking, splintering noises coming from all over. The roofs, the walls, inside, outside; everything cracked, with the sound of a crackling fire. A house burning, perhaps? My *own* house? I peered outside, inhaling a lungful of painfully searing air and letting an arctic blast into the room. No fire that I could see.

Then, I remembered a French expression used to describe intensely cold weather: *Il gèle à pierre fendre*, it is freezing to split stone. That's what was happening now! Small amounts of water absorbed by stone and roof tiles expanded as they froze. I was experiencing the stone-splitting cold of the saying. To someone used to Siberian or Alaskan winters, this might not be so disturbing, but none of the winters I'd ever known held such a thing in store.

I tried to read by the light of the last candle stub I'd been saving but couldn't keep my mind on the story. Furthermore, I had to pull my hands from cover, and they quickly became numb. After two hours, I reset the clock, pushed the logs a little closer together, and, with the entire village crackling all around me and above my head, I finally started to doze off.

Suddenly, a loud thud at my door startled me awake. Someone there, trying to come in at this hour? All other sounds drowned in the new banging on closed shutters. Again and again, the blows reverberated throughout the house—and my stomach.

"Anyone there?" I tried to cry out, strangling in terror.

Truffles, who'd been asleep, woke up with a start and let out a long, mournful wail. No, this couldn't be a visitor, rattling the walls with such relentless brutality. There *was* a robber at the door, attempting to break down the shutters, probably with an ax. He doesn't know I'm here and believes the house to be empty, but when he finds me, he's going to kill me for certain. Truffles had jumped out of her basket and stood, tail down, whining and listening with quivering ears.

More banging; two, three blows, louder and louder . . .

At home, when confronted with unexplained noises in the night, I'd normally hide under the sheets, trusting Wayne to investigate and protect me as needed. But now I was alone, in charge of my own life, no help to be expected from anyone. No other protection for me but my own resources, like battling fear to begin with. So, I pulled myself from the grip of terror-fostered paralysis, wrapped the blanket tighter around me, took Wayne's Stetson from its hook, and pulled it down over my ears. Since no other weapon was in sight, I also grabbed the antique sword from the wall.

Then, God help me, I walked to the door, Truffles cautiously slinking behind me. In spite of trembling hands, I managed to lift the massive iron hooks that hold the *volets* fast, and, fully expecting to confront a masked murderer lifting his ax over my head, I pushed the *volets* open.

Instead of a *Friday the Thirteenth* vision, I saw . . .

The mist had cleared, the moon had risen, and, in the bright moonlight, two or three roaming dogs had upset a large plastic garbage can. However, the lid, securely twisted on, remained in place. As the can started rolling down the slope, they pushed it back and forth, and each time it would hit our solid wood *volets*, sending those resounding shudders through the wood. Just as I stood in the doorway, the lid came off, scattering assorted refuse and a number of tin cans that began to roll, clattering downhill. I waved my sword ineffectually at the dogs and shooed a disappointed Truffles back inside. Oblivious to the searing cold, she apparently hoped to join those curs in their garbage forays.

So much now for assassins and murderers. But blasts of icy air had rushed in to replace my carefully hoarded warmth. I checked the fire once more, closed my eyes, and tried to fall asleep, shivering in my blankets. In vain.

Then, fear returned. This time, it had been prowling dogs. But next time? What protection can I count on here? I riffled through the pages of the thin phone book and found the number of the Pertuis Gendarmerie, as well as that of the *pompiers*, the fire brigade, almost setting fire to the pages with my candle.

I dialed the first number. Instantly, a youthful, Provence-accented voice answered: "*Gendarmerie de Pertuis, à votre service.*" I apologized for such a middle-of-the-night call. "That's all right," assured the gendarme. "I'm on night duty and not supposed to sleep. How can I help you?"

I explained who and where I was, where I had just come from. I was alone, afraid in the dark, and needed to know if they'd be there for me in case of need.

"We'd reach you in less than ten minutes. And don't

worry about frozen cars, we have gasoline engines. Tell me about California, please. It is true what they say about *les gangs?*"

We chatted for about half an hour. The young gendarme was doing his compulsory military service, assigned after training to a gendarmerie unit. A good idea, come to think of it, I said, to use military personnel for public service, without waiting for a war. But he explained that the gendarmerie—roughly the equivalent of sheriff offices in the United States—is actually a branch of the French Army. Of course, he drew frequent night duty, allowing more senior staff to sleep at home in their own beds.

Encouraged by this friendly response, I called the *pompiers*. Same cordial, instantaneous answer. They did know all about those cracking noises, it did sound like fire but it wasn't. I had correctly guessed their origin; they sounded even louder, magnified in the clear, cold, night air. One might find a few cracked stone benches, roof tiles split apart, or broken lintels in the morning. Meanwhile, I should be careful with my fireplace: Soot accumulates and may catch fire when the flue becomes overheated. If this happened, I'd hear a whooshing sound and see billows of white smoke pouring out. Be sure to call them immediately if this were to happen.

I was beginning to feel better. Those helpful, sympathetic voices told me I wasn't alone, left to freeze to death if my fire went out. I checked the embers once more, pushed the logs just a little bit closer, and fell asleep at last.

———

This time, blood-curdling screams woke me with a start. Bloody murder was being committed nearby, and it had to be a slow, painful death. After a brief respite, heartbreaking wails turned to tortured lament, then pathetic moans followed by anguished wails. How can one die in such agony? No doubt several killers were at work, for laments and screams rose from several sources. My God . . .

Only, now I knew where I could turn. Perhaps the police could arrive in time to save lives. . . . I dialed my gendarme friend. His smile came over the wire.

"People call us about that awful noise around this time of year. Especially if they're from the city, and new here. What you hear are *cats*. If you peek outside, you'll probably see a whole passel of them prowling on top of some fence, a wall, a roof. . . . They're having fun."

"Having fun?" I failed to see how fun could provoke such anguished screams.

This time, the young gendarme laughed in earnest.

"Well, you understand, those cats . . ." He hesitated. "I don't know how to put this to a lady. . . . Well, let's say their rear end is hot, and they're making love."

I had to laugh with him, while the demented racket went on, unabated. I was still laughing when I hung up, and fell asleep.

So much for that silent, quiet winter night.

To this day, however, I remember those hours with a certain amount of pride. I had dealt with all the hazards by myself, survived them, and defeated whatever demons might be lurking in the dark hours—even if they turned out to be no more than a few cats and dogs. So, it will always remain a highly charged experience. Besides, Wayne and I still laugh each time I recall that cold, cold night, when the one warm thing in an entire frozen landscape was those cats' rear ends.

By next day, I had organized.

Our regular wood man, who'd refused at first to deliver firewood, arguing a frozen diesel, was coaxed by my offer to pay *double* the going price into borrowing a gasoline truck to deliver a load of wood, with plenty of faggots and kindling. Not that it mattered, considering the situation, but with the ten-franc dollar, the price came to the same as usual.

Reports of the unprecedented European cold wave made the U.S. news, complete with dramatic images of miles of autoroute jammed with stalled trucks, so Wayne was calling frantically, beseeching me to find ways, any ways at all, to keep warm. He'd sent, overnight express, and with promise of delivery no matter what, a package of woollen dancers' leggings, ski underwear, and extra-thick sweaters. Bless his heart, he'd even dug up somewhere an electric blanket adapted to French 220-volt current that would provide toasty nights, *if* and *when* electricity returned.

With the fire now burning bright, the walls warmed a little and the thick ice crystals covering them thinned to hoarfrost. I kept a kettle simmering on the hearth, and, remembering the barbecue stored in the garage, took out the grill and placed it on its stand among the red-hot coals.

Bread toasted beautifully there, and cheese melted, brown and bubbly, so Truffles and I enjoyed some scrumptious sandwiches.

By now, I'd become used to the absence of electricity. For light, I'd run up to the church, and, with apologies to Saint Amat, who, I am sure, could understand my need, counted out the price of ten candles, slipped the coins in the box with a generous extra, and took them home. They would honor the good saint just as well, keeping darkness at bay.

The bakery lady called: Using a power-pack drill, a farmer had managed to dig a few carrots, turnips, and leeks out of the rock-hard soil. Frozen, of course, but good if used right away. He was offering them for sale at such an outrageous price (something like three dollars a pound), that she could think of no one, except this presumably rich American, as a potential customer. I bundled up, wrapped my muffler around my head and face again, pulled the anorak's hood over it, and recklessly bought all there was, vaguely ashamed to be using low-cost francs.

So, by afternoon of that second day, although electricity hadn't returned and the temperature dropped even lower—too low now to register on the outside thermometer, whose mercury had shriveled into a little ball at the bottom of the bulb of its vial—I was beginning to relish the whole exercise in survival. After all, I told myself, people had lived here for centuries with far fewer conveniences than I had now. If they could, I certainly ought to as well.

———

The frozen mist hadn't returned, and an icy blue sky turned to cobalt overhead.

That's when I looked up and saw the château.

Pipes carrying water to the upper floors had frozen and burst, so immense stalactites, maybe thirty feet high and six feet across, hung from both ends of the facade, sparkling in the sun like huge diamonds. A fantastic sight. But was the duchess there, without water as well as electricity? I dialed the number. She herself answered, with that crystal voice that never failed to enchant me.

"I am so glad to hear from you, my dear. And surprised, too. But where are you? Here, in the village? Good heavens, how do you survive in this cold?"

"I'm doing fine. My fire is roaring and I'm thinking of cooking a soup for dinner. How are things at the château?"

Her situation was a great deal worse than mine. No servants: Carlos and Maria had gone home to Spain after the holidays to visit their families and wouldn't be back for at least a month.

Meanwhile, she was all alone in that enormous pile, so high up and exposed to the winds, nearly freezing to death, all radiators cold. Fireplaces in reception rooms had long been condemned, their flues obstructed. As for the enormous fireplace in the old, medieval kitchen, it would accommodate a tree trunk, and no less. Now that the pipes had burst, she had no water, either.

"Would you come down and share the fire with me?"

And so the duchess, wrapped in her great hooded cape, walked down her ice-covered angling stairs, socks pulled over her shoes against slipping, and appeared at the door, her face blue with cold. We sat by the fire, nursing mugs of tea laced with rum, and she began, at last, to warm up. She agreed to stay for dinner, and together we peeled and chopped carrots, turnips, and leeks, and set a pot of vegetable soup to simmer on top of the embers.

"Ah," she sighed, "if only we had some fresh *pistou*, basil! We'd make a *soupe au pistou*. There's nothing better to warm you up on a night like this. But all basil is long frozen, even in the flower-pots housewives keep year-round on their window sills in Provence. A good *pistou* takes hours of pounding with mortar and pestle—only some are venturing to use electric blenders today. They will tell you it tastes just the same. You'll want to learn how to make a *pistou* before you return home."

And thus a casual acquaintance grew into a priceless friendship, so that I'd always cherish memories of the days that followed. Each afternoon, the duchess would come down from her ice-encased towers, where more stalactites seemed to accumulate as time went on. Wayne's package had miraculously arrived, so we each slipped on a pair of long ski underwear and pulled on thick wool leggings. More comfortable now, we'd sit by the fire and talk.

She told me the history of her family and episodes of the castle's thousand-year life. There were battles won and lost and a siege, long ago, where a depleted garrison made surrender inevitable, until Saint Amat worked one of his

miracles and caused hundreds of heavily armed and hel-
meted soldiers to seem to appear upon the battlements.
Panicked, the assailants fled. During the Renaissance, an
ancestor dressed the austere fortress as an Italianate palace
so that today's castle bears a Florentine facade between its
massive towers. There was her marriage to the young duke,
half a century ago, and the vow they made to consecrate
their lives to restoring the castle after half a century of ne-
glect. They had the joy, just as renovation was complete, to
see it serve as the stage for their sons' weddings, and even
that of their niece when she married into foreign royalty.

And then, his task accomplished, the duke had died, leaving her with the glowing memory of a great love. Nevertheless, she rejoiced that he'd lived long enough to celebrate
the family's thousand years' ownership of the castle.

And, as we sat by candlelight, shadows from the fire
dancing on the beamed ceiling, she grew pensive:

"I will soon turn seventy. My children are married and
gone. I carry the burden of the château as best I can, living
here rather than in Paris to pare down expenses, yes, but
also to keep an eye on things. I don't feel needed anymore,
though. So, sometimes, I long to join my dear husband,
who waits for me in our funeral chapel."

Although she kept asking me to call her by her first
name, I simply couldn't. To me, she stood as the last of the
grandes dames, in a world where breeding and grace were
becoming fast-fading memories. I couldn't accept that her
store of knowledge, her charm, her wit, the luster of a
mind that had crossed the century, and with it those memories of a world lost forever, would vanish with her.

"Do your children know the family history, and that of the château, as well as you do?"

"Not at all," she sadly admitted. "They aren't even very interested. Too young to care. Maybe when they grow older . . . but then it will be too late. As for my grandchildren, they're bound to remain in perfect ignorance of most of their heritage."

"This is why," I said decisively, "you have to write all that should be remembered. You are a wonderful story-teller, you'll bring out a fascinating book, where your children and their children, and future generations, too, can learn about their forebears, since they probably wouldn't check history books out of libraries."

"I wouldn't dare try. I never wrote anything before."

"You write the warmest, most informative and entertaining letters I have ever received," I assured her earnestly. "You have the talent, even if still untapped; the knowledge of your subject, the grace and humor. All you need is the drive. Do you *want* to write it?"

The duchess's eyes were fixed on the fire. Embers cast a glow upon her finely etched face. She smiled to herself.

"The title would be *True To Your Name*. It would mesh my own memoirs with our family history. I'll start tonight by candlelight."

So, during those weeks, in an unabating cold that killed centuries-old olive trees, split great oaks right down the middle of their trunks and sent them crashing, froze rivers whose ice pack knocked down bridge pilings—a cold that often pierced my thick stone walls—the duchess and I lived exciting, warm, wonder-filled days. She would write all morning, in muffler and woollen mittens, and so did I, on an old manual portable, shearing all my fingernails. Early afternoon, she'd walk down and we'd sit, warming up, feet resting on the fender, mug of tea in hand, while she read me what she had written. Under her pen, past centuries and people came to life in a vibrant tapestry. She told of a duchess of last century, so ugly that her gardener begged one day: "We won't save any fruit from the orchard; the birds have become so bold, no scarecrow frightens them away anymore. If *Madame la duchesse* would only be kind enough to show herself?"

The bell pull in a relative's castle near Brussels, where she'd visit as a child, remained torn to this day, because Wellington, afflicted with diarrhea on the eve of Waterloo, pulled on it too hard, calling for his pierced chair. Troops of young cousins, she recalled, would gleefully re-enact the scene, with lots of tugging on the torn pull and running up and down the halls.

An eighteenth-century admiral who ran out of ammunition loaded his guns with the family silver pieces, to pursue a losing battle against English ships. "A painting in the salon recalls the event. Always elegant, never practical; that could be our family motto."

I noticed she was writing on the back of old bills, and I offered her a box of typing paper. She refused: "There are so many of those on my desk, they should be put to good use."

She completed her manuscript, which was published with great success by a noted French house. She appeared on a few television shows, at first to promote the book, and on several more afterward, because she caught the public's interest with her simplicity, her quick wit, and her aristocratic presence—the perfect guest on many talk shows.

A signed copy of the book lies on my desk at this very moment, and I often pick it up . . . not to read it, for by now I know, almost by heart, its often poignant chapters. But as I hold it I try to recapture the warm friendship that grew between us, and something of that winter's gift remains with me, as the author's photograph smiles on, just as she smiled in the dancing firelight and murmured: "The title shall be *True To Your Name.*"

A comforting soup makes a dinner . . .

Soupe au Pistou (Pesto Soup)

This soup resembles Tuscan minestrone, but does it one better with the addition, right in your bowl, of *pistou* (the word is derived from the name for a *pestle*, but its origin is confusing, because basil is also called *pistou*). The soup recipe varies, since each family has its own version, but the *pistou*, added to the bowls, is a must.

The soup

Olive oil
1 cup sliced carrots
1 cup sliced celery
1 leek, thinly sliced
1 onion, diced
1 potato, diced
4 garlic cloves, minced
1 cup cut green beans
1 15-ounce can Canelli beans
1 15-ounce can red kidney beans
½ cup frozen chopped spinach
2 quarts chicken broth (or more, as needed for
    consistency)
Salt, pepper, thyme
½ cup small elbow macaroni

In a skillet, heat a little olive oil and sauté carrots, celery, leek, onion, and potato until soft. Add garlic and sauté a little more. Remove to soup pot, add all other ingredients. (Use little salt if broth is already salted.) Stir well, bring to a boil, and simmer on low heat for an hour or longer until vegetables are softened. Add macaroni 10 minutes before serving.

The pistou

This was traditionally ground in a mortar and pestle, but it is much quicker, today, to blend all ingredients in your blender. It tastes as good, if not better.

For a basic recipe, you'll need (but then, there never

seems to be enough *pistou*; guests spread it on their bread even after they've finished their soup):

4 Tbs pine nuts
A bunch fresh basil leaves
½ cup grated Parmesan cheese
½ cup grated Swiss cheese
4 cloves garlic
Olive oil

In a frying pan, *without oil*, toast pine nuts until golden, not brown. Place all ingredients, except oil, in your blender; process until finely ground. Remove to a bowl.

Drizzle olive oil, a little at a time, to form a smooth paste.

Serving: Ladle soup into heated bowls and drop a spoonful of *pistou* in the center of each. Pass extra grated Parmesan cheese.

And don't forget a basket of fresh sourdough bread, heated in the oven to make it even crustier.

Wine: Something red and very hearty. After all, Provence is close to Italy, so why not a solid Chianti Classico?

A New Alchemy: Turning Old Stones into Gold

To the often-asked question: Is it expensive to maintain a second home in a Provence village? the answer is an emphatic Yes.

For whatever reasons, the U.S. dollar remains low against European currencies on the exchange market. As a consequence, French prices often translate as higher than American ones. Taxes, insurance, and utilities make a dent in a modest budget, and now that we've installed electric radiators throughout the house, a winter vacation's bill runs high. Phone is expensive, if only because we all make so many long-distance phone calls. Then, one must add the cost of frequent air travel—since one wouldn't want to incur all that expense for no enjoyment—as well as that of buying and insuring a car, or renting one, but the latter turns out to be prohibitive in the long run.

Then, because these are, underneath all the restoration, *very* old houses, and also because village artisans who installed plumbing, electricity, and the pools aren't always, let's say, at the cutting edge of professional expertise, repair bills occur with predictable regularity. Also, wooden doors, windows, and *volets* protecting them must be repainted every few years. The city hall will hand you a charming booklet, titled *Palette of the Luberon*, which shows all the *volet* shades allowed in the region—designated, after all, the French equivalent of a state park. Most colors are permissible, as long as they are muted, softened by blending with a pale ocher: creamy off-white; washed out blues and gentle greens; even misty mauves and beigeish roses.

Then, one cannot abandon that beloved Provence home to the hazards of torrential rains, winter freeze, and summer heat without someone to air it, clean it, check for roof leaks or frozen pipes. Gardens and plantings must be tended year-round, pools cared for in the summer, emptied and covered in winter. The car left in the garage must also be periodically checked for deflated tires and weakening battery. Even with honest help, none of those services come cheap.

So, for most, a Provençal home is a hard-won luxury. I know of only one exception to the rule: Terry, who turns *his* old stones into gold. Furthermore, his alchemy is so potent that it overflows, brightening *his friends'* old stones with a sprinkling of the precious nuggets.

Terry is a professor of French in a respected Eastern institution. He didn't come to it by accident, or through some whim of fate, but because early in life, during a stay in Aix as an exchange student, he became entranced by the world of antiques he discovered in the region's shops. At the same time, he fell in love with Provence where, just as we did, he made lifelong friends.

So he chose academic life, with its June-to-September release, which would allow him the freedom of long summers. Later, a successful member of his faculty, Terry sought to build, or rather rebuild, a ruined house in a Luberon village. He didn't know this would lead to the awakening of a businessman's soul, long slumbering under an intellectual veneer.

Finding the ideal ruin to restore proved no easy matter. The hilltop villages had been discovered. The *rush to ruin*, as it was called, had, by then, been on for some time and the best ones already taken. Wayne, always eager to embrace someone else's plight, joined the quest with dedication. But *hélas*, nothing good turned up. Nothing in Cucuron, nothing in Lourmarin, nothing even as far as Gordes.

At that point, doubts began to assail Terry, who grew depressed and hesitant as he saw his summer slipping away and no progress made.

"Perhaps I wasn't meant to own a place in Provence, after all. If it is not in my destiny, all efforts will be in vain."

As convinced as he that fate would have a hand in the success of his enterprise, I tenaciously sought a solution to the dilemma. How could we find out whether or not Terry was meant to own a share of one of those villages' living sculpture?

In places like these, where, for untold centuries, so many people were born, had lived, and died, it is not too difficult to accept, along with the villagers, that *something* remains of those bygone lives, unseen, but very present. So, one night, I cried: "I know what to do! Whenever I walk down to our *voûtes* at night, I feel a presence hovering all around me. So, let's ask the spirits!" And that is how we held a séance, a thing none of us believed in, had ever done before, and would ever do again.

Wayne brought down a small round table with a single center leg divided into three: the three-footed *guéridon* I've always heard is the required instrument for such ghostly communications. We all trooped down to the vaulted rooms, lit a single candle in a tall candelabra, and turned off the lights. One could not dream of a more suggestive setting: the looming high arches; marks left by Roman tools darkly scarring one wall; a feeling of the ages, of a host of past lives that had breathed this very air. The spirits couldn't be far.

We sat in a circle, placed hands spread out, fingertips barely grazing the table top. After some hesitation, Terry, trying to remember what he'd read and heard about séances, addressed whichever spirit might be hovering near.

"Knock once for yes, twice for no. Spirit, are you here?"

Silence. At the fourth or fifth repetition of the question, I swear the table vibrated slightly. Yet everybody's legs were to the side, where knees or feet couldn't possibly touch it.

"Spirit, are you here?"

One foot of the table lifted slightly, one hesitant knock: Yes. I began to wonder just what we were getting into.

"Have you lived in this village?" asked Terry.

One knock, louder: Yes.

"Have you lived in this room?"

Another assertive knock: Yes.

"In this century?"

Two knocks: No.

"How many centuries ago?"

Knock, knock, knock, knock, knock. Five centuries. The fifteen hundreds, then.

"Was this the guardroom of the castle?"

Yes.

"Were you a guard?"

No.

"Were you a member of the castle family?"

Yes.

"Did you die here?"

No knock this time, but the table shuddered violently, the candle flame bent, almost went out. Shadows rose against the walls. "I think we should stop this," I said, trembling. "I'm afraid of what we're doing." But nobody paid attention. Terry, his voice strained, went on:

"Can you tell the future?"

No. Yes.

"I am Terry. Shall I own a house in Provence?"

Silence. Only a light shudder of the table.

"Shall I own a house in Provence?" repeated Terry insistently.

Yes.

"When? Knock once for each year hence."

Two years.

"Here? In this village?"

This time, the single knock struck so loudly that the table nearly tipped over, but it incredibly righted itself. I cried out loud and stood up. The candle went out, the séance was over, leaving us all shaken. But Terry had learned what he needed to know: His search would narrow down to this village.

A few shots of marc restored everybody's composure. But for weeks, I'd avoid walking down to the *voûtes* at night. We never held another séance, and never mentioned that one again.

Except once.

With renewed determination, we tried to help Terry find a ruin—asking, looking around—but nothing remotely desirable turned up. Terry, an early riser, and now growing desperate, resorted to calling us each day at dawn to check on our progress. "We have to find something if we want to sleep until a decent hour," decided Wayne.

So, we set out on a final search of the village that very afternoon. Truffles sniffing ahead, we examined all barred doors, noted the few real estate agent's signs, questioned ladies sitting on their stoops, even went in to make enquiries at the *Bar des Sports* and the bakery. In vain. We had reached the lower village, halfway down the slope and just outside the old fortifications, when Truffie, whom we'd last seen investigating cracks under barn doors for lurking cats, suddenly seemed to have disappeared. We called, whistled, looked everywhere. "Where in hell did that damn dog go?" grumbled Wayne, tired and hot and ready to blame it all on Terry and his need for a ruin.

Then, we heard hissing, followed by pained yelps. We pushed open a broken garden gate at the bottom of a steep street and found Truffles there, in a losing face-off with a large, nasty tabby defending his territory.

But mostly, we found that we'd stepped into a spacious garden, enclosed on three sides, choked with weeds and brambles, looking full south. On one side stood the shell of a house, its roof mostly caved in, windows and doors long gone, a single loose *volet* hanging askew from the last hinge, its facade devoured by still clinging, desiccated ivy.

We stepped inside and found ourselves under a vaulted ceiling of rough stones. Chutes in the walls showed where fodder had once been dropped to the sheep living there. As for the upstairs floor, we could only guess: The wooden stairs had rotted and fallen off, barring access.

Running home, we called Terry: "Get here this minute. We found what you've been looking for." Terry panted up moments later, in time to take a quick look at the property, gasp, and dash to the city hall before closing time to obtain the name of the owner. It turned out the man worked in Paris as a cab driver. He had inherited the ruin at his grandfather's death, decades earlier. "I never returned to that village since I was a little boy, more than forty years ago," he told Terry on the phone.

"Will you sell?" asked Terry, his throat dry.

The man, at his end, must have gulped, too. A little like winning the lottery, after thinking for so long that his inheritance consisted of nothing but a worthless pile of crumbling rocks, so worthless that taxes had been waived, the place being roofless and not remotely habitable. An

American wanted to buy *that?* A deranged one, no doubt. So he named a price that must have seemed demented to him and which Terry accepted without haggling.

By seven o'clock that night the deal was completed. Only papers to be drawn at the *notaire's* remained. We all congratulated Truffles, who took her triumph modestly, and celebrated late into the night—with dinner and excited conversation, Wayne not minding the delayed bedtime, now that he knew Terry would let him sleep the next morning.

Plans and restoration progressed quickly. The downstairs *voûte* would be cleaned and reinforced, but otherwise remain unchanged. Upstairs, room was found for several large bedrooms and baths, even a good-sized library. As soon as brush was cleared, excavation began for the pool to be dug out of the live rock, and pillars started to rise for a deep, shadowy porch. Setbacks? Sure, and all the scams and stings to be expected, with Terry having to be away most of the time. But at last the house was finished and the pool sparkled, blue and inviting, banked with pink oleanders.

We were all together there, on the first night that Terry was to sleep under his new roof. He looked at his calendar watch, raised his hand, asked for silence.

"Do you know what day this is? Well, it is *exactly* two years since the spirit spoke. He *did* say two years, remember? Uncanny as it may be, he was right to the day. Shouldn't we show our appreciation by believing in him?"

Then, one afternoon, Terry came over and sat on the terrace with me.

"I think I might have an idea," he began. "My place is empty most of the year. I am sure lots of people from the States would be happy to rent it for a week, two weeks, a month, to be able to spend time in the Luberon."

I was, at first, dubious.

"Won't people be hesitant to lease, sight unseen? You know the horror stories one hears about that kind of foreign experience?"

"I know, and I've heard them all myself. That's why I would send photos, plans with measurements of the rooms, full documentation on the house and the area. The lease would leave nothing unspecified. I am too scrupulous myself to cheat anyone, and I'm sure that would be quickly understood and appreciated."

"How would you advertise?"

"The travel magazines, alumni reviews of great universities, *Variety*, maybe . . ."

"How much would you charge?"

The figure he quoted seemed high for someone like me, used to housing and feeding a stream of guests for free. On second thought, it didn't come to much more than the price of a good hotel room, so a stay for up to six people was, indeed, more like a bargain. Convenient, too, for families with children. And since everyone who visits the markets of Provence longs to buy all those tempting fruits and vegetables, a kitchen is the answer. Terry might well be right. Still, I wondered how many would take the plunge into what they might read as a chancy experiment.

"More than you think," Terry assured me. "People do it all the time. Americans are adventurous, they travel all over the world and seek new experiences. I'll have all the tenants I need."

"Then," he went on, "I have another idea, too. You know of my passion for antiques. I have, through all my summers here and now the furnishing of my house, become acquainted with most of the shops and the sources for good, reasonably priced country French antiques in the area. Cost here is infinitely lower than in the States or in Paris."

"Are you thinking of importing antiques to the States?"

"No. I wouldn't have time to run a full-fledged business. But it occurred to me that there must be people back home who would like to shop here for antiques, only they don't know where to look, outside of the obvious, overpriced Paris dealers. They need someone to guide them to the right places, organize tours so they can see all there is before they make a choice. Perhaps I could do something along those lines. . . ."

I remained dubious. Too many logistics to contend with, I thought; problems would be daunting. But I didn't let on, and instead smiled encouragement.

"I'd call my business My Home in France and incorporate in the United States. Clients would come for a week and stay at my house, with everything provided. I think I could manage five or six such tours a year, during my vacation periods."

Terry is quick to follow thought with action. The fall issue of *Travel and Leisure* carried an elegantly designed ad that offered antiquing tours, staying at a lovely village home (featured in *Architectural Digest*, with photography by Wayne), Provençal cuisine served. Clients would be met at the airport and escorted every day to a new area, rich in antiquing possibilities.

By Christmas, Terry's first group had arrived, brought to the house in his smart Renault *Espace* station wagon. They found a home festive with wreaths and candlelight, each bedroom redolent of lavender sachets hung from door- and windowknobs. Trays of champagne cocktails circulated. A fire blazed in the monumental fireplace. The hay chutes now showcased fragments of Renaissance gilt sculpture, set off by indirect lighting. . . . It was all like a picture-perfect group of friends, gathering in the country for a holiday house-party. Dinner was served under the great vaulted stone ceiling, by Terry's unique cook-housekeeper, in the soft light of a crystal chandelier.

Each morning, the group set off for visits to backstreet antique shops, farmhouses turned showrooms, group shows where dozens of antique dealers gather their stock, even *brocante* fairs. A *brocante* is a sort of flea market, a hybrid between junk and valuable antiques, where great finds are possible. The largest of these *brocantes* is held on Sundays in L'Isle-sur-la-Sorgue. This is where Jack found his treasure.

Jack, an assistant curator in a large East Coast museum, sought nothing but paintings, his field of expertise. Those, unframed and dirt-encrusted, are usually stacked in boxes stored under the tables where dealers display their more promising wares. Armed with a flashlight, a magnifying glass at the ready, Jack set off to examine every dusty daub. Moments into his search, he pulled out a grimy canvas, where a sentimental scene of a girl releasing a bird from its cage was barely visible. His connoisseur heart missed a beat: eighteenth century, no doubt?

"*Hélas, Monsieur,*" cautioned the dealer, "I honestly must tell you. I am afraid this is much more recent. Look at the canvas backing." That canvas, obviously machine-made, did indeed seem too modern for the painting.

Jack, however, thought he knew better. As he told us later, over a celebratory *kir:* "The picture fairly whispered to me." He was aware, too, that often a new canvas is glued to the back of a painting when the original one shows signs of disintegrating. Keeping the knowledge to himself, he bought the painting for a pittance. Back in New York, authorities at the Metropolitan Museum of Art identified it as a Lancret, an excellent eighteenth-century French painter. A few months later, the suitably cleaned and framed painting brought a handsome figure at a Sotheby's auction.

Everywhere, low prices seduce American buyers, who purchase tables, chairs, armoires, mirrors, porcelain, silver, and crystal with wild abandon. Terry has arranged with a specialized firm that picks up, packs, and ships purchases overseas. A few of the clients, however, are content to simply enjoy the experience. No purchases are required for that.

"I can't believe I'm getting paid for this," confides Terry, "because I enjoy every minute. It's a real bonus to meet all those fascinating people, with whom I already have in common an interest in antiques!"

Over the years, his tours have met with steady success. Several clients return year after year, some bringing friends.

Many regulars are professionals in decoration or the antique business who'd feel daunted by the prospect of finding out-of-the-way places, driving alone in a foreign country, struggling with language and currency, as well as with shipment. Terry sees to everything, smiling, concerned, like the perfectionist he is.

As for renting his house the rest of the time, so many potential tenants called, eager to sign up for a week or a month, that Terry found he had to, regretfully, turn away a number of them. That's when he tapped his friends: "Would you rent out *your* house for a few weeks when you're not in residence?" An offer those friends gratefully accepted: Help with that flock of bills that descends upon homeowners? A godsend! So, our own house is now rented, in our absence, during a season that extends from March to October. I make every effort to plan for the comfort of our guests: My friend Liz is there to greet them and show them around, while our young housekeeper smilingly keeps everything neat.

After several years, our tenants have never caused *us* a shadow of trouble. Some leave little notes, like *"Love the view"* or *"A splendid terrace!,"* or tips to the next occupant: *"Don't miss the Cheval Blanc restaurant,"* and such. They enjoy both house and village according to their own desires and personalities: Those open to new experiences and attuned to the charm of old stones love both. Those who measure happiness to the square footage of their bathrooms and object to the lack of amenities, like pick-up-and-deliver cleaners in Pertuis, do not return. The Silver-Branson group is a case in point of the subjectivity of the village experience.

The village fête, on the first weekend in July, is a festive but noisy affair. Shooting galleries, bumper cars, and especially the bandstand and dance area are located directly *below* our house; sound rises and the racket makes sleep almost impossible for the four nights that it lasts. The first years, we danced on the terrace, enchanted by the spectacle: Imagine the great, black, star-studded night of the Luberon, with just that little square of light garlanded with colored lanterns way down below, filled with blaring dance music, a vocalist belting out aging American hits in approximate English ("My girl is a *weenner . . .*"). A mass of bodies moves frantically in the center, held in bounds, it looks from our vantage point, by the string of colored lights.

Those same years, we strolled to the galleries, won undrinkable *mousseux* and stuffed animals. Wayne managed to fold his long legs into one of the bumper cars and carried on a terminator-type sort of contest with Christophe that left him rubbing his knees for a week afterward. Then, as time passed, the fun waned—were we, perhaps, getting *older?*—and for us the fête eventually became those few days when it might be better to go out to dinner and come home late, or better, take a little trip.

Not so for the Silver-Branson group, whom we've never met, but who seems to be two attractive couples. They were occupying the house that week, when, back in California, I happened to look at the calendar and realized, to my horror, that this was fête time! Not only that, but French time; at this very moment, the racket would be at its most deafening. Guilt-struck and terribly embarrassed, I called to offer apologies and get-away suggestions. I was relieved to find no one home.

Instead of stopping up their ears against the din, it seems that our four tenants had walked down to the fête, mingled with the locals, danced with them, sat at a long table in front of the *Bar des Sports*, where Franco-American camaraderie was toasted in torrents of pastis, made friends who took them to their homes for Provençal cuisine, and later organized a mountain-climbing expedition and picnic parties. In turn, we heard excited reports that the Silver-Bransons invited those new friends to visit them at Christmas, and took them ice-sailing and ice-fishing on the frozen lakes of Michigan.

Now, the group has a standing reservation for that specific week, should we not be occupying the house, so they can enjoy what they call "special quality time." We are occasionally stopped in the street by people who wish to know if they'll return this year.

"They could just as well have asked for a refund," comments Wayne, "and damned if I wouldn't have given it to them."

Terry's guests rave about . . .

Thérèse's Gigot Grillé and Gratin de Courgettes (Broiled Leg of Lamb and Zucchini Gratin)

This tasty combination is one of the specialties of Terry's cook-housekeeper. You can prepare the gratin ahead of time and bake it in its *tian* at dinnertime. The leg of lamb is grilled on the barbecue in summer, or on a grill placed over the fireplace's embers in winter.

GIGOT (LEG OF LAMB)

Have the butcher butterfly it (i.e., split it open), remove the bone, and flatten it. Keep it at room temperature for about an hour before cooking. Season it well with salt and pepper. Make slits in the meat into which you push slivers of garlic—push in a little salt and pepper as well. You want the coals to be very hot, so the meat will be slightly charred on the outside, while remaining pink on the inside.

GRATIN DE COURGETTES (ZUCCHINI GRATIN)

12 medium zucchini
2 Tbs olive oil
1 pint heavy cream
Salt and pepper
Nutmeg (optional)
½ tsp thyme

3 or 4 eggs
Breadcrumbs and grated Swiss cheese for topping

Very lightly peel the zucchini, removing only the dark-green skin. Slice it on the bias.

In a skillet, heat oil and sauté zucchini until transparent, but not browned. Add cream, and stir until absorbed (if any remains, it will be absorbed during baking). Season well with salt, pepper, nutmeg if desired, and a little thyme.

Beat eggs well with fork and mix with zucchini preparation.

Remove to a shallow *tian*. Spread top with breadcrumbs and grated cheese. Bake 30 to 40 minutes at 350°F, or until an inserted knife comes out clean. If top is not browned enough, slide it for an instant under the broiler until it bubbles appetizingly.

Wine: You will need something that rises to the level of this elegant combination. A Châteauneuf-du-Pape (Château de la Nerthe, for instance) would do it proud. But should you wish to splurge even further, how about a Burgundy Château-Pommard?

Advisor to the
Marquis de Sade

The Luberon region offers perfect settings for motion
pictures and television films. Castles, picturesque hilltop
villages, squares where *boule*-playing goes on, the same as it
has for centuries, old stones, Roman monuments, all provide ready-made, authentic decor. The castle of the Marquis de Sade, standing in jagged ruin in the nearby village
of Lacoste, has inspired several movie versions of the life
of the original sadist.

Our village castle is used repeatedly, and recently lent its
gardens and salons as a background for the first French TV
series. Authorities there wish to supplant the enormously
successful, long-running American serials with shows pa-
triotically produced in France, with French actors. It must

be said that *Dallas* has become a classic, and that the country couldn't get enough of *Dynasty*. *Falcon Crest*, endlessly
repeated, held such enchantment that its characters live on
when, in the villages, one hears young mothers calling out:
"Jonathan? Fallon?" and the kids answering, Provençal
accent belying the exotic names: *"Oui, mamaing."* *Baywatch*,
translated as *Alerte à Malibu*, and *Beverly Hills 90210* as just
Beverly Hills, in turn entranced the populations. Since the
government, however, views any foreign infiltration of the
indigenous culture with the same alarm that would greet
the Chernobyl radioactive cloud, the situation is one of
concern to the Minister of Culture. So, perhaps under his
sponsorship, the four-part series was conceived, written,
and produced; a story that revolves around the saving of a
Provençal family estate from ruthless developers.

It turned out to be surprisingly good.

I happened to be in the village while one of the episodes
was shot at the château. A large tent had been set up on an
esplanade below as a commissary for crew, actors, director,
assistants, and guests. During those days, the most often-
heard question at the bakery, the post office, or the *Bar des
Sports* was: "What do you suppose they're having for *déjeuner*"? or, in the case of night shooting: "for dinner?" As
interested as anyone else, I wangled an invitation from the
duchess's son, who was supervising the situation in his
mother's absence. Dinner was served, because a night scene
would be shot *after* dinner, but, as I found out, *not* allowed
to interfere with it. The caterers in the tent produced a feast.

First, appetizers of breaded and fried Brie appeared, with aperitifs (yes, aperitifs in the middle of working hours. Did anyone think that television people are savages?). Then, at the long table, platters of assorted *charcuteries* were passed, followed by a daube, its beef tender in the rich sauce, accompanied by *macaronade*, macaroni baked in some of the same sauce. Next, salad, cheese, fruit, and coffee with cookies. A choice of white or red from the *coopérative* was offered throughout.

It was clear that in a very modestly budgeted production such as this one, and all the more modest if one has ever seen the extravaganza inherent to the same process in Hollywood, the producers had made a wise judgment-decision in heavily allocating their resources where they would do the most good: to food.

The scene to be shot that night, under a driving rain, involves the following steps: A car, driven by a young actress (the supporting female character), pulls up to the front door of the castle and stops. The girl, after many tribulations, is coming home to stay, happy and full of hope. She turns off the lights and the ignition, opens the car door, steps out, closes it, and walks to the castle. She pushes the door open and enters, closing the door behind her. What she sees once she is inside must startle and pain her, for, after just a moment, she rushes out, slamming the door behind her, and stops for an instant, facing the cameras, her face registering anguish. Then, she opens the car door, gets in, turns on lights and ignition, and backs out of camera range.

When the crew and guests return from dinner, a number of village people has gathered in front of the château.

I realize later that this is encouraged, because able-bodied men will lend a hand to supplement the shorthanded crew.

The Pertuis firemen have arrived with their tank truck and pump, plus a high tripod topped with a long sprinkler arm, from which rain will pour. It takes forever before all the apparatus is in place and spotlights are set up to pick up details. Then, the car drives up, a brand new BMW borrowed from an Avignon dealer who personally drove it here, accompanied by his son. Tests are made, some spots are killed, others added. A dulling paste is applied to the car, where reflections are not wanted. A test with rain shows the paste washes off, so, after lengthy deliberations, somebody brings out a can of shoe polish and smears it on. Then, more delays while the flow of rain is adjusted, and a new test conducted. The shoe polish resists water, should be good for a few takes, judges the assistant director.

More waiting until the actress emerges from her dressing room inside the château. She is a slight young girl, with blond hair loosely curled over her shoulders, tightly belted in a thin, silky raincoat. Helpful villagers push the car to its starting position, and she sits in it. Under the director's instructions, she turns on the ignition, switches on the lights, starts the motor, releases the clutch, and . . . stalls the engine. The same thing happens three or four times until, success at last! The car is moving forward. As a matter of fact, it *shoots* forward, and stops only after hitting the ancient carved door with a resounding thud.

Anguished protests are heard from the dealer, who sees a dent in his fender, and concern is also voiced by the duchess's son, who is rubbing a gouge in his door. Nerves from the actress, who admits she can't drive a car with a shift. A lengthy conference between her and the director follows.

"Don't worry," he tells her soothingly. "This was only a *test*. A little wax will fix the damn castle door. As for the car, it's OK. Look, they've already backed it into position. Won't you try it again?" She protests that no, she won't. She is angry because the scene was added at the last minute and she never knew until tonight that she'd have to *drive* a car. The duchess's son intervenes to support her and tactfully suggests that, personally, he'd prefer she wouldn't.

At that moment, the girl's mother arrives, who's both her real mother *and* her mother in the picture. She hugs her daughter, wipes her eyes, calms her down, and leaves, after scolding the director for his heartlessness.

"All right," decides the director. "We'll do it differently, then. You guys rig up ropes attached to the rear bumper." Amateur stagehands, keeping out of camera range, will push the car to the door, while she pretends to drive. And when she's supposed to back up, they'll simply pull the car back with these ropes. Fine, but the system causes great alarm to the dealer, who fears it might dislodge the bumper. He'll allow one take this way, no more.

Now, all is in place, ready for the real thing. The firemen are at their post. The actress sits in the car, switches on the lights. Sprinklers are turned on, and a heavy rain falls on the car's path. A good push. The car stops just in front of the door. The girl jumps out, leaving the lights on and the door open, runs into the castle.

"Cut," calls out the director. "You *must* turn off the lights and close the car door behind you. You're coming home to stay! It's only what you come upon *inside* that will make you rush out. Surely, you remember? OK, now, let's get you dried off before we try again."

She is drenched, poor thing, the silky coat clings to her body, her dripping hair is plastered around her face. On that cold March night we're not all that warm in sweaters and parkas, but she has to be freezing! She is helped inside, and an hour passes before she returns, freshly made up, hair gleaming again and dry raincoat, looking determined.

The car, meanwhile, has been pulled back into place, and the dealer is sure the bumper is being torn off, so he wants the ropes attached to the axle instead. This takes some doing, but finally, two firemen crawl out from under the car, grinning and grease-smeared, giving a victory sign.

One more take.

This time, it is the castle door she forgets to close behind her. "Remember," the director repeats patiently, "you think you're coming home *to stay*. You couldn't very well leave the front door open behind you, could you? But since you've been drenched again, darling, you must go in and get warmed up."

An hour later, one more take.

The car is pushed to the entrance door. She turns off the lights, jumps out under the downpour, slams the door. Good girl! The audience is mesmerized, rooting for her. Yes, yes, she opens the castle door, rushes in, closing it behind her. Great! This time, they have it. She rushes back out to the car, leaving the château door open behind her as she leaves. The audience lets out an audible groan.

"Cut," shouts the director. "Remember, darling: You're terribly upset by what you saw inside, so you slam the door behind you, you want to shut off that unhappy sight. . . ." The girl is shivering, wiping her face with a towel. I can see her shoulders shake.

Her make-up woman escorts her inside once more.

Everybody tries to relax, coffee is passed around. A fireman comments that a drop of brandy in that coffee couldn't do any harm. "Righto," agrees an assistant, who leaves and returns with a bottle of cognac.

The actress comes back, hair dried and coiffed, makeup refreshed, dry coat. They must have a battery of hair dryers inside.

She's back in the car. Entreaties from the director to please remember: "You think you've come home at last. You're in heaven! You open the door, walk in, and . . . Remember what you see? You haven't forgotten the script? Okay, then you get in, stay ten seconds, rush out, slam the door behind you. And don't forget to turn and stare at the camera, looking upset. Let's go."

This time she forgets to turn *on* the car lights as she leaves, before the car is pulled out of range. She couldn't very well be backing up without lights in that rain. Besides, someone *inside* the castle is supposed to spy those lights as she is driving away. They *must* be on.

One has to admit the kid has spunk. An hour later, when all bystanders are yawning away and stamping their feet to keep them from going numb, the firemen looking at their watches and shaking their heads, she is back, courageously. But she looks pale under the makeup, her jaws are clenched, tears glisten in her eyes. Regardless of the risk of pneumonia, others would have quit in her place. "Bravo, *mademoiselle*," salutes a fireman.

One more.

The rain pours down on her as she rushes in, rushes out . . . and forgets to stop and stare at the camera. Back inside for another hour. "Well," says the director, patting her shoulder when she returns, "we're getting there fast, now. Next take, we'll put it in the can."

Real rain begins to fall, and not just on her and the car, but on everybody, so the thin crowd of onlookers huddles in the shelter of doorways. Yet, no one is willing to leave; we all want to see the kid getting it right at last. Going home at this point would be like abandoning her.

"She'll do it, you'll see. Won't you, Baby? This one's for Daddy," calls out a wise guy in the audience.

One more, under a pelting rain.

The car is pushed to the door, she is helped in, under the shelter of an umbrella. There we go. She does everything perfectly this time, and, as she turns to face the camera, with rain slanting across, a stroke of lightning rips the sky and reflects in her tear-filled, haunted eyes. The audience breaks into cheers and applause.

The scene is brief on the screen, but the tragedy in the young actress's face registers so movingly that it stands out as the most powerful and memorable one in the series.

"Nothing to it, really," comments the director later. "We had it in the can in no time. Good kid, great talent. Easy to see, too, that she's had a lot of experience. It's not just anybody who could have pulled that one off the way she did."

Still, our best memory of the castle as a movie set dates from the time it was used in another television film about the life of that local pervert, the Marquis de Sade. Filming took place when we weren't in the village, so we only received echoes of all the excitement. The duchess wrote:

The film company is using the château as that of the Marquis de Sade's. Actors are housed here, too, a nice little extra income for us.

As you know, the real Sade castle, in nearby Lacoste, is in ruin and no interiors remain. No gardens, either. But *our* own topiary gardens have been lovingly maintained to just what they were at the time of the marquis's life, in the latter part of the eighteenth century. Also, it took very little rearranging of furniture and paintings for us to set up authentic rooms of that period.

Both director and producer are charming young men, constantly asking me questions about the Sade family, which still counts descendants in the region. Did I tell you that a girl from our own family married a Sade? But that was *centuries* before that naughty marquis disgraced the name. They want my advice on everything: Is this the best location for this scene? Should that painting in the background be moved?

I was thus able to contribute to some very moving confrontations between the marquis, his unfortunate wife, and his sainted father. Of course, they're only shooting here those scenes that are supposed to take place at the Lacoste castle. Most of the rest will be filmed at the studios in Paris.

Would you believe these young men even want to give me screen credit? I certainly wouldn't expect it, since I enjoy helping, but isn't it thoughtful of them to suggest it?

We had no sooner arrived that winter, when the duchess was on the phone, glad we were finally in the village, because the Sade movie was to be shown that very night on television.

"I want you to come to the château and watch it with me. We'll sit in the same salon where several scenes were shot. You'll enjoy seeing it on the screen as well. Yes, the big-screen set my son brought me from Paris last month."

At nine-thirty, all three of us were sitting in the salon, waiting for the late news to finish. The title filled the screen:

LE MARQUIS DE SADE

The topiary gardens come into view. The marquis strolls with his wife, impatiently walking ahead as she tries to cling and begs him to listen to her protestations of love. Cut to the salon, where the marquis is having a frightful row with his aging father. His wife comes in, throws herself at the older man's feet, and beseeches him to let her husband have an advance on his future inheritance. He needs to go to court in Versailles and seek the King's favor. What about her own dowry? the father wants to know. She has to admit that her husband has squandered it all, but she loves him still, and she's certain he'll send for her once he is established at court.

After a few such innocuous scenes, in the course of which many tears are shed but the advance is finally granted, the divine marquis, now in the capital and safely removed from his loved ones, is free at last to show his true colors. Sadism wasn't called that just for squandering one's wife's dowry. Accompanied by a depraved valet—with whom he clearly carries on an illicit relationship—he roams Paris in search of his peculiar pleasures. A guest at a friend's house, he corners a chambermaid, bends her over a windowsill. Screams. Blood spurts. More screams when he produces a whip and repeatedly lashes at the hapless girl, who finally manages to run away in her bloodstained petticoat. The duchess is indignant. She had no idea it was going to be *that* kind of a movie.

"Such nice young men! How dare they? They never let on, and who would have thought?"

Scenes of orgies with naked bodies writhing follow others where action is tactfully left, at least in part, to the imagination. But the good marquis is always in the midst of those happenings, and always handy with his whip. Close-up of buttocks streaked with bloody lashes. . . . When little boys are brought in by the valet, the duchess cannot take it anymore and stands up:

"Call me when these horrors are over with," she requests, as she leaves the room.

Later, the valet and his master are back in Marseille, since they are on the verge of being arrested and must escape the Paris police. In a bordello they feed wine laced with Spanish fly to a couple of prostitutes. Apparently, they're experimenting with overdose, for, instead of feeling amorous, the women moan and groan in agony, swearing they're going to die.

The duchess returns as the final scenes show the marquis condemned to death by the Aix parliament. But the sentence cannot be carried out, because King Louis the Sixteenth, mindful that Sade is an aristocrat in spite of all his crimes, has removed him from the reach of criminal justice by placing him in the safety of his own royal prison, the Bastille. Therefore, only the marquis's effigy will be burned on the Place des Prêcheurs in Aix.

The movie ends as the straw effigy hangs smoldering from the gallows in the center of the square under the jeers of a ragged crowd. The duchess is relieved.

Too soon, alas, for now the credits roll. First of all, in especially large type the duchess's name spreads across the top of the screen. The production team pays tribute, thanking her profusely:

> For her generous counsel and advice
> For her firsthand knowledge and expertise
> that helped make this
> the most accurate and best-documented life of
> **LE MARQUIS DE SADE**

Both hands over her mouth, the duchess is hyperventilating, too choked with indignation to utter more than strangled sounds. But she is forced to make a quick recovery, for her two phones simultaneously begin to ring. First, her children, who are exclaiming: "Mother! How could you?" Then, assorted relatives, prissily offended to see their noble name associated with such a revolting film—which they have clearly watched from beginning to end. Then, it's the bishop in Avignon, who hasn't missed a second either, and scolds her as he would a sheep straying from his flock.

So, resolutely, the duchess takes both phones off their hooks, firmly slams their receivers down onto the table. Then, she sits back, smiles, and winks:

"At least, all these people had double fun tonight. First, watching this naughty show; second, being holier than me. Well, if they have anything to tell me, let them *write*. Come to think of it, if my husband were here he'd be quite amused: How many people do you know who can qualify as advisors to the Marquis de Sade?"

With ravioli, or with *macaronade*, it is . . .

Daube Provençale (Beef and Vegetable Stew in Red Wine)
This is the classic beef in a dark wine sauce most people remember from a trip to Provence. The meat is tender, the sauce fragrant and satisfying. In Nice, it is served with ravioli (filled with a Swiss chard filling); in Provence, with a *macaronade*: macaroni baked in a little of the daube sauce.

3 pounds cubed, lean beef
Olive oil
1 pint mushrooms
3 onions, sliced

1 small onion studded with 5 cloves
5 cloves garlic, minced
4 carrots, sliced on the bias
4 or 5 shallots, sliced
2 beef bouillon cubes
1 bottle good dry red wine
1 Tbs tomato paste
1 bay leaf
2 Tbs wine vinegar
Salt and pepper

In a Dutch oven, sauté meat in very hot oil, so it browns quickly without rendering its juices. Set aside.

Clean and slice mushrooms (if small, leave whole). Sauté quickly, so they, too, retain their liquid. Set aside.

Adding a little oil if necessary, sauté onions, garlic, carrots, and shallots until onion is slightly caramelized (but *not* blackened). Add meat and mushrooms. Drop in bouillon cubes. Pour in bottle of wine. Add tomato paste, bay leaf, vinegar, salt and pepper to taste. Cover and bring to a boil. Then, lower heat and simmer on *low* for at least an hour. Taste to check seasonings and correct as needed. Check meat for tenderness. Continue simmering until meat is fork tender. (You can prepare the daube a day or more ahead. It only gets better.)

MACARONADE ACCOMPANIMENT

Partly cook 1 pound elbow macaroni in boiling, salted water. Remove while they are still *not quite* done. Place them in a *tian*. Ladle some of the daube sauce over. Sprinkle bread crumbs and grated cheese over the top and bake for 30 minutes.

Wine: You want a hearty red, ideally the same as used in the sauce of the daube. You can't go wrong with a Côtes-du-Rhône or a Côtes-de-Provence.

Song in the Wind

The city of Orange is festive tonight, with banners flying overhead announcing Verdi's *Aida*. Side streets leading to the theater have been closed to traffic and filled instead with dining tables decked in brightly colored cloths. Sipping our last cup of coffee, we are waiting for nightfall when the performance shall begin.

This year, *Aida* marks the high point of the *Chorégies*, a summer season of operas and concerts performed in the majestic setting of Orange's Roman theater. Tickets are at a premium, they must be purchased weeks in advance, or else scalped on the spot at outrageous prices. Indeed, it is a privilege to attend Verdi's great opera in the grandiose surroundings of this open-air theater built two thousand years ago, shortly after the Romans conquered Provence.

Earlier today, the heat was crushing. By late afternoon, the air remained languid and heavy as we drove leisurely, basking in the coolness of the air-conditioned car. The road leading to Orange, a few miles north of Avignon, follows the Rhône Valley, passing ancient villages that loom on the edge of cliffs, cut by the river geological ages ago. Now, by nine-thirty, the heat hasn't quite abated yet. I'm fanning myself with my straw hat, but we are looking forward to a little coolness as night folds down upon us. Sitting under the stars on this balmy night, bathed in Verdi's glorious music, will be a delicious, unforgettable evening.

The facade of the theater, even though depredations have robbed it over the centuries of its marble facing and its statuary, is still impressively massive. As we emerge from the narrow passages into the amphitheater, we are struck by its immensity. The semicircle of bleacherlike stone benches rises high, much as in a modern stadium. A giant statue of Augustus Caesar overlooks a stage of overwhelming width. My first thought: How in the world are they ever going to fill a stage this large?

Crowds pour in, and we are amused, if puzzled, to see most everyone walk in loaded with sweaters, blankets, down coats, pillows and cushions, thermos carriers, and even hot-water bottles. What do they expect on a night like this? Snow? Frost? Hail? A Chicago football afternoon in November? I laugh and point to a man who slogs in, wearing a pair of sheepskin boots, as Wayne shakes his head in disbelief. Meanwhile, we sit, smug, finally cooling off a bit as a breath of evening caresses us, dispelling at last the unforgiving heat, supremely comfortable now in our light summer clothes: Wayne in a short-sleeve shirt, I in a low-cut voile dress. The sight of the colorful (if strangely bundled up) crowd, rapidly filling the arena, and the expectation of music-drenched hours ahead combine into a pleasurable wait.

After every seat is occupied, a long time must yet pass, for the sky has only paled overhead, and the show cannot start until dark, which comes late on those midsummer days. Now, I certainly wouldn't want to spoil the glory of a blue twilight in such rarefied surroundings, but by now, as over an hour has elapsed, the idea of a pillow doesn't seem nearly as ridiculous. These stone benches without arm-, back-, or footrest, take a toll on your spine. Either the Romans remembered to bring pillows, as their descendants seem to do today, or else their bone structure was better adjusted than ours to the absence of upholstery. Wayne grunts, shifts uncomfortably, but doesn't complain: He wouldn't want to spoil my enjoyment with gripes, either.

Finally, lights flood the stage and the orchestra strikes the famous overture, ominously suggestive of tragedy. Trumpets blare. A huge, white staircase without banisters slowly swings to center stage, facing the looming, gold, columnated temple of Vulcan. Sets and costumes are all in gold, white, and black, a stunning combination. As the first act begins, it is close to eleven P.M.

I can see now how they propose to fill those great voids on the stage. A spectacular chorus of five hundred, all in white with gold headdresses, files onto the stage, divides into two sinuous groups, and rejoins. This is an elegant but time-consuming maneuver—just as the later extraordinary appearance of eight elephants, all painted gold and caparisoned in glittering black and white, will draw prolonged, enthusiastic applause, which, no matter how prolonged, still dies long before the last ponderous beast has been guided to its appointed place. A true showstopper, in every sense of the word. And then, each time the chorus changes its formation, its complex evolutions, fascinating as they are to watch, bring the performance to a standstill. By now, my back frankly hurts, and I see Wayne all scrunched up. Try to twist into a better position, knees under chin for a while, but above all, don't spoil the wonder of the moment with petty, selfish grousing. . . . Only now, I seem to feel a distinct chill, too. I snuggle closer to Wayne, who groans, buttons up his shirt, and wraps his arm around my shoulders.

Somebody close to me exclaims: "*Peuchère!* I can feel a mistral coming on. They were right, on the news, when they promised it for tonight! It's going to be cold in here!"

All along, I have been wondering why both voices and orchestra seem so faint. After a moment I realize there are no microphones, no sound system whatsoever. You want Roman theater, you get Roman theater, as the New Yorkers might say. I remember reading how, in antiquity, these theaters were designed in such a way that their perfect acoustics would carry sound to *every* seat in the giant, open-air hemicycles. No mean achievement, to be sure; and they do, after a fashion. Only, the Romans had obviously not been spoiled by sound amplification that carries the full depth and range to the uppermost reaches of any arena. . . . They were satisfied with a trickle of voice, a thin stream of music.

Our expectations in this regard, as well as in seating comfort, are much higher today, I reflect, as I strain to follow the slave Aida's and the princess Amneris's duet as they wrangle over the love of Radamès.

And now, the mistral has arrived! The mistral, the *master wind* in Provençal, blows down the Rhône Valley at any time of the year, always cold, whatever the season. Its unpredictably timed stints fill three, six, or nine days with capricious violence. Van Gogh's cypresses writhe under its assaults; it strips trees of leaf, flower, and fruit. For centuries it has toppled countless church steeples, and that's why one sees today so many of them replaced with open-work wrought iron, through which the mistral can just howl harmlessly. Now, a prisoner captured in the funnel of this arena, it whooshes and swirls frantically, seeking escape. Blankets flap wildly, programs take flight like crazed birds. . . .

Meanwhile, on the slowly revolving, banisterless staircase, Victoria de Los Angeles, the Spanish diva in the role of Amneris, holds onto her wig with one hand and attempts to control her ballooning skirt with the other while keeping a precarious balance, in great danger of being toppled by the merciless gusts. Nonetheless, she bravely continues singing her aria in the wind's maelstrom that rushes around her, carrying off all sound in its course.

All over the arena, people are struggling to hold down blankets wrapped around their bodies and scarves tied over their hair. My straw hat takes flight and disappears among the top rows on the opposite side. How I envy those sweaters and hot-water bottles now! The icy wind penetrates my thin dress like tissue paper, my bare legs have turned a mottled violet, hair whips my face and painfully flogs my eyelids. Wayne, who in normal times fears the cold a great deal more than I do, has slipped his program inside his shirt, in a futile effort to cut the wind, and tries to hold in whatever little warmth we still harbor by holding me tighter against him.

A plaid blanket, lifted off by a powerful gust, rises straight into the air, and, followed by thousands of eyes, sails high across the arena, flaps down upon the stage, to somersault at an elephant's feet. Startled, the animal raises its trunk and trumpets, immediately imitated by another. Are we going to witness a stampede? No. The trainers distract their charges by guiding them into their next majestic turn, as the chorus solemnly marches, robes flapping, from one side of the stage to the other.

Poor Victoria has heroically finished her aria without being swept off that steep staircase. I bet she's now in the wings, wrapped in woollens, drinking something steaming and swearing that nobody will force her back upon that damn contraption. I dream of the Great Cold Wave that I survived in Provence. A piece of cake, compared to this summer night. I had a fire, warm clothes, a roof over my head. What could I have found to complain about then?

The stone bench, so sun-warmed when we first sat, now radiates an icy current that rises to paralyze the spine. . . . Sheets of music fly straight up from the orchestra, while the maestro, tails flapping above his head, reaches out, makes a grab for them, and misses, to the titters of the audience.

Now the Ethiopian prisoners are led in: wretches in gray rags meant to look pathetic amid all that Egyptian gold. But their caps, lifted off by the wind, dance playfully at their feet. Amonasro, their defeated king, father of the unfortunate Aida, would be a commanding figure of dignity in despair, only, as he opens his mouth to sing, he is brutally slapped in the face by one of the flying *partition* sheets, which seems to stick there. Far from being moved, the audience guffaws. A few snatches of songs and instruments are swept this way and that. The smoke of tripod-mounted censers swirls erratically until one of the censers topples, rolling endlessly at the feet of the chorus, where a chorister picks it up and carries it backstage. Stagehands then come out to retrieve the others. Aida's lament when she recognizes her father among the prisoners might touch the audience's heart, if only any of it could be heard and her tunic didn't constantly flip over her head.

As Ramfis, the High Priest, raises his arms in a grand operatic gesture, holding aloft the laurel wreath to crown the victorious Radamès, his golden tiara is swept off, revealing a stocking cap over his head, to the audience's frank amusement. Nevertheless, he continues singing or at least one can guess he does, for he keeps on with his grand gestures. No matter: His voice, too, is hopelessly lost in the tornado. And I've never been as cold in my life as on this beautiful, clear summer night.

A glance at my watch, angled to catch the stage lights, shows two A.M. The show started late, and movements of the vast chorus and the ponderous elephants slowed action to its limits. When, at last, lights again flood the amphitheater, we've been sitting there for over four hours, and the second act is now just ending.

There is no element of surprise to the well-known libretto, and since the music only reaches us, if at all, in faint, isolated notes, we'll stop this torture, forget about the remaining part, and hope we didn't catch something serious like pneumonia. We shall not see Radamès condemned to death tonight. But I am sure both he and Aida look forward to that final act, when, buried alive in the crypt under the temple, that golden temple where lights have begun to glow, they await death. All the more patiently since they are now safe in the crypt's confines from the mistral's assaults. I do hope poor Amneris will be spared that crazy staircase, although the steps to Vulcan's temple do not look much safer.

As for us, we stand up painfully. Wayne is rubbing his back, and my knees are locked with cold. Crowds push and shove all the way down the narrow exits, mercifully shielding us from the wind. We won't try to fight our way to the tiny bar, already mobbed. Without a word, jaws paralyzed, we let the current carry us toward the car park. Clearly, we're not the only ones to have given up on the tragic fate of those noble Ethiopians and Egyptians, for we must now wait until the traffic jam clogging the exit gate has cleared. Though the car has retained some of the day's warmth, we turn the heater on full blast as we sink with relief into soft seats, luxuriating in regained twentieth-century comfort, too relieved to even feel embarrassed to have proved such sissies compared to the example we witnessed tonight of easily imagined Roman fortitude.

After we have warmed up some, pangs of hunger assail us. Our light dinner on that extended restaurant terrace under those festive *Chorégies* banners seems very far away.

"What was it you were baking this morning that smelled so good?" asks Wayne, pretending indifference.

I had been thinking of the same thing.

"*Petits farcis.* You know, stuffed vegetables like Madame Fabre makes. Of course," I add, and the past tense has already decided the fate of those *farcis*, "they *were* for tomorrow night's dinner. . . ."

A silence while we both wonder how those *farcis* would taste cold and how long it would take to warm them up. Then:

"Remember that hot mulled wine I made last Christmas? We still have cinnamon sticks. I saw the jar the other day," says Wayne, dreamily. "That does not take long. . . ."

It seems forever before we reach home. It is almost four A.M., and the sky shows quite pink in the east. We find the house still filled with the past day's warmth.

We will return to the *Chorégies*, we agree, and best time for that would be on a safe day, like right *after* a mistral bout has ended. Bring an ample supply of pillows and dress warmly, just in case. Then, in reasonable comfort, one can do justice to the magnificent setting and the probably glorious music.

The best seats to hear it? Directly in front of the orchestra, and low enough. Then it will be no hardship at all to stay until the last curtain. No, there are no curtains falling across that monumental stage. The last applause, then.

We certainly can think about that some other time. Right now, all we really have to decide is whether we should set the table, or carry a tray upstairs to enjoy our feast sitting in bed, watching the sun rise over the crest of the Luberon; a sliver of light that in minutes will have turned into a dazzling orange globe.

They must be caramelized around the edges . . .

Petits Farcis de Provence (Stuffed Baked Vegetables)
Farci means "stuffed with a savory filling." *Petits farcis* are vegetables, stuffed and then baked until practically melting and caramelized around the edges. Serve a small portion as an appetizer, a larger one as an entrée, arrange them all around your roast as an accompaniment. In any case, make plenty.

The vegetables
   8 small onions, center flesh cut out with a knife, then
      scooped out
   8 sweet red pepper "cups" (bottom half of pepper),
      seeds removed

8 medium tomatoes, center flesh scooped out
8 summer-type round zucchini, center flesh scooped out
   (retain all scooped-out flesh for stuffing)
Salt and pepper

Boil onions and sweet peppers, separately, in salted water for about 10 minutes. Drain well. Arrange all vegetables in a shallow baking dish (you may need two). Sprinkle the inside with a little salt and pepper and fill them with stuffing.

The stuffing
   1 thick slice ham, diced
   ½ smoked Polish sausage, diced
   3 cloves garlic
   All the flesh scooped out of the vegetables, above
   A few sprigs of parsley
   4 slices white bread, torn into pieces, soaked in 1 cup
      cream (reserve extra cream)
   3 eggs
   Salt and pepper if needed
   Olive oil

Place all ingredients (except eggs and reserved cream) in mixer. Pulse until chopped fairly fine, but *not* pureed. Remove to a bowl. Mix in the well-beaten eggs. Add rest of cream if needed to obtain a firm, manageable stuffing. Check for seasonings (the stuffing should be well seasoned).
   Fill veggies, mounding stuffing with back of a spoon. Drizzle a little olive oil over and around veggies.

Bake at 350°F for an hour, and check. If top browns too fast, cover *loosely* with tinfoil and reduce temperature. Continue baking for two or three hours, or until vegetables are very soft—practically melting and lightly "caramelized" around the edges.

Serve warm or cold.

Wine: A rosé would go beautifully with this dish.

Mistral-whipped in a Roman theater or frozen in a football stadium? Warm up with . . .

Wayne's Vin Chaud (Hot Mulled Wine)

I bottle red wine
I wine glass of port or cream-type sherry
Juice and zest of I orange
3 cloves
2 Tbs sugar
I tsp ground cinnamon
Cinnamon sticks to stir with

Place all ingredients in a saucepan and bring to a boil, but *do not let boil.* Pour into heavy, bistro-type glasses (a spoon in each glass prevents breaking). Place a cinnamon stick in each glass with a piece of the orange peel. This drink is guaranteed to raise both your spirits and body temperature to optimum level.

The Hollyhock Seeds

*I*n late summer, the duchess had taken to walking around the village's narrow streets, bending over now and then to scatter at the foot of the walls something I took to be bread crumbs. A kind attention, I thought, for the occasional bird or pigeon or adventurous chickens, free-ranging out of their yards.

"No, no," she smiled, when I commented on her thoughtfulness. "These are not crumbs. They are seeds, *roses trémières*, hollyhock seeds. They take two or three years to grow and flourish. I hope, some day soon, to see the village abloom with them. I'd like it to become known as the Hollyhock Village of Provence. I've always had a special devotion for Saint Roselyn, and the *rose trémière*, I am sure, is her flower."

As we walked together, she drew a handful of large, winged seeds from her pocket and handed them to me, so I'd help her scatter them where they would grow, tall and erect, at the foot of the old walls.

"Saint Roselyn is a Provençal saint, a great lady of her time. Surprised by her cruel and avaricious husband as she was bringing forbidden alms to the poor, he ordered her to drop the folds of her apron to show him what she was carrying. She did, expecting brutal punishment. Except that God was watching. So, there, in the middle of winter, he changed the bread for the poor into flowers. *Roses trémières*, I think they were, from the way they're always pictured. So, with every seed, I also cast a little prayer: 'May our lives be like flowers in the sight of God.' "

Before we parted in front of the bakery, she added: "By the way, it's good you're still here this late in the season. This way, you won't miss the feast of Saint Amat next Sunday. Do come to the service, and we want you for *déjeuner* afterward. Alfresco, in the park. There'll be some interesting guests and we can talk more about hollyhocks."

She accepted my offer to bring dessert. "Figure on about twenty people," she told me.

After the heavy heat of the summer, September now offered cool mornings and a gentler sun. The great cavernous church, once the castle's hall of justice—how could I ever forget that ominous little cell next to it the prince had showed me on my first visit to the castle?—had long been turned over to the village as its house of worship, the castle retaining its own private chapel. The entire village, in their

Sunday best, crowded under the ancient, high-arched vault. Even a scattering of foreigners like us stepped in timidly, unsure of the proper gestures, and stood uncertainly in the aisles until room was made for them in the pews.

As the bells pealed, the castle family filed in: Two of the duchess's sons with wives and children, her niece and the prince, and last, the duchess, elegant in cyclamen silk and a wide-brimmed hat. Heads bowed perceptibly as she made her way up the aisle to kneel in her lion-stamped pew.

The gilt busts of Saint Amat and Saint Eliabel, removed from their side chapel, had been placed at the foot of the altar, resting on a high board with four shafts, banked with flowers. As the village priest sprinkled them with holy water, the congregation sang:

> *Honneur à Sainte Eliabel*
> *Et d'Amat, chantons les grandeurs*

while three little boys, grandsons of the duchess's, with chestnut curls and in white surplices, swung their censers all around.

The monsignor, who'd come from Avignon, asked for the Saints' continued blessings upon the village and its inhabitants, as well as upon the castle and the family. He reminded all that each subsequent generation had named its eldest son Amat in honor of the Saint. As he spoke, two men of the same name stood with folded arms: the current duke, eldest son of the duchess, and her ten-year-old grandson, who are believed to be, respectively, twenty-sixth and twenty-seventh of the name. Both, however, would be the first to allow that the count might have been lost over the centuries, so it might be a little more or a little less.

The choir, trained by the duchess, sang during the ritual of the mass, she turning her head sharply each time a discordant note struck her ear. Then, she led the faithful to the communion table.

At the conclusion of the service her two sons and the prince stood up, each to shoulder a shaft and carry out the Saints. My neighbor whispered: "The duke and the *vicomte* are here today, but not the count. How are they going to manage?" The prince looked around and gestured to the mayor to come place himself by the fourth shaft. But when they lifted the board, heavy with its precarious load, it was clear that disaster threatened: The round little mayor was much too short, his shoulder too low, the Saints were tilting dangerously. He shook his head, and, grinning sheepishly, returned to his seat.

The prince scanned the audience again and spotted Wayne's head above the crowd. He winked at him: "Here, Wayne, lend us a hand," he said in English. Followed by every eye, Wayne went to stand by the shaft and lifted it to his shoulder, surrounded by a prince, a duke, and a *vicomte*, not bad for his first time inside a church.

I know I should have taken pictures of this once-in-a-lifetime event. I know it and will always regret that I didn't. Wayne's camera, hastily handed over, hung from my shoulder, and I never snapped a shot.

The monsignor, in his gold vestments, preceded by the three little boys swinging their censers, led the way. The four tall men in summer suits came next, shouldering the ancient gilded busts. The duchess with her family and the entire village followed, all singing again the hymn to the Saints, in a procession that has been repeated each year since the 1300s. Only, for the first time in recent memory, someone who wasn't a member of the family, or a dignitary, was helping to carry the Saints.

Why didn't I take pictures then? Because I was blinded by tears, tears of emotion and joy that we could be made part of such an age-old ritual, that we had been privileged to feel we belonged to this village's life. As the crowd made its way up the steeply ascending steps to the château, several people, unsure of the reason for my tears, came to pat me comfortingly on the shoulder.

In the honor courtyard, banners with the coat-of-arms of related families flew from every window, and a high trestle had been set up. The Saints were placed on top, and the villagers, one by one, led by the duchess, slipped under, each making a wish guaranteed to come true during the course of the year. As for me, slowly drying my tears, I couldn't think of a single wish to make, for there was nothing at the moment that I wanted and didn't have.

"Don't forget, *déjeuner* is at one-thirty down in the park, and we're expecting you. We'll talk about hollyhocks," the duchess reminded me, as the men once again shouldered the Saints to return them to their chapel until next year.

The walled castle park spreads way down below at the foot of the village. There, an immense stone *bassin*, fed by a cascade, once served to hold irrigation water and now, used as a swimming pool, still reflects the castle's image. A grove of tall pines shelters a space cleared for tables and chairs as well as a miniature *mas*, a farmhouse. The *mas* actually holds kitchen equipment to help with alfresco entertainment, and a spring bubbles right in the center of the room, perfect to cool bottles in. Vineyards creep right up to the edge of the lawn, and lavender fields, too, trimmed to rounded porcupine shapes now that harvest time has passed.

It seems the guest of honor hasn't arrived yet, but the company already includes the Avignon monsignor, a distinguished painter, an American scholar doing research in the château's archives, and the handsome ambassador of a country whose name I don't get. He is in conversation with the princess, who turns her angelic profile in rapt attention. The prince, meanwhile, cheerfully helps Carlos serve glasses of rosé all around, "antifreeze" he calls it, but his attention remains riveted on the spectacular au pair girl who is supposed to be looking after the boys. Instead, she lolls in a minimal bikini on the rim of the pool, in spite of the duchess's insistent frown. The prince comments: "Beautiful girl. She's an au pair. Well, I am not the *père*, but in his absence. . . ." The children help to set the tables and arrange small bouquets they gather from the flower borders.

Suddenly, the guest of honor's arrival is heralded by the sound of a horn and everyone stands to see. A low-slung, ancient car, a Rolls, perhaps, or a Daimler, white with blinding chromes, pulls up to the very edge of the lawn.

The chauffeur springs out to open the door as a male attendant in white uniform and red turban alights from the other side. In a chorus of barks, two small apricot poodles are handed over to the liveried man. The chauffeur then offers his hand for the passenger to step down. Out emerges an elegant woman, with gray-blue hair, to whom the duchess curtsies. This is, whispers the prince before he steps up to kiss her hand, the begum Aga Khan, widow of the late Aga Khan, spiritual leader of the Ismailya branch of the Muslim faith.

The begum smiles graciously and greets everyone, exclaiming over the children she apparently knows well. She is still a handsome woman who has retained much of the beauty of her youth. She chats with me in English and I cannot help but comment on her jewelry: necklace and bracelet of enormous pearls with clasps of large sapphires and diamonds.

Am I being too personal? She dismisses my admiration: "Just summer things. For outdoors, you know."

She is wearing what must be the required attire of her faith: a long tunic over pantaloons and a matching scarf she uses at times to cover her head, all in a gossamer silk chiffon, watercolored in melting shades of pale turquoise, amethyst, and cobalt. Her attendant brings a small carpet to slip under her feet when she sits, because the ground is covered with pine needles. The poodles yap and challenge the duchess's dog, an aging cocker who lies curled at the foot of a tree. In vain, for he will only raise a phlegmatic eyebrow and lazily shift his position.

His eyes still following the au pair (or was it *au père?*), the prince confides out of the side of his mouth: "The begum has the rank of a princess; she is most generous to the duchess's charities and I wouldn't swear she hasn't helped with the château's finances, too. So who would grudge her a little carpet under her feet?"

I also learn from him that the begum attracted the attention of the portly, widowed Aga Khan when, as a young saleslady in a candy shop, she won the title of Miss France. She converted to the Muslim faith and accompanied her husband on his yearly visits to Arabia, where his followers would weigh him and match his weight in gold. "No incentive for slimming down," comments the prince.

The *au père* girl, now more demurely clad in shorts and a halter, is helping to set the tables under the duchess's silent directions. But she keeps casting sidelong glances at the prince, so insistently that she stumbles over a tree root and nearly drops a tray full of silver.

Seating guests is an art: One must remember precedence as well as interests, and who would enjoy sitting next to or across from whom. The duchess has long mastered the art of distributing guests among the several round tables, each presided over by a member of the family. I am directed to the prince's table, to sit next to the American scholar, a young professor of history, who confesses that his days at the château contribute more to his understanding of French history than whatever he can find in the archives. Wayne is seated next to the begum, unaccountably, I think, until she produces a small camera, and I hear of her interest in photography with her desire to discuss cameras and lenses.

Supervised by Carlos, the little boys charmingly serve.

First, they bring small individual Cavaillon melons cooled in the spring, their seeds scooped out, and filled with Beaumes de Venise muscat wine. Next, comes a *salade de crocodile* made by the children themselves: Whole cucumbers, thinly sliced, writhe realistically on the platter, swimming in a lake of vinaigrette, sporting flirty eyelids fringed with green onion and red bowties of tomato peel. "I cut out their teeth with my new knife," proudly announces the youngest boy, displaying a fearsome pocketknife. Did the au pair summon enough interest in her charges to devise that fun recipe, someone wants to know. No, it was all the idea of the oldest boy, who'd seen it on a children's TV show. The begum beams at him. The main dish is *blanquette de veau* in a light, succulent cream sauce, with fresh peas and little potatoes from the garden. "No cheese tray," announces the duchess. "I find cheese redundant after a meal. Also, it complicates the service, especially out-of-doors."

Now the children, eyes shining, eagerly bring forth the dessert they'd helped us hide earlier in the little *mas* kitchen. When Wayne and I ordered it in Pertuis we asked for something special and the *pâtissier* promised a surprise. He has outdone himself. This is a two-foot turreted castle made of nougat, with the red lion flying from its keep, the entire confection rising from thickets of spun sugar roses, each with a candied cherry at its center. All the guests exclaim politely, a little puzzled, who knows, by this display. Would it be too gaudy? Over the top? Something only Americans would indulge in? The children certainly don't think so and crowd around excitedly demanding the roses. As I divide them up, the word sings in my mind.

Roses? *Roses trémières?* Weren't we, by the way, supposed to hear something about hollyhocks? I corner the duchess as everyone stands and walks around, coffee cup in hand. First, she must signal the au pair, now lying provocatively in a hammock, with the prince bending over her, that she should help clear the tables. Then, she brings me over to the begum, still in earnest discussion with Wayne, who has taken her camera apart and is carefully cleaning the lens with the little blower brush he always carries in his pocket.

"This is the lady we must thank if our village blooms with hollyhocks some day soon. The begum owns a villa in Egypt. . . ."

The begum's eyes crinkle. She resides most of the time in Cannes, on the Riviera, but spends a few months each winter in her splendid villa on the Nile in Aswan. There, all winter long, her gardens are filled with tall hollyhocks so plentiful they have become a sight that tourists troop to admire. When the duchess visited there last, she spent much time gathering seeds and soon had a large bagful.

There is now a faraway look in the begum's eyes, and for a moment I see the young girl she once was. "My father cultivated hollyhocks in our small garden, and to me, they always meant home. They do well in the rocky soil of Aswan, and they should prosper in the village." The eastern princess returns: "May it be the will of Allah that they flourish."

I enjoy thinking that Allah and Saint Roselyn held hands as they gamboled across the heavens, smiling down upon those seeds. For now, the village is abloom each summer with great clumps of hollyhocks, saucer-size flowers on stiff stems standing at attention against every wall, at each turn of the paths, with more springing up yearly in the most unlikely places: in a chicken yard, out of mortar crumbling between old stones, pushing between the roots of a tree, the boldest ones defying traffic in the middle of a street. They bloom on the stone steps that climb to the castle, in front of the church, on the bakery doorstep, between the outdoor tables of the *Bar des Sports*, and a large garnet one has staked the left side of our kitchen door.

They have even invaded the little enclosure where the castle funeral chapel stands, their tall heads looking, in pressed ranks, over the low wall, guarding the last rest of those who slumber there.

The Duchess's Own Recipe . . .

Blanquette de Veau à l'Ancienne (Old-Fashioned Creamy Veal Stew)

No, *blanquette* does not mean *blanket*. The word is derived from *blanc*, white, because this delicate veal dish must not show any sign of browning. It must remain deliciously creamy white, with just a touch of celadon green from the leeks.

2 or 3 leeks
2 pounds cubed veal
1 bottle dry white wine (chardonnay type)
Salt and white pepper
1 pint heavy cream
3 egg yolks
1 Tbs cornstarch
Minced parsley or chervil for garnish at serving time

Wash leeks and discard dark-green part, keeping only the light-green and white parts. Slice.

Place uncooked veal and sliced leeks in a skillet. Pour the wine over, add salt and *white* pepper (always better than black in a white sauce). Cover and bring to a boil, then simmer for about 30 minutes or until veal is *very* tender.

Add cream, and return to a boil. Remove *immediately* from heat. Beat egg yolks well with the cornstarch and just a little water. Stir the mixture into the very hot, but not quite boiling blanquette. It will thicken to a light, creamy consistency. *Do not allow blanquette to boil again, as eggs will curdle.*

If it must wait before serving, keep the blanquette warm by placing the saucepan, covered, in a large skillet, with 2 inches of water, over low heat.

PETITS POIS AND POTATOES ACCOMPANIMENT

Clean and partly peel small rose potatoes, leaving just strips of the pink skin (figure on 5 per person if very small, otherwise 3). Boil in salted water until tender. Boil peas (frozen are fine) in salted water, too, until just done (if the peas are frozen, this takes only a very short boil). Drain potatoes and peas.

Mix the two, verify seasoning (a little salt and white pepper are probably needed). Stir in enough butter to be quickly absorbed. Spoon on a little of the creamy blanquette sauce, arrange the vegetables around the blanquette in a large, not too shallow, serving dish. Sprinkle minced parsley or chervil over all.

Wine: A dry white, of course. A Côtes-de-Provence, a Chablis, a chardonnay, or a sauvignon blanc would be perfect.

Provençal Food Does Not Make You Fat

Food assails your senses in Provence, its sight and smell practically grab you in the street. But it will not make you fat.

Young people are slender here, so much so that their visitors from abroad are often hard put to find jeans they can wear, since *large* in French sizes fits like small elsewhere. With the exception of some middle-aged, belly-proud *boule* players in front of the *Bar des Sports*, adults are reasonably slim, and obesity largely unknown. Yet, thought is seldom given to fat, cholesterol, carbohydrates, sodium, or any such harmful substances, and they are never discussed at the dinner table. Appearance, aroma, taste, and texture are of considerably greater interest.

As a matter of fact, visitors from the States are sometimes aghast at such lack of concern. How can we, ourselves, in just a few weeks, have become oblivious to the
dangers that food harbors for the unwary? They are right,
of course. Only, we are convinced that the chemistry of
nutrition follows different laws in Provence.

"Olives? What's that they're in? Oil?" worries a guest.
"Couldn't they be rinsed off? You're saying they *contain* oil,
too? And . . . oh, my God, how salty! Sodium! My poor
heart!"

"Salmon mousse? What do you put in that? Not cream,
I hope? Or eggs? What, the yolk, too? Couldn't you use
cholesterol-free *Eggbeaters* instead?"

"What's that brown stuff between the meat and the
crust in your *filet en croûte?* Chopped mushrooms and shallots sautéed in butter? Did you say butter? Regular, not
light butter? And on top of red meat, too!" I don't mention port wine to *déglacer*, for we don't need Demon Rum
lurking on our plates, too.

"Roquefort? Sounds like solid cholesterol to me. Low in
fat, you say, because it is sheep's milk? Personally, I only eat
cheese made with *nonfat* milk. And why is that Brie sort of
runny around the edges? Gone bad? Ripe, you say? I'll bet
it is. Don't mind if I pass."

But then, the unanimous request:

"Butter for my bread, please."

The presentation of dessert is sure to provoke cries of
anguish. Guilt arises from *looking* at dessert, let alone from
eating it. My crème brûlée, served in small, individual
dishes, brings forth a concert of warnings.

"What's in that? Eggs again, and cream, too? Did you say *whipping* cream? Oh, no!"

"Look at that *sugar* on top! I'd blow up like a balloon, just peeking at it!"

"You'll clog your arteries with all that bad cholesterol and then you'll be sorry."

"None for me, please. I want to live."

But I have discovered that the most rabid dessert-avoiders carry candy bars, brought from home, in their purses, or hide them in their bedrooms. Two friends of Wayne's who stayed with us while on a video assignment impressed me with their diet, so sophisticated that I found myself hard put to devise nonfat, nonoxydizing, low-carb, high-protein meals that would meet its requirements. Impressed, that is, until they agreed to preview for us the footage they'd shot so far. They must have relaxed between demanding shots, for, interspersed with views of Roman monuments and interviews with guides and historians, there they were, filming each other wolfing down mille-feuilles and éclairs, or sharing a wheel-size pizza. I showed, I felt, great nobility of soul by pretending to have missed those scenes.

The only dish that never awakens suspicion in our country is salad. Everyone feels safe in a salad bar, with a salad, no matter how huge, that may contain process cheese, nuts, avocado, hard-boiled eggs, oily tuna, syrupy pickles—the whole mess slathered in a dressing composed mostly of mayonnaise and catsup. "I only eat lunch in a salad bar near my office," claims an overweight guest who has turned down sliced tomatoes and onion with vinaigrette. "I can *see* the oil in the vinaigrette!" Offered air-dried, paper-thin *jambon de Bayonne*: "Looks raw to me. Have you heard of bacterial food poisoning?" He then brags: "And would you believe they have cheesecake in my salad bar, now? Yes, slices *that* thick and as many as you want."

Since the French give so little thought to the scientific contents of their foods, why aren't they enormously fat? Sick with cardiovascular disease? Dying from lethal doses of free radicals? Instead, life expectancy there stands notably higher than in the United States, and even more important, statistics show a very high incidence of vigorous, undiminished old age.

It might be the distribution of meals: a very light breakfast, a substantial but reasonable lunch, a light dinner, and, above all, no snacks. Spoil your appetite for the next meal? Never. Or is it the institution of the family meal—a daily ritual attended by every member, with conversation and small helpings of a variety of home-cooked foods? Another view held by the French is that food you enjoy will be good for you. Worrying about it cancels out whatever beneficent effects. Often quoted is the incident in which several tourists complained of severe stomach pains after eating a mushroom dish, convinced these were poisonous, while the rest of the group, unconcerned, enjoyed the same dish as a delicacy and suffered no ill effects from the perfectly edible morels.

Another theory has it that some mysterious chemistry voids the harmful effects of your meal, as long as you remember to end it with a slice of cheese and a glass of wine. Whatever the value of this hypothesis to health, it did wonders for the wine industry, with shops reporting a sharp increase in the sale of their red wine.

There is actually no mystery to eating like the French, just a cultural difference to overcome: *quantity*. One must accept the idea that *less* and *a little* are better than *none* or *too much*. Portions are *small*. Bread? Yes, unbuttered and freshly baked. The only evidence of health concern is the presence on every French table of a bottle of mineral water. Vichy is good for liver function, Vittel for digestion, and Contrex-éville helps to slim down.

For food emergencies, our village has long offered only the resources of the *Bar des Sports*, named in honor of the traditional, if not strenuous, true sport of Provence: *boules*. The *Bar des Sports* offers two *déjeuner* formulas: a cold plate of *charcuterie*, assorted cold cuts and salads, plus cheese and a glass of wine, ordered mostly by visitors waiting for the château to open its doors for the afternoon tour. Or else a complete meal, featuring the dish of the day as its center-piece. Wayne scorns the *Bar's* cuisine, claiming to be into higher food aesthetics, but whenever I am in the village, alone or with my friend Liz visiting, I'll be sure to check on Madame Aubanel's daily special: spicy North African couscous on Thursdays, daube on Wednesdays, or my Monday favorite, *endives au jambon*: cooked Belgian endives wrapped in a thin slice of ham and baked in a béchamel sauce with a crusty topping.

A few male villagers usually stand at the bar. I am always cordially greeted, and sometimes a cup of espresso is pre-sented at the end of the meal, compliments of Monsieur So and So, who touches his cap in my direction when I smile my thanks. Needless to say, prices at the *Bar des Sports* do not dent a budget.

Now that almost all the ruins have been restored, mostly by foreigners, and that tourists converge in ever greater numbers to visit the château, a real restaurant became a must. So, our wonderful new mayor coaxed the municipal council into buying a long-abandoned building and transforming it into a restaurant, to offer for lease to some young local chef. *Le Tournesol*, under its sign of yellow sunflowers, welcomes you with blue tablecloths and yellow faience dishes. It serves Provençal food—simple, but tasty and authentic. The *tian* of lamb with eggplant is worth a detour—as the *Michelin Guide* would put it. And the chef bakes tarts so clearly homemade that they are often burned around the edges. In season, look for the cherry tart made with cherries picked from the trees you can see just below (everything in the village is always either above or below you). In summer, service is on the terrace across the street, and waiters carrying plates vie with traffic, causing minor jams, because drivers will stop to check out what looks good today. The wine list is not extensive, but *Le Tournesol* never runs out of the local red and white, and especially the famous rosé.

Ranging a little farther afield, one of our favorites remains to this day the mercifully little-known *Auberge du Cheval Blanc* in La Bastide des Jourdans, on the road to Manosque.

Driving by, we'd never paid much attention to the old building, until a few years ago we noticed encouraging signs of gradual renewal. The stone facade cleaned and mortared, sagging *volets* repaired and painted a misty green, an attractive brass-monogrammed glass door in place of a nondescript one. Window boxes filled with well-tended geraniums broke down the last of my hesitation, and I dragged in a still-reluctant Wayne. I always see fresh flowers in a restaurant as a good sign; artificial ones, on the other hand, do not hold much promise.

The *Cheval Blanc* has stood for centuries as a stagecoach relay where travelers could exchange tired horses for fresh ones, and as far as Serge, the present owner, knows, it has always belonged to his family. When he inherited it from his mother, he continued serving the traditional dishes learned in the maternal kitchen, paying little attention to the tired decor. But a breath of new life walked in when lovely Agnès happened by. Agnès had no interest or experience in restaurant operation, but she fell in love with both Serge and his old inn at the same time, so a three-way love affair blossomed: Serge, Agnès, and the *Cheval Blanc*. Now, Agnès's deft touches are everywhere: A muted carpet softens the tile floor; Provençal curtains filter sunlight; settings invite with little flower baskets, candles in antique holders, good china and silver. In warm weather, tables are set in the courtyard, its walls now covered with vines, abloom with impatiens, in the double shade of old linden trees and big market-umbrellas. Agnès, smart and slender, greets guests like welcome friends, her trademark dangling earrings sparkling. Right away, no questions asked, an aperitif of *kir* and little foie-gras toasts arrive, *compliments de la maison*, if you've been there as much as once before.

A new menu marks every season. Always trust a hand-written menu against a printed one, I say, for it tells you that dishes change to follow the availability of market produce. For our part, we know enough to order the *menu du jour*, the set menu, rather than à la carte. Menus come in a range of prices, the least expensive usually the freshest, because it is the most ordered. It is also quite sufficient, since the higher-priced ones may include only one or two more courses. As for ordering à la carte, it means, in Provence, that you want larger portions at noncontrolled prices. For instance, an order of cantaloupe à la carte may cost as much as the whole menu that includes cantaloupe as an appetizer. But, of course, you'll get a larger serving.

Serge's courses follow the seasons: To begin with, a small, upside-down flan of chopped and butter-melted shallots surrounded by an airy green watercress sauce tells you this is winter. Come spring, you'll be offered asparagus *sauce mousseline*; and you know you've just passed the greenhouse where they were picked this morning. Summer shares its special flavor with the *tian* of eggplant, *courgettes*, and sweet onion in its herby tomato sauce. And then there are the soups: the cream of sweet red pepper; the winter pot-au-feu whose broth is served first, followed by the meats, beautifully arranged with bouquets of vegetables and a bowl of aioli, an olive oil and garlic emulsion. The truffle season, in January, climaxes with the truffle soup: a rich chicken broth with grated fresh truffles and, floating on top, tiny profiterolles filled with foie-gras. On a warm summer night, iced soups of lettuce, cucumber, or spicy tomato come in frosty glass bowls.

The main dish is often lamb, since here lambs grow succulent grazing on aromatic mountain herbs of mostly rosemary and thyme. Prized above all is Sisteron lamb from the foothills of the Alps. It may be in a *tian*, baked with the traditional eggplant and tomatoes, or a roast, or grilled with plenty of garlic. *Gigot à la ficelle*, leg of lamb on a string, is cooked in a pot of broth, the string used to pull it out when pink and tender. Chicken has nothing in common with what people here scornfully call "Common Market Chicken," the kind you purchase in supermarkets. Happily raised in freedom, fed with grain rather than industrial feed, it is tasty under its roast, crackling skin and served with a garlicky *purée de pommes de terre*, whipped to a froth. Duck is *à l'orange*, basted in Cointreau and surrounded by orange slices baked in the juices. Rabbit is braised in white wine with little onions and mushrooms. And then, Serge makes the best *pieds et paquets* (literally, feet and parcels) this side of heaven, and probably the other side, too. This quintessential dish, from the Marseille area, consists of little packages of lamb meat and tripe stuffed with herbs, simmered for no less than seven hours in a hermetically lidded pot. "Every good cook has a family recipe for *pieds et paquets*," confides Serge. "I promised my mother I'd never give away hers because she worked years on perfecting the sauce." Too ethnic for me, cautions Wayne, who will not order the dish, but invariably sops up all my sauce with his bread.

Desserts make imaginative use of seasonal fruit: a baked peach, stuffed with almond paste and glazed with honey; *gratin de fruits rouges*, raspberries, little strawberries, currants, and cherries in a light cream, quickly broiled under a brown-sugar crust; a pear poached in wine and vanilla, resting on a bed of macaroons soaked in juices; a quartered fig dressed in rum custard; a small apple tart, served flaming. Serge also offers L'Art Glacier's sorbets in crystal dishes, with a splash of the matching liqueur: pear brandy over pear, apricot brandy over apricot, peach liqueur over peach, or my favorite, marc over lemon sorbet, clean and sharp, which is called, for reasons unknown, a *colonel.* Wayne remains faithful to his lavender preference, but that is, of course, best savored among the blooming spikes of our terrace.

So it is not hard to understand why back home I'll easily pass on that order of chocolate cake topped with ice cream and doused with hot fudge sauce under a ten-inch topping of whipped cream.

We once spent a week at the *Cheval Blanc,* to accommodate those tenants who didn't want to miss the village fête, and we suffered no hardships at all. The few rooms are deliciously old-fashioned, furnished with pieces from Serge's mother's attic and nearby *brocantes.* The beds are covered with crocheted spreads, and curtains billow in the evening breeze. Like most inns, the *Cheval Blanc* offers *demi-pension,* an all-inclusive price for room and breakfast, plus either *déjeuner* or dinner.

After two months in Provence, we find, upon our return to the States, that we have usually lost a few pounds. Is there a magical chemistry at work there? We often wonder whether the good Saint Amat, who knew how to feed his flock in time of famine, extends his power today to keep the same from getting fat.

A favorite at the *Cheval Blanc* restaurant . . .

Gratin de Fruits Rouges (Crème Brûlée with Berries)
This is a crème brûlée, with very little crème and a lot of fruit—the four red fruits of Provence. It is best made in individual baking dishes. You can prepare it several hours ahead of time. Serves 6.

The custard
   2 egg yolks
   I Tsp cornstarch
   I cup heavy cream
   3 Tbs sugar

Beat egg yolks and cornstarch in a little cold water until smooth. In small saucepan, bring cream to a light boil over medium heat. Stir in sugar to dissolve. Remove from heat and mix in egg and cornstarch mixture. Stir. Cream should coat the spoon. It will thicken further as it cools.

The fruit
Arrange small strawberries (sliced), raspberries, pitted cherries, and red currants (if currants are not available, use more of the other fruit or replace with a few blackberries) in individual baking dishes, filling them to ³/₄ full. Spoon custard over fruit.

The crust

Top with a nice, even layer of pressed brown sugar. Slide under the broiler until sugar bubbles all over. Remove. Allow to cool. Serve lukewarm or cold. Guests will break crust with back of spoon and enjoy the tart and sweet flavors.

The Returning Ones

"Do you believe in ghosts?" I ask Daniel.

"I have never seen one," he replies very seriously. "Never. Ghosts are sort of transparent, and they scare people, I am told. But *revenants*, the returning ones, now that's something else. I know."

Daniel is a *santonnier*, an appealing young man with gentle eyes, a cherubic face, and curly, already receding hair, although he can't be more than thirty-five. He lives and works in our village, where his shop attracts many visitors. He learned his trade—or art (isn't *art* part of *artisan* as well as of *artist?*)—from his father, first, and then apprenticed to the best master in the region, in Joucas.

Santonniers are artisans who make *santons*, the figurines used in the crèche at Christmastime. The word comes from the Provençal dialect and means *little saints*. Daniel produces, as well, some prize-winning crèches to serve as a setting for his myriad characters. For the *santons* come in an infinite variety of sizes and descriptions, which you can see at the *santon* fairs held in November and December in every city of Provence: small ones of painted clay and larger, more sophisticated ones, dressed in real clothes. They include, of course, the basic Holy Family, with Mary, Joseph, and the infant Jesus, complete with Magi, angels, and shepherds with their sheep, an ox and a donkey to stand on either side of the manger. But beyond those, Provence crèches are populated with a host of traditional village characters: the baker in his stocking cap, the miller and his flour sack, the fisherman with net and fishes, the egg woman with her basket, the laundress carrying her pile of folded linen and tiny iron, the cook, the gypsies, the pious ladies. There is also the mayor wearing his sash of office, the priest in his cassock, and always the *ravi*, the village idiot (or more accurately the "ravished one" whose mind is attuned to another world). The *ravi* is clad in outgrown vest and pants, and, endearingly, Daniel gives him his own features. Beyond all the stock characters, he also produces a *santon* we had never seen before: it is the mysterious figure of a young girl in a white dress, with dark hair over her shoulders. Intrigued, we asked him whom she might represent, but he hesitated, looked away, and we felt we shouldn't question him any further for fear of embarrassing him.

All day, in his workshop, Daniel sculpts the small figurines out of wood and clay, then, with painstaking care, constructs their accessories: the miniature scales to weigh the fish, the tiny flour sack, the half-inch loaf of bread, the thumbnail sharpening wheel, the thimble pail, the penny-sized gypsy tambourine. His mother, who is deaf, sits in the back, sewing costumes for the *santons*.

In the village, Daniel has a reputation for being sweet, but kind of remote.

"Fair as an angel as a boy," murmurs Madame Oraison, who has known him all his life. "But then, you see, something happened to him. . . ." She lowers her voice and shakes her head, looking wise, but I suspect that she just doesn't know what it is that did happen. "I heard that, since that time, he can hear the voices of the spirits. Some say he even talks to them sometimes, too."

Tonight, Daniel has walked up to our house to deliver several *santons* we'd asked him to make, some for our own crèche, others to take back home to the States as gifts. It is a cold December evening, with the mistral howling over the battlements of the castle, and when he arrives at the door, he brings with him a gust of icy air, so I ask him in to warm up a bit. We were having a drink of *vin d'orange* by the fire, listening to Wagner's *Die Walküre* on a CD. Daniel is so entranced by the grandiose March of the Valkyries that he remains standing, transfixed, until I insist that he sit down and I put a glass in his hand. He keeps silent, totally absorbed until the end of the recording. Then he lets out a deep sigh: "That was big," he says, obviously at a loss for a better word. "Larger-than-life music. . . ."

I urge: "We are going to eat soon. Please, Daniel, do stay for dinner. We're having a bouillabaisse, there's plenty of food. Meanwhile, let Wayne refill your glass."

Daniel follows proper etiquette by protesting that he couldn't possibly impose on us that way. He must be getting home soon, anyway. Well, no, he has to admit his mother isn't waiting for him; she's away for a few days, visiting an old aunt of hers near Joucas, who's feeling poorly. Still, one doesn't accept an invitation until it has been repeated and almost forced upon you. But Wayne knows the scenario, also likes the shy, gentle Daniel, so he insists with so much sincerity that the *santonnier* surrenders at last, diffidently accepting. He is intrigued, perhaps, by our exotic company, or else tempted by the saffron aroma distilled by the simmering bouillabaisse.

He talks little during dinner. It is only after the dishes are cleared, coffee and marc served, that I can see him relaxing. I have turned off some of the lights, candles on the table and on the mantel are burning low. It would be hard to remain aloof in the small, intimate room where the fire has burned down to embers. Conversation veers to last summer's episode of ghosts in the cemetery, which turned out to be nothing but a flock of small birds nestled among the wreaths on a tombstone.

"I never saw any ghosts myself," says Daniel, frowning. "So, I couldn't tell you whether there is such a thing or not." Then, we talk about a wedding celebrated in the church that afternoon, and how the mistral whipped the bride's gown and veil. Wayne had taken some wonderful photos where she looked as though she were almost taking flight with the wind. I notice then a thin, worn gold band on Daniel's left hand.

"You're not married, Daniel, are you?" I ask.

He remains silent. But I remember Madame Oraison's "Something happened to that boy. . . ." Am I being indiscreet? Daniel turns the band on his finger.

"Married? Not like in the wedding this afternoon," he says at last. "But I am not single, either. It might be difficult for you to understand. . . ."

Both Wayne and I keep quiet. I do feel the young man wants to talk, to tell us something. How can I encourage him?

"You might say I am married, in a way." Then, after a long pause: "You are foreigners, you don't gossip around the village the way people around here do. Soon, you'll be returning to your country that's so far from us. Nobody here knows just what happened, so there are rumors: Some say I asked a girl who wouldn't have me, but that's not true, she wanted to marry me. Others claim she died after we became engaged, but that's wrong, too. And she didn't kill herself, either, when her parents forbade the marriage. On the contrary, they were loving folks who treated me like a son. . . ."

"Would you want to tell us what really *did* happen?" asks Wayne, kindly concerned.

And, finally, as if unburdening himself of a long-kept secret, Daniel tells his story. As often happens with taciturn people, once the floodgates are open, he'll talk well into the night. And we listen in rapt silence, much too spellbound for disbelief.

It happened a few months after his father's death. Daniel had just turned nineteen and was apprenticing to Béraud, the master *santonnier* in Joucas, way on the other side of the Luberon. He boarded a few miles from work, at the home of his great aunt. It was a long walk, morning and night, often in the dark, along deserted paths among abandoned fields in the foothills. But he enjoyed the fresh dawn and sunrise over the mountains. Evenings, especially after being cooped up all day bending over his exacting work, he relished the exercise and the sense of freedom. He never met anybody along those remote dirt roads. Until . . .

Until one evening, in the gathering twilight, he saw a girl sitting all by herself on the low dry-stone wall, half in ruins, bordering fallow fields. Strange, he thought, as no houses were near, only silent woods, deserted land, and mountain slopes in the distance. Isn't she afraid, alone in the dark? Could she be waiting for someone? He wanted to ask her and hesitated to do so. Too shy to speak, he just nodded and went on his way.

"It never occurred to me," confesses Daniel, "to expect to see her there ever again. But there she was the next day, sitting in exactly the same spot. Since I never met anyone near, and could see no lights or sign of life, it didn't look as though she would be waiting for someone. Still, I didn't speak. But to my stupefaction, she was there again on the third day. In my surprise, I finally gathered enough boldness to greet her.

" '*Bonsoir*,' I said. She didn't answer, only turned her head toward me. Even in the dim light of dusk I could see she was beautiful, with a pale face and long hair curling over her shoulders. 'Are you waiting for someone who is late?' She shook her head, no. 'You're not afraid to sit that way, all by yourself here in the dark?' Again, no. 'Do you live nearby?' This time she nodded, yes. So I asked: 'Would you like me to walk you home?' She still didn't answer, but I waited, and after a while she slid down from her perch and silently came beside me. At first, I didn't dare turn my head to look at her as we walked, but I could feel her presence and imagine her light footsteps close to mine. And, as we went together in the enveloping night, I suddenly felt happy, happier than I knew I could ever feel. It was like a glow washing over me. I tried to question her: Why was she sitting there every night in the dark? Was she unhappy at home, perhaps, and trying to steal some moments of solitude? But she never answered. Only, once in a while, she would turn and look at me with her big eyes, so sad I thought my heart would melt.

"Eventually, we came to a point where the road meets a narrow footpath leading to what looked like a distant, secluded house. Now, I could make out a light, dimly glowing in the distance, half-hidden behind some trees. That's when she suddenly broke away, ran without turning around, and disappeared into the darkness.

"That's her home, I thought, and she's afraid her parents will see me and scold her for being out late with a boy. I couldn't fall asleep that night, and thought of nothing but her all the following day.

"Yes, she was at her usual place when I came walking by the next evening, my heart pounding in expectation. She stood as I came near. She even walked up to meet me and silently joined my steps. And the same intense burst of happiness filled my heart and soul with almost unbearable ecstasy. . . . I tried to make some conversation, but she wouldn't talk, only shook her head, no, or nodded, yes. I didn't mind her silence, found it reassuring instead. I wasn't much of a talker then, and never was later either, except for tonight, I guess. So painfully shy, as a matter of fact, that girls always intimidated me with their smart jibes to which I could think of no answer. But a feeling of peaceful intensity radiated from this girl.

"I told her my name and asked for hers. She waited a long time before answering, and when she did, it was in such a breathless voice that I wasn't certain I'd heard it. I repeated: 'Marie?' and she nodded. So I said: 'Then, we are Marie and Daniel.' It felt so right to hear our two names together, like being told a deep truth; like speaking them together put all the world in order, and they would always fit as one, that I repeated, like a prayer: 'Marie and Daniel.' I swear, then, she moved a little closer to me, but when I tried to drop my arm over her shoulders, she quickly drew away. Again that night, when we came to the crossing, she suddenly left my side, ran toward the house, and disappeared behind the trees.

"By then, I was like a man possessed. All day I worked without any idea of what I was really doing, and old Master Béraud would look at me searchingly and cluck his tongue: 'Boy, if I didn't know better, I'd say you were courting. . . .' I ruined several *santons*, trying, unconsciously, to give them Marie's long hair and fine features.

"At night, I would hurry to the place of our rendezvous, and she was always there, faithfully waiting for me. We'd walk together in the dark, my heart overflowing with bliss. I'd begun to talk in earnest, for there were so many things I felt she should know: How my apprenticeship was coming to an end; how, now that my father had died, my mother had suggested I take over his workshop and the house. I'd soon be doing well enough to think of getting settled. . . . I was so absorbed that I barely noticed her silence, but I knew she listened intently. Once, her eyes met mine and she smiled a smile so enchanting that I wanted to die. I didn't try to touch her again, since she seemed afraid of that, and I wanted her, above all, to trust me. As I told you before, bold girls scared me, and I found Marie's reticence both reassuring and comforting. But we walked very close, and sometimes her hair, blowing in a breeze, would brush my face like an angel's wing.

"We met that way for four more days, and each time she'd abruptly break away at the sight of that dimly lit house. By then, I was half-crazed with love, and such partings were harder to take every time.

"Because, during those days and sleepless nights, I'd made up my mind and decided I knew what I wanted to do. I was going to ask her to marry me. If she agreed, then she could speak of me to her parents and bring me to meet them. I would explain we'd been courting and I'd ask for her in marriage, the way a decent man would. Still, I hesitated, for I didn't want to scare her away. But on that night,

with the moon shining so bright it was almost like daylight, I decided I could wait no longer.

"I must tell you that it is the custom in our family, as
in many others around here, to pass wedding rings along
from one generation to the next. So, when my father lay
on his deathbed, and just before they came with the coffin, my mother removed the ring from his finger and gave
it to me to wear on my *right* hand. When I married, my
bride, in church, would take it and slip it over my *left*-hand
finger.

"Bending over work all afternoon, I'd made my plans: I
would ask Marie to be my wife, and if she agreed, I would
slip my father's ring on her finger to wear as a sign of
engagement until I bought her her own wedding band. Not
really the custom, but that's the way I wanted it. Then, I
could feel she was promised to me, my wife already, if not
just now, then in the future.

"She slid from that low wall and came up to me that
night, walking on air, it seemed, her hair gently lifting in the
wind. God, she was beautiful! So, as we went, I told her I
wanted her for my wife. Would she marry me? She raised
her pale face to mine, looked into my eyes, smiled, and
breathed one word: 'Yes,' I swear I heard. Only, she drew
away when I wanted to kiss her. So, I reached for her hand
instead. She let me take it and I raised it to my lips. That
little hand was so cold that its touch startled me. But this
was a winter night, after all; it's just that in my excitement I
had forgotten the frost on the ground and the snow glistening on the mountain slopes. Still holding that hand, I
slipped my gold ring on her finger and softly closed her fist

over it. So cold. . . . That's when I realized she wasn't wearing a coat. Just that flimsy dress. No wonder she was freezing! So, I took off my cape and placed it over her shoulders.

"I imagined myself, next, walking by her side to her father's door and. . . . But we had reached the crossing. Without a word or a backward glance, she broke off and ran away, as she'd done every night before.

"Petrified, I just stood there. What could the matter be? I would *have* to meet her folks, and the sooner, the better. I couldn't see why we should wait and delay speaking to them. Still, I waited a long time, staring at that single, distant lighted window. Would I dare? How would I be received? Were her parents mean and cruel folk? But I finally gathered up my courage: I would do what I had to do as an honorable man, knock on that door, walk in and face them to tell them I wanted their daughter for my wife. If they were angry, and wanted to punish her, I'd be there to protect her. So, I made my way up to the house and, deafened by the pounding of my heart, knocked on the door.

"After a moment, it opened. A man was standing there, her father, I guessed, gray-haired and kind-looking. My throat was tight as I asked him: 'Is your daughter Marie at home? I need to speak to her on a very important matter, and to you and her mother as well.'

"But he didn't answer, started crying instead with tears quietly running down his cheeks. The mother came up from the back of the room and I repeated my question: 'Is your daughter at home? I need to speak to her, because I am in love, and, with your permission, I wish to marry her.' At my words, the mother broke into sobs. I just stood there, nonplussed, until they asked me to sit down. So, we all three sat around the kitchen table.

"I told them how Marie and I had been meeting, walking home every night; how I'd fallen in love with her and asked her to marry me. Only, she'd seemed oddly afraid of me, or perhaps of what her folks would say if they found out she'd been meeting a boy in the dark. I needed to reassure her and them, too, that I was an honest young man, with nothing but the most honorable intentions and a home to offer her. Only, I wanted to see Marie and speak to her in front of her parents right now.

"All along, the mother was sobbing: 'My poor, poor child,' she kept repeating. Finally, the father wiped his eyes and placed his hand on my arm.

" 'Come with me, my boy,' he told me. 'Come with me and I'll take you to her. You'll see where she is.'

"So, together, we walked past the next village, I more puzzled all the time. He took me to a path beyond, that led to the cemetery.

" 'Where are we going?' I asked, but he shook his head and wouldn't answer. Soon, we were at the cemetery gate. He pushed it open. We walked down the main alley, turned once, and came upon a fresh grave, just a mound of earth with a plain wooden cross.

" 'This is where Marie is, my boy,' he whispered. 'She passed away last month, after a sudden fever. No time yet for a proper tombstone.'

"On that mound of freshly dug earth lay my cape in a dark heap, and in the brilliant moonlight, something on top was shining: my ring.

"I didn't even take time to pray for the soul of the woman I loved. That would come later. Because right there, taking her father as my witness, I slipped the band on my left-hand finger, and I haven't taken it off since," finished Daniel, showing his hand with the worn ring. He paused for a moment, then went on:

"You see, the dead have turned that corner, the corner that hides the future from the living, so they can see what lies ahead. That's how Marie knew she was meant to be my wife. So, she came back to try. Oh, how hard she must have tried! Can you imagine that struggle of hers against Death? Could she have hoped that she would win? But of course, death is stronger than anything, stronger than life, since it always prevails, and nobody can do anything against it. So Marie was defeated in the end. Or maybe her time of return was up, and she had only fulfilled as much of her fate as was allowed under those laws we know nothing of.

"You were asking if I am married? I am indeed. It's only that I will have to wait a while until I can be with my wife for good." He added: "Somehow, the story got around, but became completely distorted, and I never really tried before to correct those rumors. It's not something I like to talk about . . . usually."

We remained silent, and I discreetly wiped my eyes. Wayne was pale, and looked as though he, too, had met Marie and walked her home on that winter night. A night as cold as tonight. Daniel sipped his marc to cover his embarrassment at the flow of self-revelation.

"So, you see, a ghost, I have never seen. But a *revenant*, someone who returns from the dead in human form, because of an overwhelming need to? Because there is a destiny that has not been fulfilled? Why, not only have I met one, but I am in love with her."

A recipe from Madame Estaing . . .

Vin d'Orange (Orange Wine Cocktail)

After I had exclaimed several times over her *Vin d'Orange*, Madame Estaing gave me her recipe on a small piece of paper. "Share it with your friends in America," she told me.

Madame E. makes her *Vin d'Orange* with the peel of oranges consumed by her family. It is so delicious that you might want to keep a couple of bottles on hand.

8 oranges, for the peel (or 4 ounces of dried peel)
4 whole cloves
I piece cinnamon bark (or a piece from a cinnamon
   stick)
I bottle good, dry white wine
½ cup sugar
I shot glass (I ounce) brandy

Peel oranges very thinly, with as little as possible of the white part under the zest. Dry peel overnight in a low oven, with only the pilot light on, or on the lowest setting of an electric stove. Or, as they do in Provence, spread it out in the sun.

Place the dried peel in a pitcher or jug. Add cloves and cinnamon. Pour in the wine. Cover and store in lowest part of refrigerator for at least eight days but longer won't hurt.

Strain the wine. Pour 1 cup in a small saucepan. Warm it without boiling, mix in sugar, and stir until dissolved. Return to wine. Add brandy and stir.

Bottle your orange wine and cork it well. You can use it at once, but it will keep for months. Serve it very cold, with a curl of orange peel.

(Why not decorate your bottle with an intriguing, self-designed label?)

Paul and Vincent,
Brigitte and Caroline

aul Cézanne paintings shall not be acquired, accepted by, or shown in this museum as long as I live," swore the painter-sculptor Henri Pontier, contemporary of Cézanne's, curator of the Aix-en-Provence Musée Granet. Since Pontier survived Cézanne by twenty years, this oath explains why Aix, today, cannot show any of its most celebrated son's works.

Wayne and I resided, quite by chance, for the time of our Aix assignment, in Pontier's former home, the rented *Villa du Rocher du Dragon*. Dragon Rock Villa? Well, there *was*, in the vast back garden, a fountain surrounded by rocks on which sat a primitive sculpture of something that might resemble a dragon. "When I was young," an aged gardener told us, "processions would stop here on feast days, for the faithful to drink from the fountain." Not as surprising as it seems, for we knew that the dragon, in various forms, is recurrent in Provençal mythology.

"But what business could dragons have in Provence?" wondered Wayne. "Were they or their legends brought back from China by ancient travelers?" he asked Bill Hope, who is better informed of local lore than many natives.

"No," said Bill. "The dragons here seem to have been more like water monsters. They're thought to have originally been crocodiles brought from the Nile, used in the Roman arenas for fights to the death against other wild beasts. Some may have escaped their tanks, made their way to the nearby Rhône, and lived there in caves hollowed out of the banks. When the river flooded each year, they'd crawl ashore and snatch the occasional sheep, dog, or human. Popular imagination did the rest. In Tarascon, a scaly monster they named the *tarasque* would periodically appear to devour hapless Tarasconnais and spread terror among the good folks. That is, until Christianity took over. Then, Saint Martha, who happened to be preaching in the area, tamed the beast with a sign of the cross or some such thing and led it away, docile as a lamb, using her sash as a leash. Don't look to me to guarantee the historicity of the event, but I can tell you they still celebrate it every year in Tarascon, dragging a wooden, realistically articulated *tarasque* through the streets. Even the city of Nîmes shows something resembling a crocodile on its coat of arms. . . ."

So much for the dragon part. There only remained to understand the source of Pontier's bad blood. Living in his former home, we'd come to feel somehow personally involved.

Long closed off, later rented with its original furnishings, the villa had changed little in the decades since the artist's death. The present owner, an elderly recluse, cared little about the property. In the studio we found sketchbooks, fragments of sculptures, and a few plaster casts of *Boy Fishing*—adorned by a former tenant with a dangling red plastic fish—and *Young Woman Dreaming*, all competently executed but terribly academic.

Inevitably, we would hear stories of the notorious break between the two former friends. It seems that in fine weather Paul and Henri, accompanied by a few other artists, would pile into the Pontier horse buggy and ride into the countryside, seeking *le motif*, the subject that would fire their imagination.

These were congenial outings, complete with well-provisioned picnic baskets. However, the story goes, Cézanne at some point began to draw apart from the group, refusing to show them his work and remaining aloof, while his friends, glass of wine in hand, would vehemently admire or critique one another's work. As could be expected, suspicion arose, and when the others managed to steal a glance at Cézanne's canvas, they reeled in shock, enraged by his style—viewed today as prefigurative of abstraction—which they perceived as iconoclastic, an insult to reality and the Beauties of Nature. They pronounced him a "traitor to Art." A quarrel followed, and this is what led to the famous oath.

By the time Pontier passed away, Cézanne's fame had reached such heights that none of his works was available, or even accessible to the museum's budget, with the exception of a few donated drawings. This is basically why Aix-en-Provence, the city where Cézanne was born, lived most of his life, and died, from which he drew most of his inspiration, does not own a single Cézanne today.

Perhaps as a consequence of Pontier's ire, Aix, too, for most of a century, studiously ignored Cézanne. Our old gardener told us how his father, employed at the Jas-de-Bouffan, the Cézanne family farm, had once pulled, attracted by its size, a large canvas out of a trash bin. After shrugging in contempt at the somber, stiff figures painted there, he'd used it to patch a hole in his chicken coop. By the time Cézanne's fame reached his ears, he remembered the canvas that held his poultry in bounds and thought it might be valuable. But years had passed, the coop had been destroyed, and the preliminary version of *The Card Players* lost forever.

When, over a decade ago, I wanted to visit Cézanne's atelier I had trouble finding the nondescript building, and finally stepped into a marginally kept room where a scattering of dusty objects on a shelf morosely recalled those in Cézanne's still lifes. It was obvious that few people then bothered to seek out memories of the artist's life in his hometown.

The boom in tourism changed all that. Sights must be provided for tourists; they want shrines to visit. Today, those who wish to walk in Cézanne's footsteps can do just that: Bronze tenons, shaped like a C, are embedded in concrete. Polished bright by thousands of feet, they now stud the Aix sidewalks, leading the way to the well-signaled atelier.

The atelier has been refurbished, and well-meaning souls have arranged objects, just as the master did, to stand by the side of reproductions: bowls of apples, the peppermint bottle, carafes, the coffee pot, the famous plaster cherub, even skulls, as in *Three Skulls*, the inspiration of all the familiar still lifes. That and the few drawings in the museum are all that's left there of Cézanne's life, of his enormous output. In contrast, the city fathers have chosen to represent his period with two pompous statues made by the long-forgotten sculptor Truphème, which flank the entrance to the Cours Mirabeau. One represents Art and Industry, the other Letters and Science.

It is, however, in the Aix countryside that Cézanne lives on. The best tribute is perhaps a recently installed sign a few miles east of Aix, on the Autoroute de l'Estérel (French freeways have *names*, as well as numbers) that follows an inland route along the Mediterranean. There, an arrow points to "Cézanne's Landscapes." Yes, they do belong to Cézanne, these kaleidoscopic images that unfold from speeding cars: Since he taught us how to look at that group of farmhouses, that quarry, that huddled village, or those groves of pine and olive, these have taken on an existence they did not possess before. And what's to say of the Montagne Sainte-Victoire, the mountain he painted in so many lights on canvases that hang today in the world's greatest museums? Mount Saint-Victoire—not really named after a saint, but in commemoration of a great victory that Marius, the Roman general, won at its foot more than a century before Christ—is a strange geological formation. At some prehistoric time a long range abruptly broke off, revealing the chalky white of its limestone interior. The break formed a gigantic triangle that stands as a backdrop to the city of Aix. Perspective turns it into the face of a pyramid, and its ghostly pallor takes on a transparency in certain lights. Now, one cannot gaze upon the Sainte-Victoire without superimposing Cézanne's ethereal sunlight or brooding indigo on a stormy night. Cézanne opened our eyes to the Provence of Aix.

Vincent van Gogh wasn't, of course, a native of Arles, and he barely spent two years in Provence. But what years! The clear, mistral-whipped light of the Rhône Valley drove him to a frenzy in which he feverishly attempted to capture it, all of it; imprison it in the bold strokes of his brush. At the time, Arles saw him only as a disreputable figure, haunted and suspicious, existing in poverty in a sparsely furnished room. Few agreed to pose for him, and he resorted to self-portraits, executed, I like to imagine, from his reflection in the little shaving mirror hanging on the wall in the painting he did of that room.

The city never did acquire any of van Gogh's works, either. I remember, some years ago, trying to hunt down memories of Vincent in Arles, as I had of Paul in Aix. I was directed to the *Museon Arlaten*, and there, among dusty folk exhibits, finally discovered a few reproductions pinned to the wall. These pages, torn from *Life* magazine, spelled the city's only tribute! No, not the *only* one: In the public garden, at the foot of the Roman theater, stood a stela with a relief bust of van Gogh, the work and gift of an *American* artist. It was placed in the garden because at the time of its donation the museum authorities rejected that homage as unworthy of their institution. Their scorn worked out for the better, since that way the stela with its tormented profile stands in full view of every passerby.

But again, owing to tourism's hunger for places of worship, things are picking up, and Arles, at last, has awakened to her adopted son's fame. A permanent exhibition titled *Hommage à Van Gogh* offers as a tribute to the artist a number of paintings by some of today's best painters, tastefully gathered by Madame Yolande Clergue, wife of Arles's—and probably France's—premier photographer. A recent show there attracted international attention by linking Japanese prints, such as those by Hiroshige, with the paintings by Vincent that they had inspired.

In Espace van Gogh a little cloister garden has been lovingly restored to what it was when Vincent painted it in watercolors. Alas, the yellow house where he rented the famous room, damaged by bombings during World War II, has since been demolished. However, the café of the terrace view and of *Night Café* still stands on the Place du Forum. It has recently been restored, the ocher yellow of its facade a replica of van Gogh's time. It serves good, brasserie-type food, and tourists crowd its terrace.

Lucien Clergue, a protégé and close friend of Picasso's for the last twenty years of the artist's life, reminds me that Picasso donated a series of his drawings done in Arles to the local museum. These show images of van Gogh, as Picasso pictured him, either in the company of Gauguin or of Rachel, the young prostitute from the brothel at Number 1, Quay of the Rhône, whom he both liked and pitied.

"Picasso revered van Gogh," says Lucien. "As a matter of fact, he kept for years, on his bedside table, a reproduction of an old newspaper clipping." I reproduce here the text, as quoted in Clergue's book *Picasso, Mon Ami*:

> *Local News.* Last Sunday, at 11:30 P.M. a certain Vincent van Gogh, painter, and a native of Holland, showed up at the brothel at Number 1. There he asked for an inmate named Rachel, and handed her . . . his ear! Advised of the facts, which could only be the action of some pitifully insane person, the police went next morning to the man's residence. They found him in bed, barely showing signs of life.
>
> The unfortunate was admitted to the hospital on an emergency basis.
>
> (from *Le Forum Républicain*)

The article goes on to report the theft of fish from a vendor's cart.

"Most telling," Lucien adds, "is the remark Picasso made to a friend as the two were arriving at some artistic event in a chauffeur-driven Cadillac. "Can you imagine Vincent pulling up, too? *He'd* have to be in a *Mercedes!*"

Lucien, who was born in Arles and has resided there all his life, is a treasure-trove of van Gogh lore. A great-uncle of his ran a blacksmith forge right next door to the yellow house. Did he do some work, or a favor, that Vincent repaid with a painting? A portrait of the man's wife, perhaps? In any case, when the forge was demolished, a rolled-up canvas was discovered, resting on a crossbeam, much the worse for the years it had spent there exposed to dirt and smoke. It showed a woman wearing the distinctive Arles costume and headdress commonly worn at the turn of the century. Repeated requests for identification, presented to the Van Gogh Museum in Amsterdam, have always remained unanswered. Lucien's relatives, however, hang on to the portrait, intimately convinced they're the owners of an original van Gogh.

Sometimes, visitors to the Clergues' home are informed: "You are stepping on the very floor that van Gogh trod barefoot." Indeed, when the Clergues were restoring their seventeenth-century home, they heard that the Arles public baths were being demolished. The centuries-old pavers were about to be carted off to some dump. But Madame Clergue, who knows a value when she sees one, commandeered a few wheelbarrows and, with the help of friends, transported load after load of the beautiful, thick terracotta tiles. These today pave the floor of their reception rooms, glowing with the low patina of age.

"Vincent was a regular at the baths," explains Lucien, "and he certainly had to take off his shoes like everyone else. I know. I used to go there myself as a child, because we were too poor to own a bath." And then he tells of worshipful visitors who have slipped off their *own* footwear, in the hope of communing better with whatever inspiration might still linger on the tiles trod by a barefoot Vincent.

But, while the Clergues do their share, it is Nature itself that has best kept alive his spirit, faithful to the renewed eternity that Art imbues it with. Van Gogh's sunflowers bloom today in a profusion he never knew, a new cash crop whose faces crowd in countless fields. His tormented cypresses still shade farmhouses or line up as windbreaks between orchards. Haystacks still cast squat shadows under noonday sun, and drawbridges still raise spindly arms over the canals of Camargue to allow the passage of barges. We must thank Vincent, as we thanked Paul, for opening our eyes to their reality.

While it took Aix and Arles a century to recognize genius, both Saint-Tropez and Saint-Rémy capitalized instantly on the fame of *their* popular-culture icons.

Saint-Tropez, formerly a modest fishing harbor on the western edge of the Riviera, owes its present-day glory to Brigitte Bardot, who, at the height of her career, bought a seaside home there. It took no time at all for her presence to bring extravagant prosperity to the village, until then distinguished mostly by its isolation. The aging Brigitte still lives there, long retired and in near seclusion, only occasionally brought to the public's attention by her remarkable devotion to animal causes. And just as writhing cypresses, irises, and sunflowers shall forever illustrate van Gogh's name, it became difficult, in past decades, to think of Saint-Tropez without superimposing the image of a young Brigitte, clad in innocent gingham, a kerchief on her blond hair, dipping her toes in the water of her private mooring. But as expensive sleaze claimed Saint-Tropez, it fell victim to its own legend. A new *in* place had to be discovered.

And so it is, now, that Saint-Rémy is becoming the new

international rendezvous, simply, in large part, because Princess Caroline of Monaco bought a house there.

Saint-Rémy is, and has always been, an ordinary little town in the flatlands on the way to the rocky eyrie of Les Baux and Arles, the Roman city. Pretty roads shaded with arching *platanes* lead to Saint-Rémy, but the town itself attracted little interest until Princess Caroline moved in.

To be sure, the town possesses points of interest. A fountain reminds us that Nostradamus was born there in 1503. But in all fairness, stronger memories of the seer are found in Salon, where he lived most of his life. Just outside the city stands a well-preserved group of Roman monuments known as Les Antiques: a municipal arch, such as the Romans erected at the entrance to their cities, and next to it a cenotaph honoring the grandsons of Augustus Caesar.

Directly across the street, excavations have brought to light the long-buried ruins of an entire Gallo-Roman city, Glanum. And close to that, one comes upon the gates of Saint-Paul-de-Mausole, the asylum where Vincent found some semblance of serenity and spent such a fruitful year. The still-working hospital remained long closed to the public. This mattered little to most travelers, rushing on their way to the three-star restaurant in Les Baux, or the bullfights in Arles.

Then, Caroline of Monaco chose quiet little Saint-Rémy as her home away from home, the country retreat where she could escape the demands of palace life, and recover, hopefully in anonymity, from the tragic death of her young husband. And everything changed overnight.

Anonymity lasted until the media discovered her there and ecstatically published page after page of Caroline shopping at the market, sitting at a café terrace, or bicycling along the little path that led to the farmhouse restored for her. Her image, standing in line to enroll her children at the local public school, became an icon. And how democratic to register the kids simply as Andrea, Pierre, and Charlotte Casiraghi! An elegant way to disguise their princely identity. Conceal to reveal, *n'est-ce pas?* Caroline strolled hand in hand with a handsome actor, looking very plain indeed, high fashion left behind, and the press rejoiced that she seemed to be learning to smile again. If Saint-Rémy brought back happiness to the heart of a bereaved princess, imagine what it could do for lesser mortals. So it braced for the assault.

Real-estate prices soared. Since the town itself holds little architectural distinction, the place to buy was a *mas*, a farmhouse just like Caroline's. Abandoned farmhouses abound in the area, since mechanized agriculture rendered many of them obsolete. Restore the house, replace the chicken yard with a pool, plant a windbreak of cypresses, let the sun and the wind do the rest, and *voilà!* Instant Provence. Expensive, but well worth it when you realize who your neighbors might be. Luberon snobs claim that their overflow now pours into Saint-Rémy.

The words "open-air market" have taken on a new dimension, too, in Saint-Rémy. What was once a modest Wednesday market now spreads into every street in a profusion of typical Provençal wares. Bright, flouncy skirts with the matching espadrilles, in the distinctive prints made famous in the States by the Pierre Deux shops, dance in the sun, flying from overhead racks. Baskets of dried lavender stalks, olive-wood carvings and utensils, displays of assorted honeys, homemade jams, mountain ham and salami crowd one another, manned by vendors in blue smocks and red kerchiefs, so many that one begins to suspect tourist-office sponsorship. Too typical to be true, as the saying goes. The size of the crowds as well as the shoppers' country elegance and luxury cars testify to the town's newly found success and affluence.

Would it be a coincidence? The asylum that had housed van Gogh opened its doors to the public. Still in full operation as a treatment center for the emotionally disturbed, it was built, over time, to engulf the twelfth-century monastery dedicated to Saint Paul of Mausole. Visitors can pace the garden, enter the cloister, climb the winding stairs to the small room, a former monk's cell, that Vincent occupied, furnished with a narrow iron bedstead. Through the window, they'll recognize some of his best-known landscapes. One feels there as if the stark, ancient rooms have retained some of his presence, or is this evoked rather by the torrents of light pouring over the countryside?

Downstairs, under the ribbed vault of a former chapel, a gift shop offers the usual array of reproductions and postcards. There, too, an arresting exhibition will hold you: Today's inmates are still urged to paint during their occupational therapy classes. Inspired perhaps by Vincent's hovering spirit, some of them produce remarkable works.

These are displayed and available for purchase, at very affordable prices, to benefit the inmates' activities club. Each comes with a certificate of authenticity that states where, and under what circumstances, the canvas (or paper or butcher paper) painting was produced. Many—and Wayne and I are happy to number among those—feel that with such an acquisition they have come as close as possible to owning an original van Gogh.

Was it all because of Caroline? Married again, and to a bona fide prince this time, she may well abandon Saint-Rémy, but the glow will linger. A matter of changing values, to be sure, but it is ironic that Aix and Arles took almost a century before they began to pay attention to their artistic giants, while Saint-Tropez and Saint-Rémy recognized instantly the potential of a star and a princess in their midst. There is probably a moral to be discovered there, outside the fact that breathing the same—or almost the same—air as Caroline is worth any price.

The Provençal sandwich . . .

Pan Bagnat

The name means, in Provençal, *soaked bread.* The soaking is done with vinaigrette, and the filling is a close relative of Salade Niçoise. If the round, crusty *pan bagnat* rolls are not available (hamburger buns won't do; too soft), use baguettes. Count three servings per baguette on the average.

Serves 6

4 tomatoes
1 onion, thinly sliced, divided into rings
2 baguettes
Butter to spread on the bread
2 heads of Boston lettuce
2 6-ounce cans tuna, drained
2 cucumbers
13 pitted black olives, cut in pieces
2 cans flat fillets of anchovies (optional)
Vinaigrette
4 hardboiled eggs

Press tomatoes to expel extra liquid, slice. Peel cucumbers, remove seeds, and slice. Split and open baguettes; remove and reserve some of the white center part.

Spread butter thinly and evenly on both faces of the bread and line with lettuce leaves (this will prevent the vinaigrette from soaking through). On top of the lettuce, arrange flaked tuna, cucumber and tomato slices, and onion rings. Scatter pieces of olive and anchovies (if desired) on top. Soak the reserved white part of the bread in vinaigrette and spread all along the sandwich.

Wrap in plastic and refrigerate until time to eat. It will be easier to cut when cold.

For a picnic

   Pan Bagnat

   Fruit salad, or peeled and cubed cantaloupe in individual plastic bags

   Individually wrapped cheese and crackers

   Cupcakes or cookies or slices of chocolate cake

The Chicken Rustlers

A hot, drowsy Sunday afternoon. With Wayne gone off somewhere, I was lazily deciding to spend the next few hours on the pool terrace, taking in the sun, with maybe a dip now and then to cool off. I only needed to gather up the energy to slip out of my T-shirt and into something more conducive to a seamless tan. That's when the phone rang.

"Hullo, hullo," cried a British-accented voice I didn't recognize at first. "Yes, it's me, Reggie, remember? Wayne's mate? How's the bloke?" It took a moment, while I made polite noises of pleased surprise, to recognize in "Wayne's mate" a photographer acquaintance of several years ago in England. "Yes, we're in the area, and we figured, what the bloody hell! What's a couple hundred miles among friends? I knew Wayne would be put out if he found out we were in Lyon and didn't bother to look him up!" I weakly agreed that, as a matter of fact, Wayne might have been disappointed, except that tonight we were going to. . . . But Reggie wasn't listening.

"So, here we are, in our station wagon, about four hours away, I figure, and on our way to see you. I wanted to just pop in as a surprise, but my wife said no, no, give them a chance to prepare. . . . And we do know what you ladies mean when you say you want to be ready for company!"

You cannot kill through thoughts, and no doll to prick with pins happened to be handy. "So, we figure on getting there about seven or so, and we don't have any plans until the next day, when we *probably* should be pushing back to old Paree. . . ." I see. He doesn't just mean dinner, but overnight, too, with breakfast, and probably lunch thrown in for the two of them.

"And, say, you're in luck," continued Reggie. "Daphne's sister and her brother-in-law are here, too; you'll be mad about Harry, a real lady-killer." Wow, I thought, I can't wait. Hope I look like seduction material to old Harry. "And of course they brought Tony, their son; he's in university now you know, and he took his girl along, a real posh type she is. Hope your village doesn't look dirty to her, like some places we've been to; otherwise, that's it, won't touch a thing. Real particular, I'd say. By the way, don't bother to put out a spread, anything will do, you know us, simple tastes and all. Just hungry as bears, ha, ha! We'll see you later and cheerio!"

My anger subsided only with the anguished realization that on a Sunday afternoon all shops are closed. Provisions in the house were at an all-time low, because we'd planned to be away for a few days. How could I hope to feed that horde? For lack of something better to do, I opened the kitchen door and looked outside. My neighbor from just down below, Madame Janot, happened to be passing by. We exchanged greetings.

Madame Janot's house stands out in this newly restored area of the upper village. An old farmhouse, it has remained as it always was, unkempt, friendly, sitting in a garden that's been used for decades as a family dump. Unusable tools, rolls of chicken wire, torn sheets of plastic that should have been discarded long ago are piled there haphazardly, together with makeshift rabbit hutches and chicken coops covered in corrugated iron. In between grow vigorous herbs, clumps of luxuriant flowers—sown or planted at random—and the most fragrant white lilac bush ever. The roosters who bring up the sun every morning crow in Madame Janot's yard, and her chickens' plumage gleams in the sun as they peck and scratch away among the refuse.

Seeking sympathy, since nothing else was available, I confided my plight to Madame Janot.

"Six people for dinner, *à l'improviste*, unexpectedly, and not a thing to serve them," I moaned. Madame Janot clucked sympathetically and shared *her* horror stories with me: Her little grandchildren from Marseille never liked the food she served them. They only wanted *hambourgères*, and what is one to do? Then, she waddled on down to her house, like a plump pillow tied in the middle.

Shortly, a great commotion was heard in her yard: squawking, flapping of wings, Madame shouting out threats, followed by silence.

A moment later, came a knock at my door. There stood a smiling, red-faced, heaving-bosomed Madame Janot, holding in each hand an upside-down chicken, wings extended, beaks open, frightened round eyes.

"Here," she told me. "Take those. It will be plenty for your dinner. They're good-size young hens, and they'll taste good roasted." Seeing my hesitation: "Grab them by the feet. Yes, this way. You'll just cut off their heads to kill them, and they'll pluck easier afterward if you only dip them in boiling water." I tried to stammer something, but Madame brushed away my words. "Well, now, you have nothing to worry about. Your guests will be well fed." And she departed, roly-poly, cheerful, back to her messy yard, while I stood, clumsily holding out the two weakly flapping hens at arm's length.

My immediate problem had now shifted, since my premier concern had become: What do I do with these poor chickens?

I decided that it would be best to put them out in the garage for the time being. Later, Wayne would be home, and he'd surely think of some way out of our predicament. So, I carefully cracked the garage door open and slid in the two hens, who went to perch on the pile of firewood, clucking indignantly. I brought them water and a bowl of bread crumbled in red wine, to help them recover from their ordeal.

After that, frantically ransacked pantry shelves yielded

several odd packs of pasta (a medley!), cans of tomatoes, mushrooms, peas, even one of marinated artichokes. I'll call the dish *pasta provençale*, and I don't care if my reputation as a cook suffers. Two cans of tuna, a pack of green beans left over from Christmas, dug out from ice crystals at the bottom of the freezer chest, five potatoes, an onion, six eggs, all of the aperitif olives from the jar, plus a few tomatoes, and *voilà!* Salade Niçoise! Dare I throw in a raw eggplant? Enough was left in half a dozen assorted containers of ice cream and sorbet to pile in a glass bowl and declare a *giant parfait.* Wayne, who arrived thereupon, figured that if he served enough wine, the guests wouldn't be too particular about the food. He slipped into the garage to check on the hens and reported they'd eaten up all the bread and wine, and fallen asleep, head tucked under a wing.

"I know what we can do with them," assured Wayne. "We'll take care of it after our guests have retired."

Just time to prepare the guestrooms, to make up the pullout couch in the study—housing six extra people in a vacation home *does* tax your facilities—to set the table and assemble the feast, while Wayne brought up armloads of bottles from the cellar. And here they were, noisy, unloading so many bags, I feared for a moment that they were planning to stay forever, as the posh young lady asked to shampoo right away. (No, I didn't have *mint* herbal rinse, but I'd run upstairs to see what I *did* have.) She hadn't been able to wash her hair yet today and felt "yucky." All running up and down, screaming in derision at our small pool, while killer Harry cornered me to call me a "dynamite bird."

We survived the evening, and thanks to Wayne refilling glasses nonstop, bottle after bottle, they all fell asleep, practically in their plates, except for the posh young lady. She'd drunk nothing, eaten even less, but, feeling better, I guess, with clean hair, wanted to know what the village offered by way of nightlife. I was going to suggest the *Bar des Sports* as the heart of the action, but Wayne, quicker than I, warned her of rumors of a sexual degenerate roaming the darkened village streets; he also threw in, carried away by the moment, the gratuitous information that French gendarmes tend to laugh off claims of molestation. Indignant, she stalked upstairs and slammed her bedroom door.

We waited, breathless, for a long moment. But all was quiet in the house. Now!

The two hens were still sleeping off their wine, too, in the dark garage, each with one leg and her head tucked among feathers. They drowsily let me pick them up, and they felt so soft and warm that I really wished we could keep them as pets. But reason must prevail. We slipped them into my Neiman Marcus white tote and climbed in the car, left by Wayne on the Place du Château. We let the car roll down silently, and only turned on the engine *after* we'd reached a safe distance, out of earshot of both our guests and Madame Janot.

Wayne had shared his plans with me earlier: We'd find an isolated farmhouse, tiptoe with our chickens as close as we could, and release them in, or at least near, the chicken coop. This way, they couldn't fail to mix with the local poultry, perhaps, we hoped, form enduring friendships, and live happily among members of their own species. The farmer would be gaining two prime young hens for his flock, nothing to complain about. Only, it all had to be done stealthily, because, should we barge in, in broad daylight, asking him to take in those chickens, there'd be questions no end, and Madame would be certain to hear of our ingratitude and disloyalty. We couldn't risk hurting the dear lady's feelings, after she'd shown herself so neighborly and generous.

It took some searching to find just the right farm. It must be close to the road, but not too close, otherwise we risked being seen by any passing car; not too far either, so we wouldn't have to stumble endlessly along an unknown path. Finally, we spotted what looked like the appropriate target: maybe three hundred feet away from the road, a large farmhouse, where barns and service buildings stood well apart from the house. We watched for a little while, casing the place: everything dark, not a single light, and not a sound. In the faint glow of a half moon, we could make out the low roofs of what would be tool and storage sheds, an open garage for tractors, and, standing alone, separated from the rest, a smaller and lower building: the chicken coop, no doubt.

Now, if we could only approach silently, not raising any alarm, we would release our two candidates right inside the entrance, where they could quietly join the residents. We opened the car door, stepped out . . . gravel crunched under our steps and my heart pounded in my ears. The chickens made no sound, thank God, as we proceeded slowly, cautiously, in the direction of the coop. When we reached throwing distance, Wayne picked up a pebble and cast it in the direction of the darker opening. If we heard chicken noises, we'd know we had the right place. Bingo! A few muffled squawks told us we'd guessed right, and Wayne gave me a thumbs-up sign. So, we took the chickens out of the tote, put them on the ground, and tried to push them gently in the right direction. Puzzled, disoriented, they stubbornly stood their ground. So, we each picked one up and tiptoed to the doorless entrance, dropping the hens just inside.

And then all hell broke loose.

Every blasted chicken in the place started to squawk, an ungodly cacophony. A rooster crowed, imitated by several others. Two dogs (who'd been asleep, *bien sûr*, until the racket began) made up for their dereliction of duty by furiously barking and growling, straining at their chains. One light went on upstairs, then another flooded the yard, as we ran blindly to our car. While the damn machine wouldn't start right away, we could see the farmer open his door, and reflections picked off the barrel of his rifle. He shouted something about chicken thieves, and calling in the gendarmes, but then the engine caught, and we finally took off, throwing gravel under the tires.

For fear of being identified somehow, we didn't dare drive straight home, so we circled around, drove through a couple of sleeping villages, and finally returned from the opposite direction. I was vastly relieved to find no gendarmes waiting for us, only the posh young lady who couldn't sleep and complained that TV programs shut off at midnight. When she accused us of having gone out "to have fun" without her, I invented an emergency call from a sick friend, all the while furious at myself for allowing her to even question me.

We slept little, and the roosters crowing in Madame Janot's yard didn't need to remind us of the night's adventures. I was up when the bakery reopened at seven, and ran down for a solid supply of baguettes and croissants.

Several people stood already there ahead of me. While I waited to be served, a lady came in who told how, during the night, thieves had broken into the yard of the Lamour farm and stolen every one of the chickens.

"I saw the gendarmes driving there earlier, and I bet they're studying the tire marks right this moment," she declared. I shuddered.

An elderly gentleman interrupted. He'd heard the story differently. The chickens weren't stolen, they'd all been killed instead, and left lying in pools of their blood. Oh, no, not a fox. A *car* was involved, and foxes don't drive cars. Just some crazed people, like there are so many nowadays. "Wonder who'll be next, and we'd all better watch out."

And, finally, another lady walked in, greeted by the others as Madame Lamour.

"No," asserted Madame Lamour. "No, they didn't steal *all* the chickens, thank God, just a good number of them. We don't know yet what else they took, my husband is still checking that out. They were armed, you know, you could see their guns shining when my husband turned on lights. He heard them shoot, at our dogs, no doubt, but they missed. How many of them were there? Oh, four or five, at least. I am afraid the gendarmes don't have a clue, but they figure it's a bunch of rowdies from Marseille. These hoodlums drive in, do their crimes, and it's back to the city, where they couldn't be found again. We'll leave the yard lights on all night, from now on."

I tried not to cower when everyone agreed that these were times like no other before, and one would be well advised to sleep with a gun handy. Instead, all the time, with death in my soul—*la mort dans l'âme*, as the French would put it—I nodded and clucked sympathetically.

"You'd think this is *America*," growled the baker, who'd stepped in, bringing in his oven's fiery breath. "Locking your front door isn't enough these days. I bet there's going to be a run on padlocks for the coops. But those guys don't care. Since there's nothing and nobody to stop them, they'll blow them off."

By the time I left with my supplies, discussion of violence had escalated into rabbits stolen from hutches and sheets missing from clotheslines.

Back at the house, our guests were up, ready for breakfast, and Harry called me Morning Glory. Skim milk? Sweetener? Sugarless jam? Fat-free butter? The young lady also asked for mango tea, but settled for ice water instead. Still, three baguettes and two dozen croissants disappeared, with all the butter and jam in the house, too.

Then, I crept up to my room, closed the door, and,

whispering into the phone, called my friend Liz: She was to call back, ask for Wayne, and inform him that he was expected in Marseille for a business conference with publishers at eleven-thirty. She quickly made the call. We let the phone ring long enough for everyone to hear and noisily exclaimed about the nerve of those publishers. What an inconvenience, just as we were hoping to spend the day with our friends! But business is business, so we must say good-bye to our guests in the next fifteen minutes. Too bad we couldn't ask them to stay for lunch, or even longer, but you know how it is, that's life, disappointments and all.

After the last bag had been brought down and the station wagon maneuvered down the Grande Rue, Wayne and I fell, exhausted, on either side of the ravaged table, too spent even to want to laugh.

Later in the day, Madame Janot knocked on the door, full of expectation, wanting to know how the dinner went. By now, a few more lies hardly bothered me at all, so I invented a feast with crackling-skinned roasted chicken drawing the delight and admiration of our famished guests.

"They'd never *seen*, much less *tasted* such plump and tender ones, and they ate every last bite. It was the most delicious chicken we've ever had, and I can't thank you enough."

Madame beamed. "Next time," she said conspiratorially, "you just let me know. I'll bring you a couple of rabbits, and you'll be in for a treat."

The chicken rustling story died hard. It was mentioned in the village newsletter, published monthly by city hall. The mayor was aghast to relate that a band of "desperate bandits" had invaded Monsieur Lamour's property, stolen *hundreds* of his chickens, plus some valuable farm implements, and that only Monsieur Lamour's heroic action drove them away. The culprits were hereby warned that next time, they could expect to be shot on sight. No protection in numbers.

Wayne and I didn't tremble, since we were not about to repeat our daredevil deed. Over the course of the next few days, we wondered how our two hens had adjusted to their new surroundings and hoped they'd developed a satisfactory social life. Wayne, especially, was concerned, until one day, driving by the Lamour farm, he swears he recognized them in the company of some new friends, happily scratching in the dirt by the roadside.

This one is the real . . .

Salade Niçoise

Pale versions of this wonderful salad are served everywhere. But a true Niçoise must include potatoes and green beans, as well as tuna, tomatoes, and olives.

You can prepare it several hours ahead of time and keep

it refrigerated, covered with plastic film. Add final dressing at serving time.

Serves 6 to 8

5 or 6 medium potatoes, firm (Yukon Gold, for instance)
2 cups vinaigrette dressing
Salt and pepper
I pound fresh or frozen green beans, preferably whole
3 cloves garlic, minced
I 6-ounce can tuna, drained
2 large tomatoes, peeled or unpeeled, sliced
I medium sweet onion, thinly sliced and divided into rings
20 pitted black olives
6 to 8 hardboiled eggs

Peel, then boil potatoes in salted water until tender. Slice them into a bowl. Mix in ½ cup vinaigrette, which they'll absorb. Salt and pepper to taste.

Cook green beans in salted water until just tender. Drain. In a bowl, mix with ½ cup vinaigrette and minced garlic. On a large serving platter, spread potatoes. Place tuna, flaked, at center. Arrange green beans in circle around edge of dish. Form rings of alternating tomato slices and onion rings around the tuna. Arrange olives around tomato and onion. Decorate with hardboiled eggs (for an extra touch, mix yolks with *tapenade*, p. 34). Sprinkle a little salt and pepper over all. Pass a bowl with the rest of the vinaigrette dressing.

As an alternative to canned tuna, use a grilled, sliced tuna steak.

Wine: An unpretentious white would be good, a Côtes-du-Rhône or a sauvignon blanc. But a rosé would be very interesting, too.

A Flame for a Spirit

erry Christmas, my dear," smiled the duchess when I opened the door. She offered the armload of holly and mistletoe she had brought us. "I cut the holly myself from a bush in the park. As for the mistletoe," she shook her head, "it is a parasite that grows on untended trees and, heaven knows, we have enough of those! It's ours for the climbing, so Carlos set up his ladder and knocked down whole clumps."

She had driven herself from Paris the day before, in great form, flushed with her new-found media fame.

We took a long walk in the woods; found some spectacular red mushrooms all speckled with white, half-hidden under dry oak leaves; gathered evergreen branches, lichens, and moss to decorate the crèche. She spoke of plans taking shape for a second book, focusing on the history of the château and the village rather than the family, this time.

I had no idea this was the last time I would see her.

After I returned to California, we exchanged a few notes, and she sent me clippings of her television appearances. In June, as I was on the phone, checking up on our village house with the housekeeper, the girl mentioned the duchess hadn't been well. I called the château immediately. The crystal in the duchess's voice was intact.

"It's probably nothing, nothing at all, only my children wanted to be certain that I am all right. So, they insisted I spend a week in the Marseille hospital, undergoing a full battery of tests. As expected, all the results came in negative, they tell me. So I'm not to worry. I'm fine, really fine, God be thanked."

Her *children* tell her she's fine, I thought, but haven't the doctors shown *her* the test results? I tried to dismiss the nagging concern as probably a matter of semantics. Still, I wasn't satisfied, and insisted:

"Please tell me what happened."

"Oh, it's just that I had a fainting spell last month, as I was stepping into my car. Then, it happened again, a few days later, standing in the courtyard, talking with Carlos. I don't know what happened, it seems I just fell. . . . Oh, it was only an instant, I regained consciousness immediately, and was rather embarrassed by the incident, believe me.

That's when the children became worried. But I've been perfectly fine since."

"I'm reassured," I said, "and glad you're well. I hate to tell you, though, that we'll only come later in the summer this year, probably not before September."

"Well, make haste, both of you, it's always a joy when you're here," she assured me. Then, lowering her voice, and after a pause:

"Please, tell me something, my dear: Do I sound normal to you?"

A chill ran through my heart, while I affirmed, truthfully, that she did sound exactly the same as always. What did she know that she wasn't telling me? What alarming symptoms was she keeping to herself? I wanted to question her further, but didn't dare, afraid to be seen as prying. So, I would never know, because next she gaily stated that, thank God, she'd always enjoyed the best of health and continued to do so. And we rang off, I still not reassured at all.

I sent a note, but tried not to call too soon, for fear of worrying her unduly. So, I waited for several weeks and finally dialed the château. A man's voice answered the ring. I identified myself, and told him I wished to speak with the duchess. He told me he was her youngest son, whom I'd only briefly met.

"I'm sorry, but she cannot come to the phone."

"Should I call again a little later, perhaps?" No answer. A disconcerting pause instead. So, I went on, hesitantly:

"How is the dear duchess?"

"She is resting and doing as well as can be expected."

I was aghast. "As well as can be expected!" I read a stunning finality in the words. She must be very ill, indeed. At a loss, unwilling to end the conversation without learning more, I persisted:

"Would you please tell her that I look forward to seeing her next month?"

His hesitation was audible over the miles of ocean. Finally, he stammered:

"Uh . . . well . . . as a matter of fact . . ." Then, obviously gathering his courage: "It is not to be wished, madame."

The duchess was dying. I gathered from his carefully controlled words that his mother had been stricken by a fast-developing cancer of the brain. Medical tests performed in Marseille had revealed such extensive organic damage that any surgery would prove useless. Only, her children, in common accord, had decided to reassure her instead of telling her the truth, in the hope of giving her a time of peace, since nothing else could be done for her. Afterward, it had all gone very fast. She had trouble finding words, and suddenly didn't seem to recognize familiar, everyday objects. Now, she remained unconscious most of the time, doctors only able to make her as comfortable as possible with morphine. But they left no hope, and she could go at any moment.

Appalled, I begged:

"Couldn't I fly over, see her? Perhaps she'd be glad . . ."

"There's no point. As I told you, she is in a semicoma from which she seldom emerges completely. She wouldn't even recognize you. Nothing can help her now, except God's mercy."

Helpless, desperate for news, I called friends in the village. I learned that the princess, her niece, was frequently there, but couldn't remain all the time because of her concert dates. Instead, the youngest son's wife had moved to the sickroom, slept there on a mattress on the floor, and nursed the dying woman with unstinting care.

I remembered now. Several years earlier, the duchess had mentioned the marriage of her youngest son, which, at the time, seemed to have caused tension in the family because the bride—while from an excellent family—wasn't of aristocratic birth. Then, over time, the duchess began to speak admiringly of the young woman for whom her affection seemed to grow. She was, declared the duchess, an exemplary wife who gave her husband four strapping sons, the only male heirs so far to carry on the family name. Red, perhaps, instead of blue, but it certainly looked as if the family had been blessed with more of that good blood that will remain true to itself.

Village sources spoke highly of the young woman's role, caring for her mother-in-law with a devotion few daughters could match. But, they all added sadly, a pall had descended from the castle, to spread over the whole village.

I knew the duchess to be a staunch believer in the afterlife, in paradise earned by a lifetime of faith and worthy deeds, and damnation being the wages of sin. Long unfamiliar with prayers myself, I had masses said for her in a bright California church, and attended them, in tears, hoping God would lend an ear to my halting entreaties.

And then, the inevitable call came: I was informed that the duchess, dear to all of us, had departed this world for the rewards of heaven. Her granddaughter broke into sobs as she spoke the formal announcement phrases. Composing herself, she was able to tell me how the duchess had died peacefully, after moments of fully regained consciousness during which she gave instructions and expressed the wish that her youngest son and his family would take over the demanding care of the castle.

No one expected me to attend such a distant funeral, but nothing could have kept me away. Wayne spent most of the night on the phone to travel agents and airlines. Flights were all booked up, for this was the height of summer, when everyone takes to the air, seats reserved long in advance.

At long last, a ticket was obtained: I'd fly a tortuous route, from Los Angeles to San Francisco, on to Atlanta then to New York. From there it was London, and a few hours' wait for a flight to Paris, where I'd catch the last Air Inter plane of the day to Marseille. It would be a long trip, with those five layovers, but I'd still arrive on time, late on the eve of the funeral.

In Marseille, I found to my dismay that Air Inter, the government domestic airline, had failed, in Paris, to transfer aboard my bag that held the mourning clothes I'd wear the next day to the funeral. I sought the employee in charge of luggage, and begged that my missing bag be brought on an Air France flight coming in later that night. Naively, I mentioned I had come to attend the funeral of the duchess. He sneered:

"Air *France* does *not* carry Air *Inter* cargo. Furthermore, this is a socialist country, lady, haven't you heard? Personally, I vote communist and believe in equality. We don't recognize titles, it is the comrade workers we honor instead. Your luggage can't be here until tomorrow sometime, or the day after, and you'll be notified when you can pick it up."

A taxi took me to the village, strangely silent on that warm summer night. No groups conversing on doorsteps or strolling down the steep streets, no music or television sounds filtering through open windows. Several women, heads covered with dark scarves, were stepping out of the church, still open at this late hour. The castle loomed above, silent and somber, no lighted windows in evidence, its flag hung limply at half-mast in the night-blue sky.

I climbed once more the wide, angling steps, and was led into the chapel I had first visited on that day the prince took me on a tour of the castle.

There, lying in stark simplicity, rested the bier of the duchess. All flowers had been piled around the altar, and in my sorrow I found some comfort in the fact that the single wreath of lilies at the foot of the catafalque was the one I'd sent.

The princess came over and kissed me. I found her almost unrecognizable, suddenly aged and drawn. "The coffin is open," she whispered, "but please, don't look at her the way she is now. She'd want to be remembered as you saw her last."

I understood so well. I wouldn't want, either, to be retained in memory as an illness-wasted death mask. By the same token, I'd keep my own image of the woman I'd known and loved. As I knelt on one of the tapestried prayer chairs, I buried my face in my hands trying to conjure the duchess on that last winter holiday, her face glowing in the cold sunshine of a December day, white hair shining like spun candy between the boughs of red-berried holly.

When I mentioned later to the prince, as he walked me home, that my luggage hadn't followed, he offered to call the Air Inter office. I regretfully explained that it wouldn't do any good, for it seemed the personnel were socialists, or even communists. I doubted they would take kindly to a call from *him*. He was amused.

"Communists? The personnel, probably, but not the airline directors. *They* wouldn't be communists."

So, he made a few calls and in no time had on the line one of the airline's top executives, at home in Paris and probably in bed. He began the call thus:

"Here, Prince Louis of . . . Tell me, my friend . . ."

Somehow, Air France must have accepted Air Inter cargo that night because two hours later the bag was delivered to my door by special messenger. So much for the universality of socialist conviction. Tradition dies hard in French hearts and the title of prince undeniably carries more seduction than that of comrade. In spite of the republic's motto of *"Liberté, Égalité, Fraternité,"* more power still remains with those who are less equal than the others.

Next day, the funeral showed all the simple grandeur of an ancient rite. A vast crowd had massed in front of the castle's crenellated entry. When the gate slowly rose, the bier appeared, draped in the red flag struck with the gold lion of Provence, carried shoulder-high by the duchess's three sons and her nephew the prince. The crowd fell mute as many knelt and crossed themselves, with only scattered sobs breaking the silence.

Directly behind the bier marched the duchess's twelve-year-old eldest grandson, carrying the ducal coronet on a velvet pillow. The daughters-in-law and the rest of the family followed. The princess stood out, looking suddenly emaciated, bare-headed, no dark glasses to hide her tear-swollen eyes, a picture of sorrow as haunting as the despair-wracked heroine of a Greek tragedy. She had loved the duchess and felt her loss deeply. The crowd formed into a loose, somber cortege that met with an even larger group in front of the church.

The entire village attended, and most of the neighboring ones, as well as dignitaries from Aix, Avignon, and Paris. Religious orders had sent delegations—figures from a distant past in their cowled robes—and the several charity groups headed by the duchess were represented.

All along, television cameras mounted on high tripods whirred. Hand-held mini-cams captured the scene for the evening news. And the next day, the striking picture of the red-draped coffin made the front page of the press.

In spite of my tears, I couldn't help noticing some disarray, confusion in the church seating, lack of a guiding hand. All the condolence cards had been left on the floral offerings, so there was no way, I thought, the family could express thanks later. Then, I remembered what the duchess told me at the time of Grace of Monaco's funeral:

"Nothing was done quite right. I felt some confusion all around, because, for the first time, *she* wasn't there to see to every detail." The duchess left the same empty place, and no one yet had stepped in to assume the responsibilities she had always carried.

The choir she'd trained sang, and the bishop in tall miter and purple vestments sprinkled holy water over the catafalque, promising that her eyes, closed to this world, would reopen to the light of eternal life and eventual resurrection. The Catholic faith may be a demanding one to live with, but how comforting to die in, for it promises so much: Heaven and reunion with your loved ones in bliss and glory, with resurrection in the end. All this for those who believed, and the duchess *had* believed.

The crowd carried the coffin, now brought downhill by village men who took turns, so that many of them would have the honor of having assisted their duchess to her final rest. At the private funeral chapel near the cemetery, the coffin paused while the gate ceremoniously opened for it. Then, it was taken up the few steps and we saw that the heavy stone that formed the floor had been slid back, revealing several other coffins lying in the small crypt. One must be the duke's, departed fifteen years earlier, and whom she had sometimes longed to join. Sobs choked everyone, as the bier was lowered with ropes and the stone slid back into place.

The duchess had left us forever.

No reception followed, simply, I suppose, because the only person who would have organized one wasn't there, so the mourners returned home.

Later that evening, as I lay exhausted and dozing on my living-room couch, knowing I was to leave early the next morning, I must have dozed off, when I thought I heard a timid knock on my door. Nobody was there when I opened it, so I realized I'd simply dreamed it. No one would be strolling through the grieving village tonight.

Awake now I kept thinking I should walk down to the funeral chapel. Perhaps I could just stand outside its grounds for a moment, saying a final farewell to my friend before returning to my distant country. So I went.

To my surprise, the gate had been left open, and I stepped inside the enclosure. Darkness was just replacing twilight. I walked on the trampled grass and the unswept petals. All was silent, no breath of wind, even the cicadas had interrupted their sawing melody tonight.

I sat on the stone bench where I'd sat before with the duchess, on a day she was reminiscing about the great love that had brought her and her husband together, about his funeral and how she, too, would be laid to rest there someday.

And then . . . a few feet from the chapel's wall, a tiny blue light seemed to rise from the ground, unsteady, as it shone through blades of grass. No larger than a struck match, it hesitated, went out, lit again, vacillated, became stronger, leaned in an imperceptible gust of breeze, rose again, then straightened and seemed to float a few inches above the ground. There, it burned brighter for an instant before going out. It hadn't lasted for more than ten seconds. I waited, breathless, but it didn't return. I sat motionless for a long time, fixing the spot where I had last seen it.

In vain.

A will-o'-the-wisp! For the first time in my life, I had just seen the faint blue dancing flame that has nourished ancient folk legends. It is said to appear occasionally in swamps, or else in places where unembalmed bodies have been buried in plain wood coffins, in graves simply dug out of the earth without the protection of a crypt or cement vault. It occurs supposedly when bubbles of methane gas produced by organic decomposition rise from the ground and spontaneously ignite, especially on warm summer nights.

Looking around, I noticed several wooden crosses I hadn't discovered before: A number of servants, retainers, distant relatives maybe, were buried there in the ground, close by, in the chapel enclosure.

In any other place, back home in the States, for instance, I certainly would have accepted a rational cause for the faint light I'd seen rise from the ground, and clung to it. But Provence is such an ancient land, where myth and magic are never far removed and often found entwined with reality, that I gave no thought to the possibility of some chemical process at work. Folk wisdom had taught me better.

I knelt in gratitude and thanked the duchess for allowing a flame to show that her spirit remained with us still. And I saw that all around the walls of the little enclosure, tall hollyhocks stood as her honor guard, just as they do each summer, in every nook and corner of the village.

And now, that spirit is still with us, several years later, and glows upon the village. The duchess's son's young family has brought renewed life to the castle. Family dinners are served in the immense, vaulted medieval kitchen, firelight dancing on the hundreds of copper pots and pans, rather than in the formal dining room. The boys help with the service. Bicycles and rollerskates sometimes mar the majesty of the honor courtyard and in summer, the great *bassin* that reflects the château is the scene of rousing, splashing parties. Elegant alfresco luncheons in the park are often replaced with picnics the boys carry in big wicker baskets. They are all studying English, and we help by reading the *Herald Tribune* with them and "forcing" them to "*causer Ricain*," talk *Ricain*, as they say to tease me. And I am never happier than when they are allowed to come and visit us in California.

I often think the duchess must be smiling upon her four grandsons, growing into fine, tall young men, who will ensure the continuation of their proud name.

Getting There: On the Trail of the Red R's

*A*fter landing in Paris, getting to Provence can be half the fun, for one must still cross most of France and that is a trip in itself.

In our early years, after landing at Charles de Gaulle Airport, we used to simply walk over from the overseas arrival section to the domestic Air Inter departure lounge. If Air Inter wasn't on strike, the next flight would land you in Marseille in just over an hour. However, Air Inter strikes were not infrequent and were often scheduled, for greater effectiveness, during periods when air travel was heaviest. Such a strike—employees demanding that their days of sick leave count for more on their retirement package, or some such exigency—happened once, on a beastly hot day when we were arriving in France for the summer. (Air Inter has since merged with Air France, but its employees' labor negotiation methods do not appear to have changed much.)

Although we held tickets, we were rudely informed that all Air Inter flights from CDG that evening and next day were canceled, with no resumption of service expected at any time soon from this airport. We could, however, board a company bus to Orly—the older Paris airport, way on the other side of the city—stay overnight at the Orly Hilton, easily the worst of the chain, and eat there the meal prescribed for airline reimbursement. Next morning, it would only be a matter of rushing out at five A.M. to sign in and then wait, in a crowded departure lounge, in the hope that at some time a flight to Marseille would be announced that would agree to squeeze us on board. It finally happened in the late afternoon. None of this represented what we come to France for.

So now, we rent a car instead (no more costly than two airline tickets) and, exiting the airport, drive about fifteen miles toward Chantilly, to the Château de Chaumontel, in Luzarches.

Chaumontel, a small, white castle surrounded by age-old trees, reflects its turrets in the still waters of a flower-banked moat. The rooms are romantic, smell of beeswax and lavender, and one always finds a crystal jug of the house cologne in the bath. Dinner is served by candlelight near a blazing fire in winter, or, in fair weather, under pink umbrellas in the garden. The moment we enter the gates of Chaumontel, we do remember why one would take that long, tiring flight, and rejoice that we did.

The next morning we get up early, because our biological clocks are still on California time, even if our watches have been set nine hours ahead. After that, it is only a matter of deciding whether to take a swing through Chantilly or through Paris before hitting the open road. We usually opt for Chantilly in the summer, Paris in the winter.

Chantilly, only a few miles from Chaumontel, is famous for its castle-museum surrounded by an incredible waterscape. We have visited it several times and even given up on trying to feed the hordes of ravenous carp, after we saw a small truck pull up, loaded with day-old loaves of bread and huge containers of fish food. "We do this twice a day," said the men. "Those carp'll leave food floating on the water, but they'll still surface to beg visitors for more." Everyone has heard of crème Chantilly, a sweet whipped cream, and it is served in town on every conceivable dessert. Chantilly lace, alas, the gossamer handmade kind, is found only in museums today. Chantilly is also the self-proclaimed "horse capital," with its racetrack and sumptuous stables. These were built under the reign of Louis the Fourteenth in a grandiose design reminiscent of Versailles, and horses live there in equine splendor, worth visiting at least once, if only to catch the morning dressage show. We have done that several times, too.

Above all, perhaps, Chantilly is known for its magnificent forest, which begins just at the edge of the castle's waterscape. And we are eager to plunge straight into that forest, still mist-strewn at this early hour.

After the sere California landscape we have just left, it is a jolt, in May or June, to pace the moss-lined walks, to duck under arching branches dripping with dew, covered with unfolding leaves. Sometimes, riders out for an early-morning gallop overtake us in a rhythmic pounding of hooves. We have come upon acres of bluebells and stands of lily-of-the-valley in bloom. Once, venturing far from the path, we found a carpet of wild strawberries glistening scarlet at the foot of oaks, ripe for the tasting.

In winter, we eschew the forest, and drive instead directly to Paris, entering the city at the Porte de Bercy, to follow the Seine into the heart of the city. We stop at a little café on the quay, and inhale a *café noir*, with a croissant from the basket on the counter. We catch a glimpse of the Louvre glass pyramid, and wave at the haughty Eiffel Tower. Through the Place de la Concorde, with all its freshly gilt lampstands, up the Champs-Elysées, all spruced up now with blue-striped sidewalks and almost traffic-free at this hour, down the Avenue de la Grande Armée, and here is the *périphérique* with signs to A6, Lyon, and Marseille, our very own Autoroute du Soleil that will lead us straight to Provence.

From that point on, Wayne's total concern is focused on *déjeuner*, still several hours away, but it is never too early to start planning for a meal that we see as a celebration of return. And for many years, he remained fixated on three-star restaurants.

The *Michelin Guide*, our travel bible, rates top restaurants by granting them stars, from one to three (these stars are not to be confused with *hotel* stars; those indicate only degree of comfort). Wayne long thought that one and two stars meant little more than higher prices than the next lower categories. There are hundreds of one- and two-stars, he'd say, disdainfully. Ah, but the *three stars!* This rarefied, elite group seldom numbers more than twenty for all of France, and several lie near our autoroute, in Burgundy or in the Lyon area. One must admit that, for years, the extraordinary quality of food and service made them worth their price, which remained, after all, reasonable, all things considered.

Still, a game had to be played. It was tacitly understood that after checking guide against map, I would timidly suggest Lameloise in Burgundy, for instance, and that Wayne, after grousing about time wasted and calories consumed, would grumpily consent to stop, to oblige me—not because *he* wanted to, heaven knows, but in order to make *me* happy, since I showed such insistence. So, we'd go, and we would *both* be happy.

Still, we had never tried Bocuse, the most famous, the original three-star, who pioneered the genre. Why? Simply because, situated just north of Lyon, it was a bit too far south for travelers who've been up since dawn, on the road for hours, thinking of nothing but food.

But that year, we'd taken delivery the day before of a new car to replace little Chipper; a much larger, better-powered, and air-conditioned Citroën, with an economical diesel engine. Four of us were traveling that time. Truffles the dog, a veteran of "Francing" as Wayne calls that sort of travel, plus Peter, a novice on his first trip.

Peter was our other pet, a white angora rabbit, the nicest, fluffiest little guy, with tasseled ears and impressive, British-colonel mutton chops framing a pink, constantly twitching nose. The lady who usually stayed at our house to care for him was unavailable, and since there are no facilities in our area that will board rabbits, we were left with no alternative but to bring Peter along. Not that we minded, but it turned out easier decided than done.

First, I learned that rabbits, not being among recognized pets, need permission from French authorities to enter their territory—over and above routine vaccination certificates. No one, however, could tell me *who* held the power to grant that authorization. At the French consulate, the commercial attaché helpfully agreed to consult his books of import regulations and found: *Rabbit, Frozen Meat,* and *Rabbit, Fur for Industrial Use,* but no entry under *Rabbit, Beloved Pet.* Still, I kept badgering him, so he eventually suggested (to get rid of me, I thought) that I personally appeal to the director of quality control at the Ministry of Agriculture in Paris. To my stupefaction, the dear man faxed right back, declaring Peter a *"lapin de compagnie,"* companion rabbit, officially recognized as such by his office, and authorized thereby to travel with us to France. In one of those typically French gestures—after they have driven you to distraction with their Byzantine regulations—he ended his note with *"hommages"* for me and wishes for a happy trip to the *lapin.*

Upon arrival in Paris, carrying Peter in as elegant a carrier as I could find, I expected to meet with suspicious scrutiny from customs, immigration, perhaps even the *lapin* police, who knows, mobilized for the occasion. Instead, Peter's passage through customs raised not the slightest interest, and no one so much as cast a glance at the sheaf of papers, with the Ministry of Agriculture fax on top, that I held out in evidence. There still remained to cross the gauntlet of a few yawning gendarmes. Didn't *they* want to examine the documents I was waving at them, proving my *lapin* was coming in legally?

"Messieurs," I called out, "I have a *lapin* here. Don't you want to check his papers?"

One of the gendarmes shrugged:

"You don't have to bring *lapins* to France, Madame. They're better here than anywhere else, and we know how to cook them right. Little onions and white wine's the secret." I swear I saw Peter shudder. . . . So much for that absolute need for such hard-to-get permission.

As soon as we took possession of the car, Peter settled in his portable sandbox on the back floor, and stayed there when the car was in motion, for stability, I guess. Only when we played a Dave Sanborn tape, the sweet sound of the saxophone brought him to the flat space between the front seats (no transmission bump: Citroëns are frontwheel drive). With forefeet crossed and plumy ears swaying, he stayed, listening attentively until the music ended, and then hopped back in his box. (That is why we took him later to the Montreux Jazz Festival, but that is another story.)

Driving down the autoroute, the three-star game had to be played, of course, and since we'd left very early, by one o'clock we were just nearing Lyon. I checked both map and guide, and pointed out to Wayne, in the prescribed tenta- tive tone:

"Should you wish to get off at the next exit, you'd be minutes from Bocuse, just in case you're interested."

"What's so great about Bocuse?" snarled Wayne. "Just another of *your* three-stars, isn't it?"

"Not just another! This one's supposed to be the greatest, the pioneer of the genre, the three-star that would be four if. . . ."

"If you're so eager to go," sighed Wayne, "I guess there's no getting away. We'll have to . . ." And he burned rubber turning off the autoroute.

Bocuse's restaurant still occupies the building that used to house his father's modest fishermen's café on the bank of the Saône, which rhymes with Rhône of which it is a tributary. It has been extravagantly embellished, the outside unaccountably painted red, with green Japanese architectural motifs, a tribute, perhaps, to the success of Bocuse's Tokyo branch? Under a broiling July sun an attendant was guiding arriving cars to parking places, all located on heat-reflecting gravel.

"Can't you find us a spot in the shade?" I asked. "We have a dog in the car."

"Don't you prefer to bring the dog inside? He can have *déjeuner*, too."

"To tell you the full truth, we also have a rabbit. Look." I showed him Peter, unrealistically furred and fluffy. The young man oohed and aahed and wanted to know why we were traveling with a *lapin*, a good question, by the way.

"Well, we live in California, and we're going to Provence for the summer. So, we brought both the *chien* and the *lapin* with us."

"A *lapin* from California! Is he an animal actor?"

Not exactly an actor, perhaps, but Peter *has* appeared in a few commercials and ads, in particular one for silk lingerie, in which the art director nestled a soft little animal in billows of tulle at the feet of each model: a dove, baby chicks, a white kitten, and, splendid in full angora, Peter. So I proudly admitted to a few credits. This won us the privilege of seeing the great gate opened for us, and we drove in, parking right next to the kitchens, under the canopy of a giant chestnut tree. Peter, busy chewing the *stems* from a bunch of grapes and scattering the grapes all over the floor, didn't mind staying put. So, Wayne and I, with Truffles on her leash, marched into the temple of superlative cuisine.

We were given a table near an open window. Menus were brought, the fabled Bocuse menu emblazoned with his portrait on the cover (the master will autograph it upon request), and a smaller one (without the portrait) for dogs. Choices on the dog menu include, among other entrées such as chopped raw lean steak, a mixture of lamb and chicken served lightly sautéed, tossed with brown rice, grated carrots added upon request. Truffles didn't hesitate to pick the latter, no carrots, please, which arrived almost immediately in a silver bowl, slid under the table. Since she didn't finish it, the leftovers were handed to us as we left, packed in an elegant box shaped like a small suitcase, with a handle and illustrated with a dog. A three-star version of the common doggie bag. One poodle, in fact, was walking out just ahead of us with its owners, carrying *his* box in his mouth.

We had barely dug in to our *amuse-gueules* and aperitifs, when, through the window, we spied the parking attendant beckoning to someone in the kitchen, and Paul Bocuse *en personne* came out, a commanding figure in his chef's whites, tall hat, and tricolor ribbon around his neck holding the medal of *Meilleur Ouvrier de France*, Outstanding Artisan of France, the prestigious award granted by the state to those who have reached a true pinnacle in their chosen artisanship. Both looked into the car window, and the attendant pointed to our table.

Sure enough, Monsieur Bocuse came in, shook our hands, graciously thanked us for stopping at his place, and asked:

"Is it true that rabbit in your car comes straight from California? Why don't you bring him in?"

So Wayne went out and returned, carrying Peter, haloed in his angora cloud, plumy, frothy, tassel-eared, and mutton-chopped. Bocuse sat at our table.

"Here, put him on my lap." He called out to a waiter: "Bring a bowl of lettuce."

Great cuisine holds, of course, an element of showmanship. Bocuse—whose portraits adorn, besides menus, walls and napkin rings—is a master of the game, plays his image to the hilt, and welcomes any chance to provide a show alongside the meal. Diners at every table craned their necks, cameras clicked, camcorders whirred away, and people exclaimed at the charming picture of the greatest chef in the world—the universe, probably—holding that cute rabbit (remember that, to the French, rabbits are food, not pets) on his lap. Peter may have felt apprehensive, but he didn't let on, and played his part with poise, delicately placing his forepaws on the damask cloth to nibble at a lettuce leaf.

Two years later, when we stopped by, this time without Peter, Bocuse recognized us and asked about the *lapin angora*. Wayne was deeply moved.

Over the following years, though, we acquired perhaps greater restaurant sophistication, and concurrently we saw some of the three-stars degenerate progressively into tourist traps, as quality went down and prices skyrocketed. Too many marble floors, too much gold fringe on velvet drapes appeared in what used to be honest country inns before fortune struck. Arrogance tinged the smiles of welcome at the desk: "*Non, Madame*, you *cannot* wear your coat into the dining room. Coats stay *here*," I was told, as I hoped to warm up progressively on a very cold day. Menus gained in pretentiousness what they lost in taste. A *Merveilleuse Surprise de Truffes* turned out to be a surprise, indeed: a mound of very ordinary potato salad topped with a few slices of white, canned (i.e., tasteless) truffles. The price? Enough to keep you in *good* food for several days.

Slow learners that we are, we came to realize that the hundred and fifty kinds of cheeses, presented on a succession of immense trays, means essentially one thing: SHOW. For, indeed, how many different cheeses will you eat at the end of a large meal? One, two slivers *at most*. In *La Ronde Folle des Desserts*, the Mad Saraband of Desserts, four carts are wheeled to your table, one loaded with sorbets and ice creams in frosty silver icers; another with spectacular arrays of fruit—fresh, in an astounding pyramid, candied, compoted, in elaborate confections; another with a wild assortment of never-before-seen cakes; and the last with a variety of *entremets*—custards, puddings, floating islands, mousses, creams, and flans, all beautifully decorated. Still, how many desserts will you actually eat? One? Two, with an effort? The twenty-dollar bottle of mineral water and the fifteen-dollar cup of espresso got to us, too. I felt sorry for the terrified young waiters, who could not bring you a glass of water without permission from a haughty, overbearing maitre d', who, by the way, had long ceased to intimidate *us*. Thus, little by little, the three-stars lost their magic.

At the same time, we discovered the real treasure of French cuisine: The Michelin red *R*'s restaurants.

The *Michelin Guide* added, a few years ago, the feature of indicating with a red *R* (for *Repas*, Meal) those restaurants that offer unusual quality-to-price ratio. We found the legendary Michelin inspectors to be right every time. So, whenever we travel in France, we follow the trail of the red *R*'s. These are often a husband-and-wife operation (with family or local help), always flowery, impeccably and charmingly kept. Most specialize in fine cuisine with emphasis on dishes of the area, the best local wines, and all at more than reasonable prices. Most offer a few rooms, too, in tune with the establishment: not overly luxurious, but attractively comfortable, with beautiful baths. So, now we plan our meals and overnight stays around those red *R*'s.

Driving down from Paris, Burgundy is the first province crossed by the A6 autoroute. In the northernmost part of Burgundy, one comes upon Chablis, eight miles from the

Auxerre exit. There, an excellent red *R* just before the town offers a chance for a worthwhile *déjeuner*, after which it makes sense to do a little wine shopping, having noted, as best references, the vintages offered by the restaurant's list, completed by tips from the owner.

While in Burgundy, it would be unthinkable to entirely miss the great wine road from Dijon to Beaune and on to Chagny. Not a big detour, and worth it, if only to read the village names by the roadside, like some utopian wine list: Romanée-Conti, Morey-Saint-Denis, Gevrey-Chambertin, Aloxe-Corton and Corton-Charlemagne, Nuits-Saint-Georges, Château-Pommard, Meursault. . . . Since one cannot stop everywhere and buy everything, we settle on only a few bottles of sublime Château-Pommard, together with one or two of their marc, an eau-de-vie that breathes all the concentrated fragrances of this great vintage.

Getting closer to our destination, we leave the autoroute at Orange, and take a swing through Châteauneuf-du-Pape for a little more wine shopping, and while so close, push on to nearby Tavel and the rosé vineyards. Unlike our more elusive village rosé, which neither keeps nor travels, Tavel lines up with the top vintages and will age, although we never did get to find out how long it actually keeps.

After that, it is Avignon, the ancient city of the popes, still girded in its crenellated fortifications, painted pink by a setting winter sun or tinged umber on a summer evening. A quick stop for provisions: the most tempting fruit, especially the small, musky melons, a baguette, and *charcuterie* to fill out any little hollow spot in our stomachs left by the splendid *déjeuner*. Then, the familiar expectation sets in as we near the village, knowing it will soon appear, silhouetted against the evening sky.

Blessed be that Air Inter strike! Had it not happened that year, we might not have experienced the ever-renewed adventure of getting there. We might still be flying over Burgundy, instead of experiencing it. And now . . .

Hello, Provence, we have returned; open your arms to those who find such pleasures in your land! We keep emotion at bay by recalling with a laugh the first time we came, firmly determined *not* to buy a house, and thanking fate that brought us here.

A relaxed way of entertaining a group . . .

Apéritif Dinatoire (Drinks-into-Dinner Party)
In the laid-back atmosphere of our village, this is a favorite mode of entertaining.

There is no exact translation for *apéritif dinatoire*. It describes the sort of before-dinner-drinks-party that gradually turns into an informal dinner. The guests are glad not to have to go home to a cold kitchen, when they're relaxed and enjoying themselves. So, why not prolong that delightful twilight hour in the company of friends?

Drinks
 Pastis
 Kir
 Wine (white, red, rosé)
 Fruit juices
 Mineral water, etc.

Snacks to start
 Olives
 Nuts
 Cocktail crackers
 Vegetable dip with *tapenade* (see p. 34)
 Assorted canapés (Roquefort mixed with butter, bone-
  less sardines mashed with butter, smoked salmon
  and cream cheese, etc.)

A little later, set out
 Vegetable tarts
 Pizzas
 Salami and baguettes to slice on a board
 Crocks of pâté and bread
 Assorted cheeses

Well into the evening, serve
 Chocolate cake (the Duchess's own recipe, p. 66)
 Pots of coffee, regular and decaf. Set out cups and
  invite guests to serve themselves.
 Set out brandy and assorted liqueurs. Suggest mixing
  brandy with a little fruit liqueur in a balloon glass—
  a sort of after-dinner version of the *kir*.

Let the aroma of Mediterranean Provence waft
from your plate . . .

Bouillabaisse

They'll tell you that bouillabaisse must be made with fish from the Mediterranean, namely *rascasse* and *grondin*, plus a variety of little rockfish. You also need a shellfish called *araignée de mer*, sea spider. Well, *rascasse* and *grondin* are, respectively, according to my dictionary, scorpionfish and gurnard, and I don't recall seeing those in the markets. As for that indispensable sea spider, I have had bouillabaisse many times in the best places in Marseille (like Chez Fonfon) and no sea spider was in evidence. As for the little rockfish, yes, they were there, but mostly bones and little flesh.

My friends, however, all make bouillabaisse with fish commonly found in markets in America as well as in France. And there has to be some leeway in a bouillabaisse recipe, if one is to believe the old story: When the Marseille fishermen returned home with empty nets, their wives would simply replace fish in the evening bouillabaisse with a nice rock, picked from the tideline, well covered with seaweed. Just season the broth well with saffron (now, *that's* indispensable) and your bouillabaisse will taste *almost* as good.

So, here is a recipe that does away with those impossibly named fish and shellfish, using instead excellent, tasty, readily available ones. They have few bones, which are easy to remove. You can use, with equal success, frozen fish and shellfish (just let it thaw before cooking). And, whatever you do, do not forget the saffron.

The broth

You can prepare it ahead of time. Just bring it to a boil before you add the fish.

Serves 6

1 can tomatoes, peeled and diced
2 or 3 onions, thinly sliced
2 fennel branches, cut into pieces
1 piece orange peel (about ½ a peel)
5 crushed cloves of garlic
Saffron or Knorr's Bouillabaisse Mix
1 bottle dry white wine
1 quart chicken broth
Salt and pepper

Saffron is the pollen of a flower, so it is rare and costly. Many markets keep it under lock and key with the caviar. The contents of one envelope will be enough, though. You might also find (especially in Italian and Spanish markets) *stigmas*, or threads of the saffron crocus; much less expensive. The aroma is less concentrated, but it is good, too. Also, Knorr's makes a Bouillabaisse Mix that contains saffron and that you can add to your broth instead.

In a soup pot, place the tomatoes, onions, fennel, orange peel, and garlic. Sprinkle in saffron powder (or Knorr's Mix). Pour in the wine and chicken broth. Let simmer, covered, for *at least* 40 minutes. Check seasonings, add salt and pepper (you may not need any if you are using Knorr's Mix).

The Fish and Shellfish
   I pound sea bass
   I pound salmon fillet
   I pound John Dory or orange roughy or monkfish
      (remove any skin and visible bones)
   I2 medium (or 6 large) shrimp
   I2 scallops
   Clams and mussels, if desired

If the fish and shellfish are frozen, allow to thaw. Cut fish into I-inch cubes and add to the broth. Bring to a boil, then reduce heat and allow to simmer for I0 minutes. (Remember, fish should not be overcooked.) At this point, the bouillabaisse may be allowed to cool and sit for a couple of hours.

Just before serving, reheat, and drop in shrimp and scallops (and clams and mussels if desired). Allow to cook on reduced heat for 5 minutes, no more—just until shells open. (Shellfish should be *just* cooked through.)

TO *ACCOMPANY THE BOUILLABAISSE*
Sauce Rouille (a rust-colored, spicy mayonnaise)
   ²/₃ cup mayonnaise
   I Tbs tomato paste
   ½ tsp (or more) cayenne pepper
   3 cloves garlic, well mashed

Combine ingredients and mix well. The rouille should be very spicy and hot. Adjust amount of cayenne to your level of tolerance.

Toasted baguette slices: Real garlic-lovers insist on rubbing their bread slices with fresh cloves of garlic, so have a few peeled cloves in a saucer on the table.

A bowl of grated Swiss cheese

SERVING THE BOUILLABAISSE

Ladle fish, shellfish, and broth into *heated* soup plates, and pass a basket of toasted baguette slices, the bowl of rouille, and the bowl of cheese. Guests will spread rouille over baguette slices, float them on top of their bouillabaisse, and sprinkle cheese over it all.

Note: If any guest, having overestimated his/her capacity for cayenne (in the rouille), turns red, starts spluttering, with or without smoke coming out of the ears, I am told that a teaspoonful of grated coconut will counteract the effect of too much spice and restore serenity.

Wine: The ideal here is a flinty white, a Cassis or a Bandol. But a sauvignon blanc or a Pouilly-Fumé would be great as well.

Bon appétit et au revoir,
Yvone

A Reader's Guide

Reading Group Questions
and Topics for Discussion

1. Did you think Yvone and Wayne were insane to purchase their house and then have it remodeled while they were away in California? Would you have trusted Madame Arnaz? What prompted them to make such a potentially foolish purchase?

2. On their first day in their new home in Provence, Wayne and Yvone encounter a prince and a garbage collector. How is this day emblematic of their future in Luberon? What do they learn about the village from their first two visitors?

3. Luberon is living atop its own history, as can be attested by the presence of ancient stone vaults beneath its houses. How do you see Luberon's history interacting with modern civilization? Do you think it is a healthy interaction? What remnants of the old world are being preserved? What evidence do you see of medieval Luberon asserting itself into contemporary culture? What role do Yvone and Wayne play in all this?

4. At her first dinner with the duchess and her family, Yvone notes a delicate exchange between the prince, his

wife, and the duchess in regard to who should proceed first into the dining room. Yvone describes their courtesies as "evocative of centuries of tradition, a tradition whose evidenced survival today enchants me. It is a flicker of grace in an increasingly graceless world." What are other "flickers of grace" in Luberon? How would you describe the value of grace in today's world? Are there "flickers of grace" in your hometown?

5. The duchess's reaction to seemingly paranormal activities in her home is to say, "Why, this is just one of those things you'll come face to face with in a place like this. In a thousand-plus-year-old castle, you should expect a few unexplained events now and then." How is Yvone's perception of unexplained events changed by her ancient surroundings?

6. How does Luberon treat the Americans in its midst? Why do you think the town is so welcoming to Yvone and Wayne? In what ways does the village slowly incorporate these foreigners into its community? What are some signs of their deepening acceptance?

7. What are some other signs of globalization reaching the quiet hilltops of Provence? Do you think these changes are healthy, or dangerous to the village communities?

8. How are men and women treated differently in Provence? How does Yvone navigate these somewhat anti-

quated gender relations? Do you find the men's behavior toward women to be stuffy and stifling, or charming and quaint?

9. Why is Yvone faced with such a serious dilemma when a neighbor presents her with two live chickens for the night's feast? Do you approve of her and Wayne's solution? What would you have done in her place?

10. Could Yvone find a village with the same charms elsewhere in Europe, or the world? What are some attributes Luberon shares with other such villages? What are some of the charms unique only to Luberon? What is the "Magic of Provence"?

Suggestions for Further Reading

Marcel Pagnol: *My Father's Glory and My Mother's Castle*

Colette: *My Mother's House* and *Sido*

Frances Mayes: *Under the Tuscan Sun*

Peter Mayle: *A Year in Provence*

Adam Gopnik: *Paris to the Moon*

Susan Loomis: *On Rue Tatin*

Mort Rosenblum: *A Goose in Toulouse and Other Culinary Adventures in France*